Eagle Day: The Battle of Britain

Richard Collier

EAGLE DAY
THE BATTLE OF BRITAIN

August 6 – September 15 1940
Picture Research by Chaz Bowyer

NEW EDITION

E. P. Dutton ■ New York

For information contact: E.P. Dutton, 2 Park Avenue,
New York, N.Y. 10016

Library of Congress Catalog Card Number: 80-65191

First published 1966
New edition published 1980

ISBN: 0-525-09650-7

10 9 8 7 6 5 4 3 2 1
Second Edition

TO HONOR THE POLISH GENIUS
NICOLAUS COPERNICUS
500TH ANNIVERSARY 1473 · 1973

Copernicus' greatest contribution to universal progress is in his laying the groundwork for a systematic planetary theory. Making his own astronomical instruments and developing his own trigonometry, his monumental treatise "De Revolutionibus Orbium Coelestium" demonstrated the heliocentric theory of the solar system as we know it today. He "stopped the Sun and moved the Earth" — the theory that pioneered our space program, making him the Father of Modern Astronomy.

This Polish astronomer, Mikolaj Kopernik, better known by his Latin name, Nicolaus Copernicus, was born February 19, 1473 in Toruń, Poland. He was one of the most versatile men of his time. After 14 years of university studies in Kraków, Poland and Bologna, Padua and Ferrara in Italy — he became a physician, geographer, economist, churchman, statesman, soldier, poet, painter, besides being a mathematician and scientist. He was a linguist and humanist undaunted by the narrow thinking of his time and driven by a burning dedication to individual freedom by which to develop and prove his theories and then to give unselfishly to build a better world.

The above illustration shows a Polish coin (1 silver grossus) which was in circulation during Copernicus' lifetime.

This bookmark issued under the authority of Calif.-Arizona Copernicus Regional Committee.
Designed by Leon S. Kawecki
This Terra stock Donated by Mead Papers, Div. of the Mead Corp.

Contents

Preface

The Battle of Britain has been subjected to as much debate among military historians and air strategists as any campaign in recent history. However, this book is not intended to be a full history of the Battle of Britain in that sense. Instead it is the story of a handful of people who lived out their lives against the Battle's six most fateful weeks; it tells of their hopes and fears, and of how the Battle felt and sounded to them. I therefore make no apology for the numerous personal accounts and recollections which I have included. None of the conversations recorded are imaginary; they all represent a genuine attempt by the individuals concerned to remember what they said at the time.

There is still considerable disagreement among leading authorities as to the time-span of the Battle. The official Ministry of Defence viewpoint is that it was a five-phase campaign starting on July 10. Other schools of thought give the start as August 8 or August 11. The end of the Battle is varyingly given as September 15, October 5 and October 31. Many German historians place the Battle's climax as late as May 1941. For the purposes of the book I make no apologies – again – for my arbitrary choices of August 6 and September 15 respectively. For these were the six crucial weeks in 1940 when the eyes of the world were upon the frail defences of London and the south-east corner of England, and the safety of Britain lay with a handful of RAF pilots.

1. The Calm Before the Storm

August 6–7

1. Pilots of 32 Squadron relax in the hot sunshine of 31 July 1940 at Hawkinge forward airfield. Behind them a Hurricane stands ready for start-up.

The house named Karinhall was silent. It sprawled in the dawn, as still as a slumbering animal, a vast unwieldy pile of hewn stone, forty miles north-east of Berlin, amid the sandy plain called the Schorfheide. The overlord of this feudal complex, forty-seven-year-old Reichsmarschall Hermann Göring, Commander-in-Chief of the Luftwaffe, was in benevolent mood. For today, Tuesday, August 6, 1940, all the omens were good.

It was just nine weeks since Dunkirk, six since the fall of France – yet still there was no indication that Great Britain would realize the true hopelessness of her position and sue for peace. Three weeks earlier, even before Winston Churchill's outright rejection of a peace offer, made through the King of Sweden, Hitler, angered by the stalemate, had issued his famous Directive No. 16: since England seemed unwilling to compromise, he would prepare for, if need be carry out, a full-scale thirteen-division invasion of the island on a 225-mile front – from Ramsgate on the Kentish coast to west of the Isle of Wight. The code-name for 'this exceptionally daring undertaking' was 'Sea-Lion'. But, the directive stressed, prior to any such landing, 'The British Air Force must be eliminated to such an extent that it will be incapable of putting up any substantial opposition to the invading troops.'

To Göring, sipping breakfast coffee, this seemed no insuperable task. The French collapse had given his Luftwaffe fully fifty bases in northern France and Holland; even the short-range planes which accounted for half of the 2,550 machines immediately available – Messerschmitt 109 fighters, Junkers 87 (Stuka) dive-bombers – were now within twenty-five minutes striking distance of the English Channel coast. Since the end of July, no British convoy had dared to run this formidable gauntlet – and as Göring had warned the world through an interview on July 28 with an American journalist, the Luftwaffe's strikes to date had been child's play, 'armed reconnaissance only'.

And to the top commanders whom he had this day summoned to mull over final details, men like Generalfeldmarschall Erhard Milch, the Luftwaffe's Inspector-General, and Generaloberst Hans-Jürgen Stumpff, commanding Air Fleet Five in Norway, it seemed that Göring hadn't a care in the world. Both Air Fleet Two's Generalfeldmarschall Albert Kesselring, and Generalfeldmarschall Hugo Sperrle, chief of Air Fleet Three, found him benign, even cocky. Resplendent in his sky-blue uniform, Göring seemed more eager to show off the Renoirs in his art gallery than to discuss tactics.

Pacing the tapestry-hung corridors in Göring's wake, neither Kesselring, Sperrle, nor the other members of the party were much taken aback by such diversions. Though a stream of memoranda countersigned by Göring flooded almost daily from Karinhall, the brunt of planning aerial missions in detail rested as squarely as ever on the Air Fleet chiefs and their staffs. As a thrusting Minister of Aviation whose drive, from 1934 on, had made the Luftwaffe into the world's most powerful air-arm, Göring's disdain of technical detail had still been such that he met his inspector-general, Erhard Milch, just once every three months.

It wasn't that his Air Fleet commanders didn't raise objections over the forthcoming battle – but Göring, in euphoric mood, brushed them cheerfully aside. To Sperrle, the target selection seemed faulty; if Britain was 100 per cent dependent on sea-borne traffic, shouldn't ports be the main target? Kesselring maintained that one swamping attack on a key target – say London – was the answer.

As things stood now, the main attack plan – *Adlerangriff*, or attack of the Eagles, to come into force on receipt of the code-word *Adler Tag* (Eagle Day) – was scattered along the whole invasion front: airfields, ports, even aircraft factories. Following hard on this, more mass-attacks – code-named *Lichtmeer* (Sea of Light) – were slated to wipe out all the RAF's night operational bases between the Thames and the Wash.

Poring over a map, the three men checked over key targets . . . the radio direction-finding (later called radar) stations on England's south coast, for a start, though their true function was still something of a mystery; the coastal airfields, naturally – Manston and Hawkinge in Kent and Warmwell in Dorset; and the major airfields like Biggin Hill, lying inland, eighteen miles south of London.

As yet no final date could be fixed – from August 5 onwards meteorologists predicted a high-pressure zone moving slowly

towards the Channel from north-west England – but on one score Göring was adamant. By the yardstick of the Polish and French campaigns, the Royal Air Force should be out of the picture in four days flat.

Across the English Channel, where twenty-three RAF fighter squadrons were defending a 250-mile front against odds of three to one, most people yearned for a break in the monotony. At Biggin Hill airfield in Kent, Corporal Elspeth Henderson had pined for action for eight long months – yet though experts warned that the field was on the direct bomber route to London from the south-east, life at the

2. (*Left*) Air Chief Marshal Sir Hugh Dowding, AOC-in-C RAF Fighter Command from July 1936 until November 1940.

3. (*Right*) Hermann Wilhelm Göring, supreme commander of the Nazi Luftwaffe.

450-acre hilltop site called 'Biggin-on-the-Bump' was as uneventful as pre-war Edinburgh, where Elspeth, a Scottish law professor's daughter, had passed her childhood days.

Aged twenty-six, a petite, determined redhead, Elspeth had swiftly rebelled against the stifling routine of life as a volunteer nurse. She yearned to be in the thick of things, so within three months of war's outbreak, armed with little more than a suitcase containing two evening dresses, she had set off from Edinburgh to join the WAAF. Now, eight months later, she knew every corner of Biggin Hill's Operations Room, which controlled four fighter squadrons over a crucial 2,800 square-mile sector. As a trainee plotter she'd worked with the long-handled magnetic plotting rods, tracing suspected German raiders on the big glass screen that showed Biggin Hill's operational area; on night watches she had even slept beneath the Operations table.

Yet for three long months, while Biggin's runways were constructed, there hadn't even been a squadron to control – and for the most part Elspeth and her friends Barbara Lecky and Yvonne Simmons could only spread their knitting patterns on the table and gossip. The officers whiled away tedium with a card game called 'Up the River' for penny stakes. And during the hot, sultry nights, penned behind the black-out curtains, not one solitary German bomber showed up to enliven the watch – only moths and cockchafers battering against the electric lights, to fall writhing on to the controller's daïs, the maps and the telephone keys.

Often, as much for encouragement as anything, Elspeth would re-read the notice that Group Captain Richard Grice, the Station Commander, had posted everywhere, the words of the Prime Minister to the nation as long ago as June 18: 'What General Weygand called The Battle of France is over. I expect The Battle of Britain is about to begin. Upon this battle depends the survival of Christian civilization. . . .'

Much of Churchill's indomitable spirit infused the pilots of the Royal Air Force: as yet, many were still unblooded and they ached to prove themselves in action. At Kenley airfield, outside London, Squadron Leader Aeneas MacDonell, commanding No. 64 Squadron, summed up the spirit of many such outfits: 'It's like holding in a team of wild horses to keep them in formation when there are Germans near.'

The more seasoned pilots took a graver view: how long before one saw death as in a mirror? At Tangmere, on the Sussex coast, Hurricane pilot Tom Hubbard likened it to a game of roulette: 'It's like backing black all the time. Our luck can't come up for ever.' Pilot Officer George Bennions, a fiery Yorkshireman, felt differently; it seemed that life had never offered more. In the officers' washroom at Hornchurch, Essex, he burst out to Harry 'Butch' Baker: 'My God, life wouldn't seem right if you didn't go up to have one scrap in the morning and another in the afternoon.'

Most were lighthearted – uncertain of how they would stand the strain, it seemed safer to play it cool. At Warmwell airfield, Dorset, Pilot Officer Eugene 'Red' Tobin joined in the private joke of No. 609 Spitfire Squadron: the lull of these first August days was easily explained. Göring had given the Luftwaffe a whole week's rest, before facing the RAF. Posted to 609 Squadron only four days

4. The mainstay of Fighter Command throughout the Battle of Britain, the Hawker Hurricane. Here an example from 32 Squadron taxies out from a Hawkinge dispersal on 31 July 1940.

earlier, along with his friends Andy Mamedoff and 'Shorty' Keough, Red Tobin could rarely resist a wisecrack. And to Red, in any case, the fact that three native-born Americans should be here in England fighting with an RAF squadron had an especially humorous slant. Just six months earlier, at Mines Field, near Inglewood, California, an agent had been busy signing up both Red and Andy Mamedoff as fighter pilots for the war in Finland. The bait: all their expenses to Helsinki and 100 dollars a month while they lasted. A twenty-three-year-old real estate operator's son from Los Angeles, with blue eyes and flaming red hair, Tobin had assented cheerfully – undeterred by the fact that he'd never flown a fighter in his life.

Neither Red nor Andy had turned a hair when the war in Finland folded before they had even left Los Angeles. As Red put it reasonably, 'If you go looking for a fight, you can always find one.' Ten

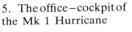

5. The office – cockpit of the Mk 1 Hurricane

days later, as embryo pilots of the French Armée de l'Air, they had boarded a freighter in Halifax, Nova Scotia, along with Brooklyn-born Vernon 'Shorty' Keough, a professional parachute-jumper they had met along the way, bound for the French port of St Nazaire.

But hard as they looked, the Americans found no fighting in France. All the way from Paris through Tours to Bordeaux they stayed just one jump ahead of the German advance, living on unsweetened coffee and potato soup, bedding down on piles of damp hay, unable even to cadge a combat flight in an antiquated Potez 63. At noon on 22 June 1940, they reached St Jean de Luz on the Spanish frontier to tumble aboard the *Baron Nairn*, the last ship to leave occupied France. Two days later, still seeking that fight, Red Tobin and his friends disembarked at Plymouth.

Now, thanks to a chance contact with a friendly Member of Parliament, they were on the point of finding it; after four weeks brief indoctrination at No. 7 Operational Training Unit, Hawarden, Cheshire, they had adopted the sky-blue silk scarves of 609 Squadron and were ready for action. Already, they found, their fellow pilots held them in some awe; to gloss over his inexperience, Red had generously credited himself with five thousand flying hours. Yet never once did the Americans seem conscious that in a space of months, in Europe, they had seen more action than any other squadron member. Red Tobin would shrug off such exploits as their hair-raising ride to Bordeaux on an ammunition train with his favourite wisecrack: 'We had a million laughs.'

One man, however, was in no mood to laugh; he and all his squadron were filled with cold implacable hatred. At thirty-six, Major Zdzislaw Krasnodebski, joint-commander of the newly-formed 303 Polish Squadron, had seen his world turned upside down. Since that September day in 1939, when he took off from Zielonka airfield to see the German warplanes raining bombs on Warsaw, Krasnodebski had known the end was predictable in days. Shot down in flames on his first day of combat, he and his men had soon travelled as tortuous a road as Red Tobin's – to Bucharest, where the Rumanians impounded their planes – to Italy, via Belgrade – at last to France, to find all the heart for fighting gone. Each day as the German bombers circled Tours and Lille unmolested, French pilots relaxed in the bar, sipping their vermouth, ignoring the brand-new Curtiss fighters parked on the tarmac outside.

Now that this world was past, Krasnodebksi was like every Pole

6. Spitfire – the aesthetically-beautiful creation of R. J. Mitchell which was to become synonymous with RAF Fighter Command throughout the war years.

7. Plt Off Colin Gray's Spitfire of 54 Squadron at Hornchurch, April 1940, with trolley accumulator plugged in and ready to start.

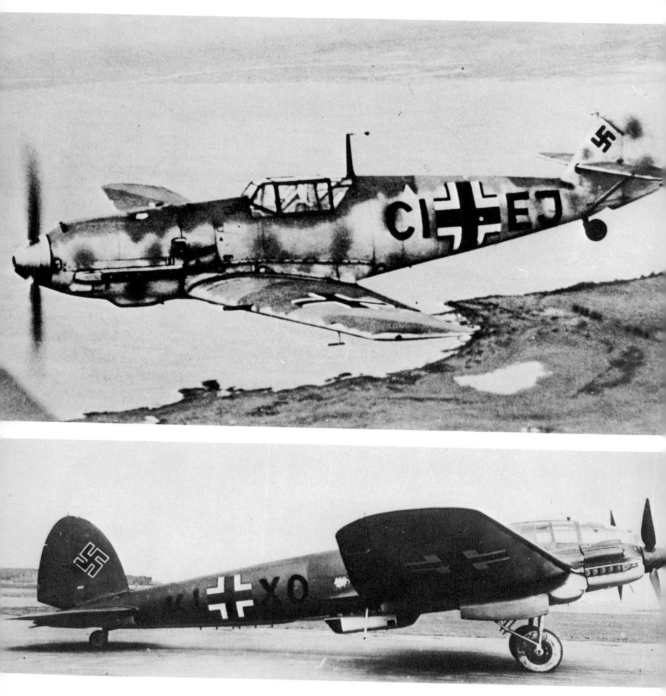

who had elected to continue the fight from English soil – a man living on memories. They flooded back to him this August morning as he stood in the bar at Northolt airfield, ten miles west of Hyde Park Corner, toying moodily with a whisky . . . the rolling acres of his father's vast estate at Wola Osowinski, the sleek Arabs he'd ridden as a young nobleman destined for the cavalry, the time when he was nine years old and looked up to see his first Russian plane circling low on manoeuvres, and his sudden boyish decision, triumphantly fulfilled: 'Flying will be my life.'

Krasnodebski was, in one way, supremely lucky: the years had taught him much-needed patience. For the eager young Poles he commanded, thirsting for combat, their reception at Northolt had come as a bitter blow. No doubt the Hurricane fighters were fine planes, superior by far to the obsolescent P 11s they had flown in Poland – but who'd ever heard of planes with retractable undercarriages? The airspeed indicators registered miles, not kilometres – and the altimeters showed only feet. Some of the British officers assigned to them, like Squadron Leader Ronald Kellett, the joint-commander, had fluent French – but the Operations Room officers spoke only unfamiliar English.

As training mishaps mounted steeply, Group Captain Stanley Vincent, Northolt's station commander, laid down a flat ultimatum: 'Until this squadron understands English, it's grounded. I'm not having people crashing round the sky until they understand what they're told to do.' Then to a junior officer, in a rueful aside, 'Their spirit's magnificent – I think they hate my guts now more than they

hate the Germans.' It wasn't easy for pilots with 2,000 hours flying behind them to cool their heels in the mess ante-room, thumbing through *1,000 Simple Words in English*. They prayed for nothing but the chance of combat. Yet before they killed they must sit dutifully like schoolboys, studying their English grammars.

As he drank up his whisky and strode in to lunch, Krasnodebski was sure of one thing. When they did become operational the Germans – *and* the British – would see exactly what a Polish squadron could do.

The mood wasn't universal; in these last hours before the battle, some men were racked by doubts. At Hawkinge airfield, Kent, within sight of the blue-grey Channel waters, Pilot Officer Geoffrey Page, sprawled on the grass, exchanging banter with the pilots of No. 56

19

Squadron, hardly seemed to have a care in the world – yet a small, hard core of fear was lodged within his mind. Only recently, as his Hurricane closed in on a Stuka over Dover Harbour, Page had felt a sudden frightening shock of exultation as he thumbed the firing button. Yellow flame had whooshed from the Stuka's wing-roots – yet as it plunged like a comet towards the sea, Page was still firing, appalled yet knowing he had enjoyed this kill.

A sensitive, fair-haired twenty-year-old, Page gave few outward signs of his inner secret: that his life had been one long battle against fear. Page, a pupil of the RAF College at Cranwell before the war, had told himself time and again that a fighter pilot's was the one career worth the winning. How could the World War I fighter ace, Captain Albert Ball, vc, whose portrait seemed to dominate the college's art gallery, ever have known the doubts and insecurity that tortured *him*?

Rarely free from such doubts after a sheltered childhood in his mother's home, Page had seen a life modelled after Ball's as the only answer. Nothing had dashed his hopes more when the college's top brass flatly disagreed: though he had a great future as a flying instructor, he just didn't possess a fighter pilot's temperament. Overnight, Hitler's invasion of the Low Countries had reversed his luck: trained fighter pilots were needed, and fast. And after three months with 56 Squadron, Page was, by August 1940 standards, virtually a veteran – and daily, in secret triumph, he noted each victory over the inner self that cared and doubted. But now, frightened that he'd reached a point where only killing had the power to stir him, Page was fighting to brush the fear aside. Defiantly he told himself: This is what they call drinking the red wine of youth – so enjoy it while it lasts. The battle hasn't started yet – it can't last long.

At Ladwood Farm, forty-year-old Robert Bailey was doing what he did every day soon after mid-day: scrubbing down the dropping boards of the poultry house where some of his 1,500 hens were kept. His farm, cupped in a shelving green valley flanked by tall groves of beech trees, lay only two miles north-west of Hawkinge airfield – a priority target for the Luftwaffe when they came.

On this sultry August day, Ladwood's hundred acres, where the loudest sounds were the sheep in the fold and the soft scolding of wood pigeons, were outwardly peaceful. But there were small signs about the farm that showed the crisis at hand: those long black poles,

10. 'Greetings to Winston' – the message being chalked on a bomb destined for London by this Heinkel He 111 *Staffel* in the summer of 1940.

11. The Junkers Ju 88 bomber fared badly during the 1940 air assault on England, but was later, in myriad modified forms, to see extensive service with the Luftwaffe in many roles.

for instance, placed to repel glider landings, jutting from the ripening wheat in Raikes Hole field. Robert Bailey knew all about those anti-invasion poles. As local secretary of the National Farmers' Union he had hared round the district in his old Ford 8, urging each farmer to set up makeshift obstructions – hay elevators, waggons, even sheep huts – on every stretch of level ground. Many were unwilling to accept the worst – yet when it came to the pinch, few could resist the urgency of this gentle blue-eyed man who had farmed Ladwood all his life and had taught their children in Sunday school for as long as they could remember.

Like hundreds of farmers across southern England, Bailey was carrying on in the heat of the driest summer for seven years. Rations were low, and would be lower yet – two ounces of tea a week, four of butter, one and tenpence worth of Argentine meat – but determination didn't waver. The girls of Britain's 80,000 strong Women's Land Army bent to stooking the last of the harvest. The London Cockneys

12. Scramble! Spitfire pilots of 19 Squadron arrive at dispersal at Duxford.

who garnered most of the hops for British brewers were back in Kent as usual – and wearing steel helmets as they picked.

Yet each day hundreds of people were leaving the coastal zone. Five miles from Ladwood Farm, in the Kentish port of Folkestone, removal vans cluttered every street; in Margate's deserted shopping centre, Northdown Road, grass sprouted from the kerbside. House after house stood as empty as a ghost town's, often with beds unmade and ham and eggs congealing on the stove. Westwards, from low-lying Romney Marsh, 100,000 prize sheep had been evacuated. The children had gone, too, with Mickey Mouse gas-masks for the toddlers to make it all seem like a game.

Others, however, wouldn't budge. At Folkestone, eighteen-year-old Betty Turner, garbed in swimsuit and steel helmet, still wormed through a chink in the beach's barbed wire for her morning bathe. Near by, in George Lane, Mr Pink's grocery store carried on with just eight customers – seventeen less than the official qualifying number, but eighty-year-old William Pink had personally convinced the Minister of Food, Lord Woolton, that a grocer had a duty to those he dealt with. And somehow Robert Bailey's neighbours on Firs Farm, Arthur and Mary Castle, still took thirty gallons of milk to market daily – in an old Morris Oxford topped with straw bales to ward off shrapnel.

When it came to adversity, most people perversely looked on the bright side. At Wateringbury, Kent, when a blast from a stray bomb stripped an entire apple orchard the farmer exulted – it was the quickest picking he had ever known. At Hayling Island, Portsmouth, families still took picnics to the beach; it was nice to say they had seen the barbed wire. Petrol may have been short but one Romney Marsh farmer, John Hacking, still escorted his wife Anne weekly to dances – in a horse-drawn cart. For Mrs Martha Henning and her friends, a shopping trip to Dover was always good for a laugh; sometimes a uniformed provost checked your identity card over morning coffee.

To Robert Bailey, however, life wasn't all humour; his love for Ladwood, with its leaded windows, the red Kentish brick that had endured for two centuries, its black oak beams, went too deep for that. Somehow, it all added up to a heritage he must stay on and cherish. Bending again to the dropping boards, he reflected wryly that thanks to the war, farming Ladwood was profitable again after twenty years penury – yet 2,500 German planes were massed just twenty-five minutes flying time away.

23

In northern France, the Germans were in relaxed mood, too. With the sun dazzling on the Channel waters, the weather seemed too wonderful for war – and despite Hitler's Directive No. 16, the prospects of invasion seemed remote. Had not Oberst Werner Junck, regional fighter commander for Air Fleet Three, told his pilots the British must sue for peace? His source seemed impeccable, too: the former German Ambassador to Britain, Joachim von Ribbentrop.

It wasn't that any German pilot doubted ultimate victory; when one of his fliers sought leave of absence to marry, the fighter ace Werner Mölders, twenty-five victories to his credit, counselled: 'Why marry now, when only England's left? Marry later to celebrate the victory.' For by noon on August 7, twenty-four hours after Göring's crucial Karinhall conference, it was nine days since a destroyer, let alone a coastal convoy, had moved in the English Channel.

After the rigours of the French campaign – often eight sorties a day – most were content to take life as it came. Major Hennig Strümpell's pilots at Beaumont-le-Roger, in Normandy, were taking time off to brush up their tennis; Major Martin Mettig's 54th Fighter Group were almost a fixture on Boulogne's Berck beach; and any day now, grouse shooting would be in season. Many had brought pets to divert them on the Channel coast – often just a dog, to add the home-from-home touch, like Hauptmann Rolf Pingel's dachshund, Raudel, who'd even flown on reconnaissance flights to England. But others had fauna strange enough to stock Stuttgart's famous zoo: the 3rd Fighter Group with their owl, their tame hawk, and Oberleutnant

13. (*Left*) The Three American Musketeers – 'Red' Tobin, 'Shorty' Keough, and 'Andy' Mamedoff – all of whom fought with 609 Sqn during the Battle, and all three of whom were killed later in the war.

14. (*Right*) 151 Squadron pilots at North Weald, July 1940. Fourth from left is E. M. Donaldson, DFC (later, Air Commodore); while fifth from left is Wg Cdr F. V. Beamish.

24

Franz von Werra's lion cub, Simba; Major Hennig Strümpell's group tended a menagerie of ravens, goats, parrots, even donkeys. Some units had their own pet bear – like 'Petz', the 27th Fighter Group's shaggy black mascot, who'd recently disgraced himself by playfully nibbling the thigh of a visiting concert party soubrette.

Those homely touches seemed essential for, with most airfields little more than landing strips, conditions were as primitive as might be. At Guines, near Calais, Oberleutnant Hans Ekkehard Bob's unit had a pasture so furrowed with sheep-tracks that tyros almost came to grief at the moment of take-off. At Desvres, near Boulogne, Leutnant Erich Hohagen's men first had to harvest an entire wheatfield, then roll it level.

In this first week of August, the German pilots, much like the British, were living from day to day and relishing such creature comforts as came their way. At Crépon in Normandy, Hauptmann Werner Andres, heading No. 2 Wing, 27th Fighter Group, had welcome news; tomorrow, August 8, his unit was on twenty-four-hour stand-down, one whole day's freedom from the cramped gipsy caravan that served him as billet. Hans-Joachim Jabs, a twenty-two-year-old Me 110 pilot, checked over his laundry; if combat threatened, he always liked a clean white shirt to fly against England.

One man was bent on action – a welcome relief after weeks of sitting cooped in the stuffy omnibus that was his headquarters at Cap Blanc Nez, near Wissant, dwarfed, ironically, by the memorial to Louis Blériot, the first-ever cross-Channel flier. After days of fiddling paper work, the stocky, smiling fifty-year-old Oberst Johannes Fink, newly-appointed *Kanalkampfführer,* or Channel Battle Leader, knew just what he had to do. Before each mission, Fink would tell his crews: 'Each sortie is a dedication – you must put all your past life behind you' – advice that angered the irreligious Göring beyond all reason. Yet none could deny Fink's mastery of his job. Posted to the Channel one month earlier, with orders to win and keep air superiority over the Straits of Dover, Fink had fulfilled that task in twenty-seven days flat.

Today, Wednesday, August 7, he was tense and excited; returning post-haste from the Karinhall conference, Generalfeldmarschall Albert Kesselring had called a top-level conference at his headquarters nearby. Straight from the shoulder, Kesselring had told them: 'Things are going to be different from now on. We're going to attack the airfields.'

25

2. Early Encounters

August 8–1

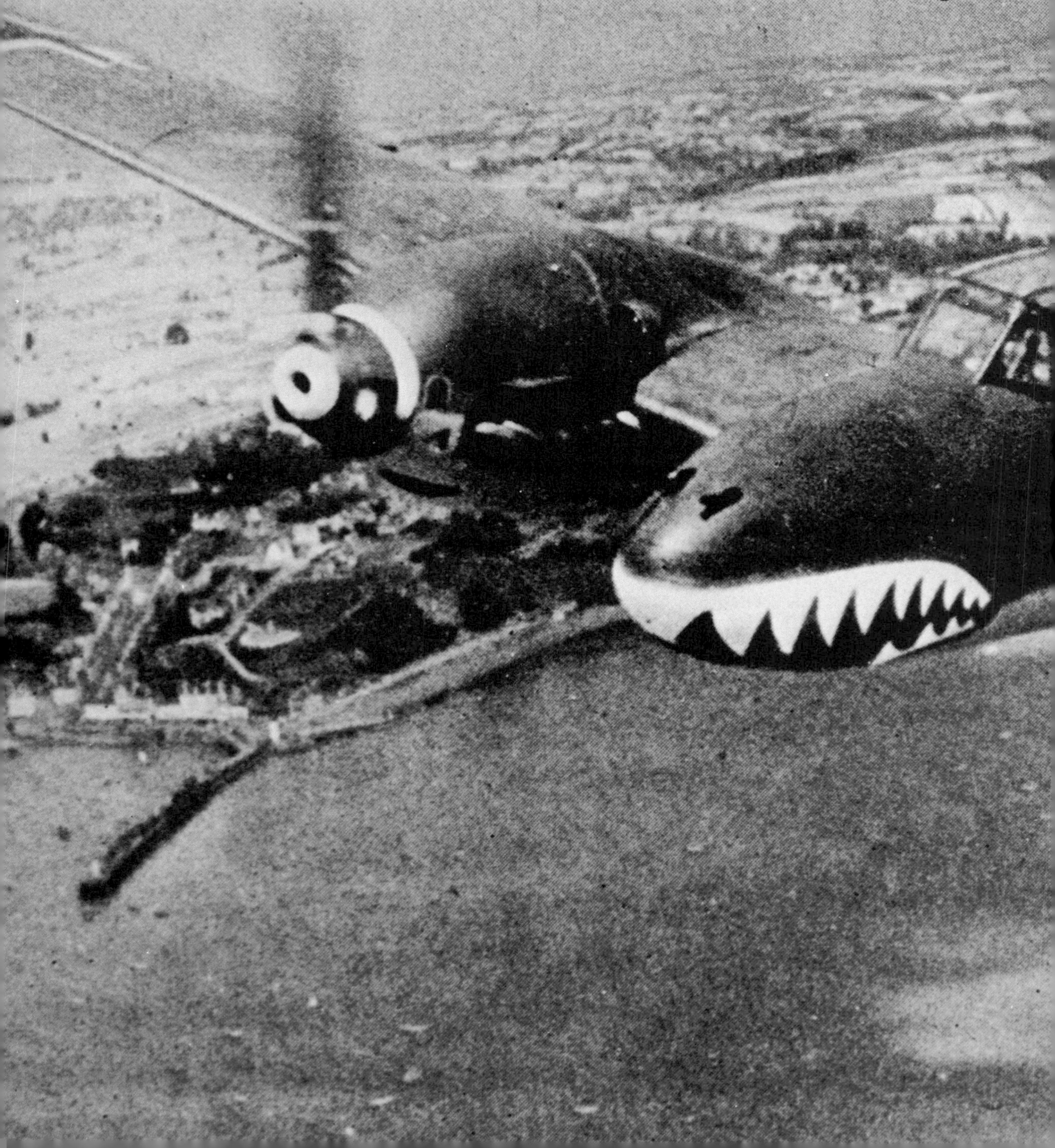

15. *Zerstörer*—Messerschmitt Bf 110 of II./ZG 79 *'Haifischgruppe'* ('Shark Group') over the English coast during the summer of 1940. As Göring's vaunted *Zerstörer* ('Destroyer'), the Bf 110 failed lamentably to live up to its reputation as a killer.

Hauptmann Werner Andres saw the waters of the English Channel racing to meet him, faster and faster now at over 300 miles an hour. He tensed himself for the crash. Already he had thrown back the cockpit hood and released his parachute harness. With white steam pluming furiously from the shattered radiator of his Messerschmitt 109, it would be all over in seconds. Then a wash of grey water swamped the plane and Andres was scrambling; as he dived he felt the icy water knife through the blue-grey gabardine trousers the pilots called 'Channel pants'. Striking out away from the wreckage, he saw the fighter's nose tilt steeply. Within sixty seconds it had vanished from sight.

Swimming steadily, Andres fumbled for the packet of fluorescine strapped to his belt above the right knee. He ripped it open, and the yellow-green patch of marker dye spread sluggishly outwards, like ripples from a tossed stone – a sure guide for the rescue planes that would be cruising even here, thirty miles north-west of Cherbourg. Now his thoughts furled rapidly back over the day just past, Thursday, August 8, one of the most disastrous he could remember – a day that had cost Göring's Luftwaffe thirteen planes for a loss of twenty-two British ships.

In the small hours of August 8 had come the astonishing news that the British were daring once again to force the Channel passage – twenty-five merchant ships under armed escort were steaming from the Thames Estuary towards Falmouth in Cornwall. At once, from his Cherbourg headquarters, the 8th Flying Corps' Generalmajor the Baron von Richthofen had sent positive orders: 'This convoy must be wiped out.' By noon, 300 planes – the 8th Flying Corps' Stuka dive-bombers, escorted by fighters of Major Max Ibel's 27th Group – had wiped out close on 70,000 tons of shipping. All the way from Dover to St Catherine's Point, the Channel bobbed with rafts, hatch-covers, life-jackets, the empty shells of abandoned British ships glowing red-hot. Still von Richthofen wasn't satisfied; despite

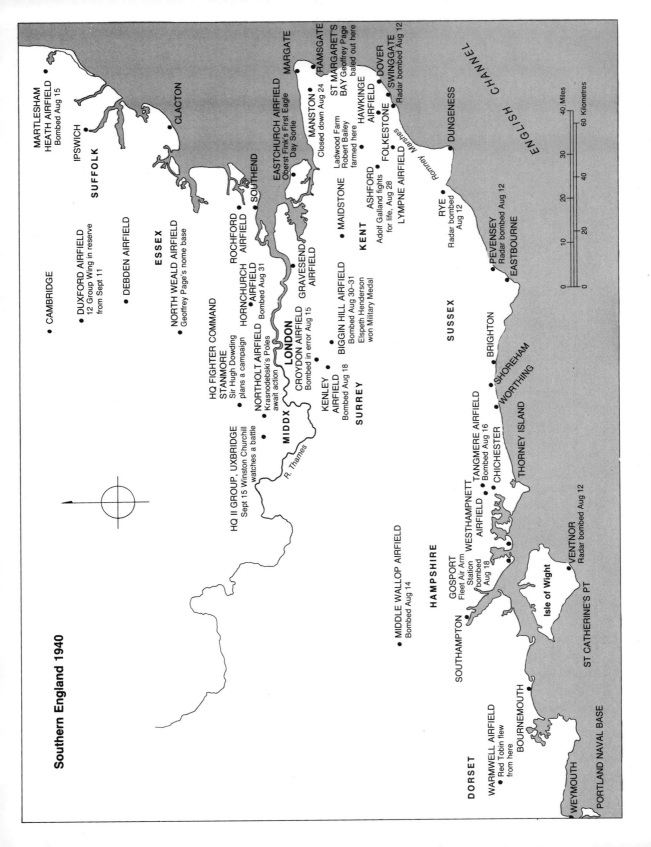

Southern England 1940

DORSET
WARMWELL AIRFIELD
● Red Tobin flew
from here

BOURNEMOUTH ●

WEYMOUTH ●

PORTLAND NAVAL BASE

ST CATHERINE'S PT

HAMPSHIRE
● MIDDLE WALLOP AIRFIELD
Bombed Aug 14

SOUTHAMPTON ●

GOSPORT
Fleet Air Arm
Station
bombed
Aug 18

WESTHAMPNETT
AIRFIELD

TANGMERE AIRFIELD ●
Bombed Aug 16

CHICHESTER ●

THORNEY ISLAND

Isle of Wight

VENTNOR
● Radar bombed Aug 12

WORTHING ●

SHOREHAM ●

BRIGHTON ●

SUSSEX

EASTBOURNE ●

PEVENSEY ●
Radar bombed
Aug 12

RYE ●
Radar bombed
Aug 12

DUNGENESS ●

Romney Marshes

ENGLISH CHANNEL

40 Miles
60 Kilometres
0 10 20 30 40
0 20 40

HQ II GROUP, UXBRIDGE ●
Sept 15 Winston Churchill
watches a battle

HQ FIGHTER COMMAND
STANMORE
Sir Hugh Dowding
plans a campaign

MIDDX

NORTHOLT AIRFIELD ●
Krasnodebski's Poles
await action

R. Thames

CROYDON AIRFIELD ●
Bombed in error Aug 15

KENLEY
AIRFIELD ●
Bombed Aug 18

SURREY

BIGGIN HILL AIRFIELD ●
Bombed Aug 30–31
Elspeth Henderson
won Military Medal

GRAVESEND
AIRFIELD ●

HORNCHURCH
AIRFIELD ●
Bombed Aug 31

ROCHFORD
AIRFIELD ●

NORTH WEALD AIRFIELD ●
Geoffrey Page's nome base

DEBDEN AIRFIELD ●

DUXFORD AIRFIELD ●
12 Group Wing in reserve
from Sept 11

CAMBRIDGE ●

ESSEX

SOUTHEND ●

EASTCHURCH AIRFIELD ●
Oberst Fink's First Eagle
Day Sortie

LONDON

MAIDSTONE ●

ASHFORD ●
Adolf Galland fights
for life, Aug 28

KENT

LYMPNE AIRFIELD ●

FOLKESTONE ●

HAWKINGE
AIRFIELD ●

Ladwood Farm
Robert Bailey
farmed here

MANSTON ●
Closed down Aug 24

ST MARGARET'S
BAY Geoffrey Page
baled out here

SWINGATE ●
Radar bombed Aug 12

DOVER ●
Radar bombed Aug 12

MARGATE ●

RAMSGATE ●

CLACTON ●

IPSWICH ●

SUFFOLK

MARTLESHAM
HEATH AIRFIELD ●
Bombed Aug 15

the first two all-out attacks, observation planes reported that six ships still remained defiantly afloat. In the early afternoon of August 8 he ordered yet a third strike.

Though head of the 27th Fighter Group's 2nd Wing, Werner Andres hadn't flown on those first sorties; his machine had been stripped down for overhaul. Now came final orders; overhaul or no, the mechanics must reassemble his plane and his wing must fly with the rest. It was small wonder Andres blazed: 'Are they mad – or must the German public have good news every day of the week? However stupid the English are, they'll have guessed our target by this time.' And by 3 pm on August 8, cruising with the Stukas across the drifting waste of jetsam, Andres knew he had been right. He never even saw the plane that hit him.

At Headquarters, Fighter Command, twelve miles north of London on the Hertfordshire border, Air Chief Marshal Sir Hugh Dowding paced his high Georgian office facing south towards the spire of Harrow Church. The Luftwaffe may have suffered severe losses but Dowding knew that the British losses of August 8 – nineteen planes – were higher than Fighter Command had ever been called upon to bear. And Dowding cared deeply because Fighter Command was his life. At fifty-eight, a widower, the pale, austere man they nicknamed 'Stuffy' was still a mystery to his officers; never once, in four years at Headquarters, had he been known to enter the mess. Instead, his punishing routine never varied: four hours desk-work until 1 pm, lunch at 'Montrose', the rambling gabled house in nearby Gordon Avenue, where his sister Hilde kept house for him, more paper work and home again for a quick dinner at 7.30 pm, then back to his desk until it was time to set out for a small-hours visit to one of the new night-fighter stations, still grappling with the unsolved problem of intercepting the night-bomber.

It was no new role for Dowding; even the 1,434 pilots and the 708 fighters that were this day available to him – two-thirds of them Hurricanes, which Luftwaffe fighters saw as easy meat – had involved a hard-fought battle. As far back as early May, Dowding had warned Squadron Leader Theodore McEvoy, of Air Ministry's Directorate of Operations: 'I tell you, McEvoy, every Hurricane we send to France is a nail in our coffin.' On June 3, standing alone before the entire War Cabinet, Dowding had made plain what a near-run race it had been: the French campaign had cost him nearly 300 trained

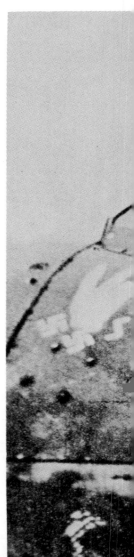

16. Geoffrey Page in his 56 Squadron Hurricane, 'Little Willie'.

30

pilots. Further to weaken defences at home by despatching yet more squadrons to France, as Churchill had urged, would have been fatal. Passing along the ranks of Cabinet Ministers to set a graph squarely in front of the Prime Minister, Dowding had told him: 'If the rate of wastage shown here had continued for another fortnight, we shouldn't have had a single Hurricane left in France or in this country.'

Fortunately, due to the intercession of the Chief of the Air Staff, Air Marshal Sir Cyril Newall, the ten Hurricane squadrons that France's Paul Reynaud had demanded to stem the German breakthrough had never been forthcoming. But even those machines still

17. Stalwarts of 56
Squadron; Sgt Peter
Hillwood, Flt Lt E. .
'Jumbo' Gracie, and
Sgt F. W. 'Taffy'
Higginson.

available in England on June 3 had needed vital modifications.

No man to mince words, Dowding was constantly at odds with authority. Yet despite all opposition Dowding, in four years flat, had built the formidable machine that was Fighter Command, pressing for all-weather runways on six airfields, which now had them, urging for one whole year that only the dispersal of planes on airfields could safeguard squadrons against low or high level attacks, even pioneering bullet-proof windscreens for fighter planes. Since May he had known a valued ally in Lord Beaverbrook, whose get-up-and-go had now pushed fighter production to an all-time high of 496 machines a month – yet so often did the Air Staff still threaten to retire Dowding, that he confessed: 'I feel like an unsatisfactory housemaid under notice.'

And now, with the Luftwaffe's arrival on the Channel coast, his whole defence system was in some ways outmoded; to intercept German formations approaching at over 200 miles an hour, RAF fighters, which needed close on twenty minutes to reach operational height, would have to climb from coastal airfields laid down when the Rhine was the frontier. Only recently Dowding had gone on record

32

that: 'The Germans could lay large areas of our big towns in ruins at any time they choose to do so' – and how his pilots would fare now he did not know, if the losses of August 8 were a harbinger of what was to come. For, as 'Stuffy' Dowding studied the flimsy green combat reports the pilots had scrawled at the day's end, the carnage was plain. From Hornchurch in the east to Middle Wallop in the west, the six Sector Controllers who manoeuvred the squadrons into battle over southern England had scrambled them too late and too low.

Just one unit – Squadron Leader John Peel's No. 145 Hurricane Squadron – had had the lucky height. At 9 am on August 8, patrolling 16,000 feet above the haze-shrouded waters off St Catherine's Point, the Isle of Wight's southernmost tip, they had seen the Stukas streaking like furies for the packed, black mass of shipping. Appropriately, breaking radio silence, John Peel gave the fighter pilot's war cry: 'Tally ho!' At once, as if on cue, twelve hump-backed Hurricanes altered course – heading not for the shattered convoy but for the brassy orb of the sun that swam above them. If they dived from the sun, Peel knew, the Germans' vision would be dazzled from the start. Eighteen thousand feet above the water Peel's voice rasped through the intercom – 'Come on, chaps, down we go!' – and suddenly, as the Hurricanes swooped, ninety-six 303 Browning machine-guns were chattering as one, marking the first shots fired in the Battle of Britain.

It was a breath-taking sight . . . a tanker splitting clean in two with a mighty mushroom of smoke, everywhere parachutes blossoming white, rocking in the slipstream of hard-diving 109s, barrage balloons dripping flame towards the shining water, the pale fire of Very lights bursting red against the sun.

For every pilot of 145 Squadron it seemed a field-day all the way; even a novice like nineteen-year-old James Storrar, whose cheery take-off cry was 'Fuel and noise – let's go!' felt himself a world-beater. Opening fire on a Stuka, Storrar did not even know he had hit it, until its rear machine-gun spun crazily skywards: the gunner lolling dead. Then, as he watched, what seemed 'like liquid fire' rippled along one wing and down the leg of the Stuka's undercarriage. Flying level only yards distant, Storrar could see the German pilot watching with almost clinical detachment as the orange flame engulfed his wing. Without warning, the Stuka nose-dived, spreading blow-torch fire across the sea.

Convinced they had knocked down twenty-one German planes single-handed the squadron that night threw an all-ranks party to end them all – as Storrar recalls it: 'The floor literally swam in beer.' Quietly confident, John Peel inscribed one swastika in his log-book. To the men of 145 Squadron, it seemed the battle was almost over.

The fact was, however, that while this one squadron had gained needed height, most hadn't come within an ace of it. Although Air Chief Marshal Dowding's twenty-odd radar stations, stretching from the Isle of Wight to the Orkneys, could pick up a German formation's course, even gauge its strength, their estimation of height was almost always unreliable. Then, too, the Germans timed each sortie to strike with the dazzling sun behind them – yet the Sector Ops Rooms didn't even plot the sun's position on the board.

To most of Dowding's pilots, it seemed the Luftwaffe held the sky as never before. Even at mid-afternoon – around the time Hauptmann Werner Andres was ditching his 109 in the Channel – 43 Hurricane Squadron, from Tangmere, saw a sight to turn them cold: von Richthofen's third and last sortie, an umbrella of German planes filling the sky all the way to Cherbourg. To Pilot Officer Frank Carey it was 'a raid so terrible and inexorable it was like trying to stop a steam-roller'. Within minutes 43 Squadron, two wounded, two injured, were out of combat.

The day's losses weren't surprising. Though the War Cabinet had yielded to Dowding, withholding his precious squadrons from France, recently they'd hampered his efforts in another way. As early as July 10, urged by Professor Frederick Lindemann (later Lord Cherwell), Winston Churchill's scientific adviser, they had drastically reduced the pilots' operational training – from six months to four scant weeks. Faced with a dearth of trained pilots, a glut of operational machines, they had seen no other solution. Confident that the monthly output of pilots could be boosted from 560 to 890 per month, Lindemann challenged: 'Are not our standards of training too high? The final polish should be given in the squadrons.'

Westwards, over the shattered convoy, more and more men acquired that 'final polish' on August 8 – through a cruel baptism of fire. One Hurricane squadron, No. 238, operating from Middle Wallop airfield, Hampshire, had been formed so quickly that they had never done a training flight together; sighting the Germans over the Channel they opened fire half a mile out of range. Pilot Officer Vernon Simmonds, as green as any, did not even realize that battle had commenced until empty cartridge cases showered him like hail.

When two of his pilots were reported missing in the Channel,

Squadron Leader Harold Fenton flew gamely off to search for them – only to find himself outduelled and shot down by a German observation plane. Hauled aboard the trawler HMS *Bassett,* Fenton spent a damp, unhappy afternoon drying out in the boiler-room – along with a German pilot so confident that he had flown over England with nothing more lethal than a Very pistol and a packet of prophylactics.

Hence Air Chief Marshal Dowding's unease, for as he leafed through the combat reports, it was plain that 145 Squadron's success was as much due to luck as judgment – and soon many squadrons, down to half-strength after the débâcle of Dunkirk and costly convoy patrols, must be pulled out to rest and reform. If Reichsmarschall Göring stepped up the pressure, what could Dowding do ? In southern England, he had just twenty-three squadrons and he could not afford to strip northern England of the fighter units guarding the vital industrial areas of the Tyne and Clydeside. If Fighter Command's losses could be assessed at a steady drain of twenty per day, could even Lord Beaverbrook's Ministry of Aircraft Production keep pace?

For so many thousands, as yet, the battle had barely started – and Dowding couldn't know.

Pilot Officer Geoffrey Page awoke with a start; dawn still hadn't broken on August 12 and for a second he couldn't even recall where he was. Then, abruptly, it came back to him. He sat bolt upright in bed and, by the light of a torch, tried to set down all he felt in a letter to an old Staff College friend:

> I sometimes wonder . . . if the whole war isn't a ghastly nightmare from which we'll wake up soon. I know all of this sounds nonsense, but I'm slightly tight, and it's only an hour to dawn. . . . To me, it will mean just another day of butchery . . . it makes me feel sick. Where are we going and how will it all end?

Page, like most other pilots, felt this sense of expectancy he couldn't quite define – that something big would break at any minute; on the previous day, August 11, the RAF had lost an all-time high of thirty-two planes.

Across the Channel the Germans too were awake early, and with reason. This morning, following days of frustration, the battle would move away from the Channel and over England itself. Bad weather had already led to one postponement of the big strike but now, at least, the meteorologists had so far unbent as to make a positive

35

prognosis. On the morrow, there would be fine clear weather over the United Kingdom.

Alerted by Göring's headquarters, OKL (Oberkommando der Luftwaffe), Air Fleets Two and Three had been ordered to clear the decks. The all-out attack, the Sunday punch – Eagle Day – was timed for 7 am on Tuesday, August 13. But first, leaving nothing to chance, those giant aerials, towering 350 feet above the Kent and Sussex coastlines and clearly visible by telescope from France, must be neutralized. Constant monitoring of British radio had made plain to General Wolfgang Martini, the Luftwaffe signals chief, that RAF fighters kept in touch with their bases by ultra short wave transmissions. And these coastal aerials must somehow link up with this, for Fighter Command always seemed to know when German formations were approaching.

Martini didn't quite know how, but he had pounced on one salient fact: the detector stations virtually ruled out any chance of a surprise

18. RDF – 'Radio Direction Finding' – the contemporary name for the radar network which was the 'eye' of RAF Fighter Command, 1940. Transmitters (left) and receivers (right)

attack. As early as August 3, his appeal to Generaloberst Hans Jeschonnek, Chief of Staff to the Luftwaffe, had borne fruit. Then Jeschonnek had ruled: 'Identified British detector stations are to be attacked in force and put out of action early on.' Only one man, Oberst Paul Deichmann, the 2nd Flying Corps' Chief of Staff, voiced a minority view. Surely the whole aim of Eagle Day was to destroy the British fighter force? In that case, was it not better that this system *should* warn them, so that they came up to be destroyed in the air?

Among the pilots, reactions varied, but if morale was at a peak, none saw the struggle ahead as a walk-over. The British would prove formidable adversaries. Hauptmann Walter Kienzle, newly arrived on the coast, had it straight from Oberst 'Uncle Theo' Osterkamp, the regional fighter commander for Air Fleet Two. An Anglophile, to whom the British were always 'the lords', Osterkamp warned: 'Now we're going to fight "the lords", and that's something else again. They're hard fighters and they're good fighters – even though our machines are better.'

At group commander level, there were reservations; victory might be assured, but they still distrusted the High Command's airy optimism. Like many commanders, Major Hans Trubenbach felt that Göring, weak in logic, pinned his faith in the wrong planes – above all, the twin-engined Me 110. Christened the Zerstörer (destroyer) the twin-seater fighter, meeting only token opposition, had first won easy laurels in the French campaign – yet all through July, as Oberst Fink's units triumphantly swept the Channel skies, its losses had mounted steeply.

A long-range escort fighter, designed to clear the way for mass bomber attacks, the 110 looked foolproof on the drawing-board; against the Me 109's maximum cruising range, 412 miles, the 110 could clock up 680 miles. Yet, loaded, the 110s outweighed the streamlined 109s by almost 10,000 pounds. Their lack of manoeuvrability and speed was a byword with every pilot. In combat, their stock tactic was what the RAF called 'the circle of death' – a defensive gambit which had the machines circling warily, each guarding the other's tailplane, perilous to friend and foe alike. Only recently, Major Hennig Strümpell had found himself in one such circle dog-fighting with a Spitfire – while 110s blasted tracer at both of them impartially. Yet to all arguments, Göring was obdurate: 'If the fighters are the sword of the Luftwaffe, the Me 110 Zerstörer is the point of that sword.'

Göring's unswerving belief in the Stuka troubled his commanders too. Unrivalled in precision-bombing and close infantry support when the Luftwaffe held the sky, they now made up one-third of the Luftwaffe's bomber force – for maximum success at minimum cost of material the Reichsmarschall saw them as unbeatable. Yet to most, the heavy losses of August 8 had presaged the shape of things to come.

One man was quietly confident; with luck, the element of surprise would come to his aid today, August 11, just as it had done yesterday. At thirty, Hauptmann Walter Rubensdörffer, a tall, dynamic Swiss with an infectious sense of humour, knew that he held a unique command in the Luftwaffe; as leader of Test Group 210, a task force of twenty-eight hand-picked pilots, he had spent long weeks of trial and error at the Luftwaffe's experimental station at Rechlin on the Baltic, proving that fighters could not only carry bombs but could hit their targets. Only the day before, swooping on a British convoy fifteen miles south-east of Harwich, his unit had met only desultory ack-ack: how much more harm could fighter planes do to shipping?

As he drank his breakfast coffee at Calais-Marck airfield, Rubensdörffer was confident, yet tense. By now, Test Group 210 was Kesselring's most cherished unit and this morning its mission was the most crucial yet: to knock out four key radar stations on the Kent and Sussex coasts. On this mission might hinge the whole success of the battle.

The targets were vital indeed. Set amid the Kentish apple orchards and the flat salt marshes, the brick-built radar stations, girdled by barbed wire, were a mystery to all except the screened personnel who lived and worked there. And the sinister latticework of steel aerials rearing 350 feet above them lent colour to that mystery – some country folk swore they housed powerful rays, which could cut out the engine of a hostile aircraft at one flick of a switch. But the truth, if more mundane, spelt equal danger to the Germans. Once the echo of approaching aircraft showed as a V-shaped blip of light on the convex glass screen in the station's Receiver Block, the news flashed like wildfire, from detector station to Fighter Command's Filter Room, from Filter Room to Air Vice-Marshal Keith Park's HQ 11 Fighter Group, controlling southern England, from 11 Group to the sector stations directing the fighter squadrons. The whole intricate structure of Dowding's Fighter Command must stand or fall by this high-

19. Hurricane pilots of 615 Squadron, AAF, relaxing at dispersal at Kenley in August 1940

pressure plotting, which from the first blip on a screen to a squadron racing for its planes had a time-lapse of just six minutes.

So on the morning of August 12 every coastal radar station was gripped by tension. At Rye, near the old Kentish seaport, Corporal Daphne Griffiths, one of the morning watch of four, had just taken over the screen in the flimsy wooden Ops hut from her friend, Helen McCormick, a pretty New Zealander. Now, as Daphne mechanically intoned plots to Fighter Command's Filter Room at Stanmore, Corporal Brenda Hackett stood by to keep record of every one – its time, range, bearing and grid reference.

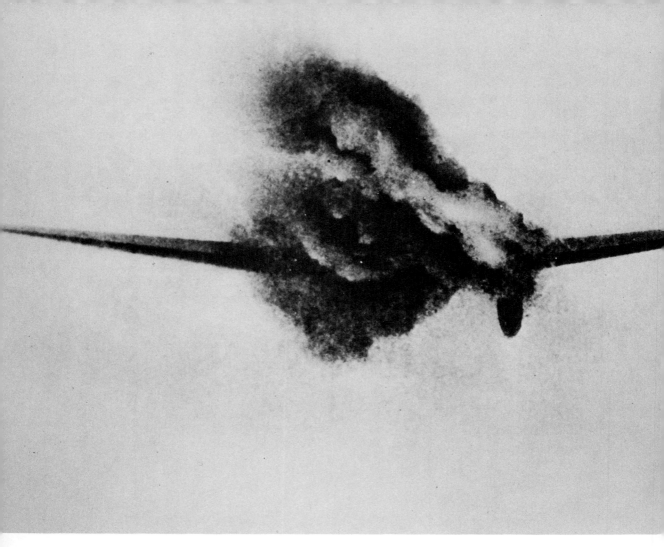

At 9.25 am, Daphne was alerted by a V-shaped blip of light registering suddenly off northern France. Calmly she reported: 'Hullo, Stanmore, I've a new track at thirty miles. Only three aircraft – I'll give you a plot.' Seconds later, the thought struck her: were other stations plotting these same planes? But the Filter Room assured her that she alone had registered them – and could they please have a height? As Daphne Griffiths reported back – 'Height, 18,000' – she noted that the range was fast decreasing, too. Was there any identification? The Stanmore plotter's voice was metallic in her headphones: 'No, there's nothing on it yet.' By now, Daphne was perturbed: two more plots had made it clear that if the planes con-

tinued on course they would pass clean overhead. Again she queried: 'Stanmore, is this track still unidentified?' The Filter Room seemed unruffled: they had that moment marked the plot with an x which signified doubtful, to be watched and investigated.

There was less doubt on the coast. Behind Daphne Griffiths, the station adjutant, Flying Officer Smith, one of several officers who had drifted in to watch, recalled that the Ops hut was protected only by a small rampart of sandbags. He told Corporal Sydney Hempson, the NCO in charge: 'I think it would be a good idea if we had our tin hats.' At that moment the voice of Troop Sergeant Major Johnny Mason, whose Bofors guns defended the six-acre site, seemed to explode in their headsets: 'Three dive-bombers coming out of the sun – duck!'

It was split-second timing. All along the coast, Test Group 210, split now into squadrons of four, came hurtling from the watery sunlight – Oberleutnant Wilhelm Roessiger's pilots making for the aerials at Rye, Oberleutnant Martin Lutz and his men streaking for Pevensey, by Eastbourne, Oberleutnant Otto Hintze barely a thousand metres above the Dover radar station, flying for the tall steel masts head-on in a vain effort to pinpoint them, Rubensdörffer himself going full throttle for the masts at Dunkirk, near Canterbury.

Suddenly the Ops hut at Rye shuddered, and glass and wooden shutters were toppling; clods of earth founted 400 feet high to splatter the steel aerials. Prone beneath the table, the WAAF crews saw chairs and tables spiral in the air like a juggler's fast-flying balls – everywhere the sites were under fire. At Pevensey, tons of gravel swamped the office of the CO, Flight Lieutenant Marcus Scroggie, only minutes after he'd left it; at Dover, a bomb sheared past recumbent operators to bury itself six feet beneath the sick quarters. At Dunkirk, one of Rubensdörffer's thousand-pounders literally shifted the concrete transmitting block by inches. All along the coast the tall towers trembled, and black smoke rose to blot out the sun.

But by mid-afternoon, General Wolfgang Martini, Luftwaffe signals chief, knew bitter disappointment. Operating with stand-by diesels, every station except Ventnor – a write-off for three long weeks – was reported back on the air. To Martini, it seemed now as if radar stations could not be silenced for more than a few hours at a time.

They had been crucial hours, even so. At noon, with the radar stations still inoperative, the coastal airfields had lain open to the worst the Luftwaffe could do – and they lost no time. Already at

20. A Heinkel He 111 victim of Sqn Ldr Adolph 'Sailor' Malan of 74 Sqn.

41

12.50 pm, Rubensdörffer's Test Group 210 were back over Kent's east coast: twenty bomb-laden Me 109s and 110s dived at 375 miles an hour on Manston, the 530-acre forward base, code-named Charlie Three, pitting it with scores of craters.

That Manston was caught unawares was almost symbolic. An all-grass field. lacking runways, its largely civilian staff still viewed daily life in terms of peace, not war. For instance, hard-pressed flight mechanics, lacking a spanner, found that Main Stores did things by the book: emergency or no, only the right form, duly countersigned worked the oracle.

One squadron, No. 65, was caught at the second of take-off: from 3,000 feet Oberleutnant Otto Hintze glimpsed their Spitfires clearly, lined up in neat V-shaped formations of three, engines turning over. Then Rubensdörffer had peeled off, a hangar went skywards in a spawning cloud of rubble, and the planes were lost to view, taxi-ing blindly through choking smoke. Only one pilot, Flight Lieutenant Jeffrey Quill, was airborne amid the bombs – far too late to exact revenge.

Another Spitfire squadron, No. 54, saw it all from first to last: only sheer misfortune stopped Flight Lieutenant Al Deere, this day leading the squadron, from a classic intercept. A chunky New Zealander of twenty-one, whose split-second baleouts were legendary, Deere was at 20,000 feet when he saw Rubensdörffer's planes streaking from Manston. At once, breaking radio silence, he hailed Pilot Officer Colin Gray, a fellow New Zealander leading Blue Section: 'Do you see them?' As Gray exulted, 'Too bloody right,' Deere knew they were all set. Then suddenly, as Squadron 54 loomed within striking distance of the raiders, everything was wrong. Despairing, Deere saw Gray's section was no longer with him; only now did he realize that Gray had sighted a second formation instead, approaching Dover, and was already in combat. Vainly, Deere yelled, 'Where the hell are you?' then saw a vast white cloud of what looked like pumice pressing slowly upwards from Manston. He didn't realize it was chalk dust, whirling from scores of craters; he thought Manston was on fire.

By now the airfield itself was a thundering horde of blue-clad men seeking shelter. Planes passed like black shadows, and Corporal Francis De Vroome, priding himself on his cunning, leapt for a brand-new bomb-crater: they wouldn't strike twice in the same place. Within seconds, he had clawed his frantic way out; the walls of the

21. London's Newhaven Docks in August 1940.

crater were glowing red-hot. Manston's medical officer, Squadron Leader John Dales, racing for the main camp in his staff car, slewed suddenly on screaming tyres; the car's right window had burst across his arm. Later he found that nineteen bullets from a low-level dog-fight had ricocheted from the road.

Inland, at Biggin Hill, the pilots of 32 Hurricane Squadron heard of Manston's ordeal over lunch at dispersal – with one spontaneous unsympathetic guffaw: 'Let's hope that bloody cook had to run for it.' At Fighter Command, Dowding's staff officers heard the news more

gravely: the airfield attacks had barely started, yet Manston's morale was in doubt. Whether or not the cook had run for it, hundreds had – to the deep chalk shelters that wound like catacombs beneath the airfield – and here many, despite their officers' exhortations, would stay for days on end, contracting out of the battle for good and all.

At Rochford airfield in Essex, the old Southend Flying Club, now a satellite aerodrome for Sector Station North Weald, news of Manston's plight took time to reach Geoffrey Page and the pilots of 56 Squadron. Stretched out on the cool grass at dispersal, in the aerodrome's farthest corner, Page, his eyes closed, was more conscious of

22. Messerschmitt Bf 109E of 2./JG52 which was shot down near Berwick, Sussex, on August 12. An airman helps himself to a 'souvenir'; the 'Little Devil' insigne alongside the nose.

44

the bird-song than the muttered conversations of his friends. He was within inches of drifting off to sleep. Suddenly the telephone rang and 'Jumbo' Gracie grabbed for the receiver: 'Scramble . . . seventy-plus approaching Manston . . . angels one-five.' In the fighter pilots' jargon, 'angels' signified height per thousand feet, so the message was plain to all: more than seventy German aircraft were approaching Manston at 15,000 feet. It was 5.20 pm on Tuesday, August 12.

There was no time for further reflection. As he pelted the fifty yards to his waiting Hurricane, the suspense was banished and Page's mind was clear and alert, with only physical action to preoccupy him. Right foot into the stirrup step, left foot on the port wing, one short step along, right foot on the step inset in the fuselage, into the cockpit. Deftly his rigger was passing parachute straps across his shoulders, then the Sutton harness straps . . . pin through and tighten the adjusting pieces . . . mask clipped across and oxygen on. He had primed the engine, adjusting the switches, and now his thumb went up in signal to the mechanics. The chocks slipped away, the Rolls-Royce Merlin engines roared into life, flattening the dancing grass with their slipstream, and Page was taxi-ing out behind 'Jumbo' Gracie.

The Hurricanes climbed steeply, gaining height at more than 2,000 feet per minute, and the voice of Wing Commander John Cherry, North Weald Controller, filled their earphones, calling 'Jumbo' Gracie: 'Hullo, Yorker Blue Leader, Lumba Calling. Seventy-plus bandits approaching Charlie Three, angels one-five.' Then Gracie's high-pitched voice acknowledged: 'Hullo, Lumba, Yorker Blue Leader answering. Your message received and understood. Over.' One of the squadron's pilots chipped in: lack of oil pressure was sending him home. Again Gracie acknowledged, and now ten Hurricanes swept on to intercept seventy German aircraft. Page thought idly, odds of seven to one – no better nor worse than usual. As they followed the serrated coastline of north Kent his altimeter showed 10,000 feet.

Suddenly, what looked like a swarm of midges was dancing in the top half of his bullet-proof windscreen. But Page, craning closer, knew better. They were several thousand feet higher than the Hurricanes, and more deadly than any insect – thirty Dornier 215 bombers escorted by forty Messerschmitt 109s. He heard 'Jumbo' Gracie call, 'Echelon starboard – go', and saw Constable-Maxwell's Hurricane slide beneath Gracie's. Cheerfully Page thumbed his nose at Constable-Maxwell, then took up position slightly to the right and astern. Habit prompted him to lock his sliding hood in the open position – for a hurried exit, if need be.

The Dorniers turned north, setting course over the sea, but the Hurricanes were gaining on them banking, in pursuit; minute by minute, the distance between the fighters and the slim pencil-shaped bombers was closing. To Geoffrey Page, it was suddenly like an express overhauling a freight train: there was time for bomber and fighter pilots to exchange silent glances as the Hurricanes forged on

for the bomber leader. Swiftly, Page glanced behind and aloft, but no – the Me 109s weren't pouncing yet.

At 600 yards, too far away to register, Page opened fire on one of the leading machines, then abruptly stopped short. One moment there had been clear sky between himself and thirty Dorniers. Now the air was criss-crossed with a fusillade of glinting white tracer-cannon shells converging on the Hurricanes. He saw Gracie's machine peel from the attack; the distance between Page and the leading bombers was only thirty yards now. Strikes from his machine-gun fire flashed in winking daggers of light from a Dornier's port engine; it was suddenly a desperate race to destroy before he himself was destroyed.

As a thunderclap explosion tore at his eardrums, Page's first reaction was: I can't have been hit. It could happen to other people, but not me. Then all at once fear surged again as an ugly ragged hole gaped in his starboard wing. And then the petrol tank behind the engine, sited on a level with his chest, blew up like a bomb; flames seared through the cockpit like a prairie fire, clawing greedily towards the draught from the open hood. A voice Page barely recognized was screaming in mortal terror: 'Dear God, save me – save me, dear God.'

Desperately he grappled with the Sutton harness, head reared back from the licking flames, seeing with horror the bare skin of his hands on the control column shrivelling like burnt parchment in the blast-furnace of heat. Struggling, he screamed and screamed again. Somehow – he would never know how – he extricated himself from the cockpit, and began falling like a stone, powerless to stop.

23. Hurricanes were rugged. Tail damage from a Messerschmitt's heavy cannons did not prevent this Hurricane from returning to base safely.

24. (*Over the page*) '*Achtung Schpitfeuer!*' – an attacking Spitfire viewed through a Heinkel He 111's nose cupola as the fighter jinked its way through the German formation.

3. Eagle Day

August 13

At dawn on Tuesday, August 13, Oberst Johannes Fink was as puzzled as any conscientious commander could be. At first, as eighty-four bomb-laden Dorniers gained height over airfields ringing Arras, everything had seemed set fair for the long-awaited Eagle Day. All reports suggested the previous day's softening-up attacks by Rubensdörffer's Test Group 210 had gone according to plan. Yet Fink was both puzzled and angry. Over Cap Blanc Nez, a cold, marrow-damp bank of cloud was rolling in over the Channel – something the weathermen had never predicted. Worse, there was no sign at all of the fighter escort.

Suddenly the Me 110 of the fighter group commander, the wooden-legged Oberstleutnant Joachim Huth, loomed dead ahead of them. For a second Fink wondered whether Huth had taken leave of his senses – for the Messerschmitt, instead of setting course for England, swept clean past the Dornier's nose in a series of jinking dives, then curved steeply away towards the ground.

Outraged, Fink couldn't make head or tail of it. Why choose such a dangerous and unconventional way of letting him know that the raid was on? Then, abruptly, he shrugged it off. The cloud was now so dense the fighters had vanished completely, but Huth's weird aerobatics at least proved they had kept the rendezvous. Now, as leader of the attack and navigator of his own plane, Fink set course for Eastchurch airfield, Kent, the first of many Eagle Day targets.

At 5.30 am on August 13, Johannes Fink had no way of knowing that through a freakish chain of mishaps only three units were, in fact, launching Eagle Day. Early forecasts routed to Göring's headquarters, OKL, revealed that overnight the weather had changed; across the English Channel, at any height between two and four thousand feet, the cloud had thickened to ten-tenths. Accordingly, Göring had postponed the strikes until 2 pm.

Incredibly, this message had reached only the fighters – and since no radio link existed between fighters and bombers, Oberstleutnant

Huth's antics had been a last vain attempt to tell Fink that Eagle Day was *off*. Nor did Fink even realize the long-range radio in his plane wasn't functioning; the frantic *Angriff beschranken* (Attack cancelled) sent out by Kesselring's headquarters went unheeded. Only one radioman, on the plane flown by Major Paul Weitkus, 2nd Wing leader, picked it up, and again the unit's luck was out. Muzzy with 'flu and a high temperature, the Radio Op logged the message as 'A.A.' – *Angriff ausfuhren*, or Carry on.

Innocent of all fighter cover, Fink's *Kampfgeschwader* (Bomber Unit) 2 droned on through fleecy cloud towards east Kent. Peering to right and left, Fink kept a wary eye open for stragglers. In weather like this, his prime concern was always for the inexperienced few who might lose contact – what he called his 'straying sheep'. Suddenly all anxiety left him; he couldn't believe his luck. Abruptly, the clouds had parted, and there, 10,000 feet below and three miles ahead, lay Eastchurch airfield, planes lined up in neat rows, wing-tip to wing-tip, almost inviting a bombing raid. As one, eighty-four bomb-aimers, prone on their stomachs, began setting the five complex readings of the bomb sight. Oberleutnant Karl Kessel, of the 1st Wing, was only one of many to warn his crew: 'In three minutes, down go the bombs.' To achieve the maximum effect from carpet bombing, Fink insisted every bomb-aimer must pinpoint his own target.

Thanks to the vagaries of the weather, the airfield was still unalerted. Though the radar stations had charted Fink's progress, his destination was still in doubt – and the low-lying cloud had so far given local Observer Corps posts no chance of a visual check. At 6.57 am, Bromley's Observer Corps Controller Brian Binyon had asked Fighter Command's liaison officer: 'Have we a large number of aircraft near Rochford?'. The answer was prompt and disconcerting: 'No.' But within minutes, at 7.02 am, Controller Binyon had brought them up to date: 'Raid 45 is bombing Eastchurch drome.'

On the airfield, men could scarcely take it in. The station commander, Group Captain Frank Hopps, awoke in bed to the telephone's strident jangle, to find HQ 16 Group, Coastal Command on the line: 'We think there may be some bandits bound for you.' Barely had Hopps pulled on his flying boots and dived for a slit trench outside than from 9,000 feet the bombs came screaming down. As plaster dust seethed like fog across the airfield, Hopps could only think

51

25. Jagdgeschwader (JG)26 crews take breakfast under the improvised camouflage netting of a dispersal 'hut'.

despairingly: my God, the station's worth millions – some accountant's got a job to do writing off this lot.

As the aerodrome quaked with the force of the bombing, instinct drove men to strange feats of self-preservation. Pilot Officer Robbie Roach and five others scrabbled like climbing-boys up the enormous chimney of the mess ante-room; they emerged caked in greasy soot to find all the water mains severed. Sergeant David Cox, a seconded Spitfire pilot, was hustled bodily into a urinal by an elderly flight sergeant, who warned him, 'Son, this is no time to be squeamish.' With that, both men hit the deck face down. Minutes later, Cox staggered out to fall almost headlong over the bloody remains of an airman on the concrete path outside. As he recoiled, his stomach heaving, a senior officer contemptuously turned the body over with his boot: 'Haven't you ever seen a dead man before?'

26. The colourful leader of JG26 was Adolf Galland (in white jacket), one of the many outstanding Luftwaffe fighter pilots of the war.

In a bungalow on the airfield's perimeter, Mrs Eva Seabright, an Army wife newly-arrived to join her husband, complained tearfully above the bombardment: 'I haven't even unpacked yet – and you said this was a quiet area.' Concern for her safety drove all thoughts of tact from Private Reg Seabright's mind: 'It was, ducks, until you came here.' No one had yet grasped that quiet areas were a thing of the past: from this moment on, civilians were in the front-line too.

But Oberst Fink's advantage was fleeting; within minutes of the raid passing, *Kampfgeschwader* 2 was itself in trouble. The sun had earlier troubled Oberleutnant Heinz Schlegel and the pilots of the rearmost formation but it now proved a godsend to the pilots of Squadron Leader John Thompson's 111 Squadron. From high in the sky, Thompson saw ten of Fink's Dorniers, lacking all fighter cover, speeding for the mouth of the Thames Estuary and the open sea. At

27. Fighting pair – the smallest tactical 'formation' used by the Luftwaffe's Bf 109 units was a pair, the senior pilot having a No. 2 or wing-man to protect his tail while he concentrated on attacking. After the Battle the RAF adopted several Luftwaffe tactical ploys for air fighting.

once, his Hurricanes were diving in an all-out, head-on attack; ten more Dorniers, coming up from astern, ran into the same wall of fire. Under the scything shower of tracer, engine cowlings exploded like shrapnel; the bombers which hadn't found their target now jettisoned their load to gain height and speed. The rout was over within minutes. By 7.40 am, claiming five of Fink's Dorniers, 111 Squadron were breakfasting at Croydon airport, feeling that the day had begun well.

To Oberst Johannes Fink it seemed, by contrast, that the High Command had wantonly sacrificed his crews' lives; as the returning raiders touched down in the fields circling Arras, he was so shaken by anger he could scarcely speak. All along he had striven to minimize the risks for his men, yet now, only six days after Generalfeld-marschall Albert Kesselring's ebullient pep-talk on the coast, criminal negligence had cost him five crews, twenty experienced men – dead or taken prisoner, he couldn't know. Hastening to a phone, he demanded a priority link-up with Kesselring's Cap Blanc Nez H.Q..

As Kesselring came on the line, Fink forgot he was talking to a field-marshal; anger and grief for those who had gone swept all discretion aside. He kept shouting: 'Where the hell were those damned fighters, then? Just tell me that.' Patiently, Kesselring sought to mollify him, explaining the details of the last-minute cancellation, and Fink grew angrier still: 'Well I don't understand this any more than the other thing – a major attack can just be cancelled then, can it, at one moment's notice? Has anybody down there ever taken the trouble to estimate how long it takes my *Kampfgeschwader* to get across?' An aching silence followed, then Kesselring said: 'Well, let's leave it for now. I'll come over and see you.'

Kesselring was as good as his word, but as Fink listened in silence to his chief's halting apologies, it was plain that Eagle Day had started badly. The sudden thick cloud, the amazing speed of the radar stations in setting up standbys, the Luftwaffe's inexperience of promoting large-scale coordinated aerial missions, these factors had cost the High Command all too many men.

It wasn't only Kesselring and Fink who were dismayed: in many places on this day, German pilots abruptly found their worlds turned upside down. Oberleutnant Heinz Schlegel, of Fink's rearguard formation, had seen Eastchurch looming ahead but hadn't dropped a single bomb; the Spitfires of 74 Squadron had swooped from the sun too swiftly. There was a rending clatter, and the starboard engine spluttered and died; the Dornier was yawing violently to the left. A

28. Bf 109E of Galland's JG26 '*Schlageter*' forced down during the height of the August battles.

29. Another August 13 victim – a Dornier – which ended in a Kent hedgerow.

30. 'Vic' of three Spitfires from 610 Sqn, AAF, patrolling from their base at Biggin Hill.

hot, yellow light flashed before Schlegel's eys, and now the port engine was in trouble too. Breaking for cloud cover, Schlegel fought to keep the Dornier airborne, steering what he hoped was due south. Then the clouds parted and his spirits rose exultantly, only to sink again as quickly; land loomed beneath them but it wasn't familiar terrain. Cautiously, Oberleutnant Gerhardt Oszwald, the navigator, voiced what all of them felt: 'I don't think *this* is France. Shall we make it?' Schlegel realized they wouldn't so, grimly, he set the Dornier careening for the flat English pastures, seeing too late that the one unobstructed field for which he had aimed was scored by a deep trench. Swaying from side to side like a truck out of control, the bomber ripped like a juggernaut across the meadowland, then, with a sickening half-swing, wrapping its starboard wing round a tree, smashed to a halt.

To the crew's astonishment, they barely had time to crawl from the plane before ten British soldiers came storming through the grass to disarm them, whooping like Comanches on the warpath. Bewildered, Schlegel was taken to an outpost of the London Scottish Regiment, near Barham, Kent, and confined in a small office adjoining the unit canteen. At a counter, a long line of men was queueing unhurriedly to buy regimental cap-badges and tartan stocking tabs; from somewhere he heard the far keening of bagpipes. Still dazed from the shock of the forced landing, Schlegel puzzled: If England's due to be conquered in three days, how can they take time off for this?

By noon on August 13, it was plain that Eagle Day had totally gone awry. To the west, the 54th Bomber Group, slated for a second sortie, against the naval base at Portland, got word that the main strike was delayed and didn't fly – but their fighter escort, the vulnerable Me 110s of Zerstörer Group 2, had no such message. Forging on for Portland, vainly seeking the bombers, they lost five planes in as many minutes – among them Unteroffizier Kurt Schumacher, who was harried to the end by three Spitfires.

To Schumacher's chagrin, the odds and the sudden shock of failure proved all too much for his gunner, young Obergefreiter Otto Giglhuber; hunched over his machine-gun, the boy could only weep brokenly. All at once there was a sound as if a giant paper sack had been blown up and burst behind their ears. The Me 110 shook all over, and there was a noise like hail striking a tin roof. Sick at heart, Schumacher ordered: 'Bale out.'

From the clifftops, above the shining waters of Kimmeridge Bay,

Dorset, scores of people had a grandstand view. It was just past noon when Mrs Ivy Marshall, a lobster fisherman's wife, saw the crippled Messerschmitt pass overhead 'like a black bird shedding feathers'. As it dropped from sight, plunging out of control towards Swalland Farm, close by, twin parachutes flowered like giant chrysanthemums over the water. As Kurt Schumacher drifted towards the water, he was surprised and relieved to see a motor boat puttering its way towards him. Mrs Marshall's husband, Anthony, tending his lobster pots on Portland Roads, a mile and a half from the shore, had watched the descent, too; at once he veered his boat, *The Miss Ivy,* in the Germans' direction.

The rescue was so unexpected and the day had gone so badly that Schumacher, whose English was fluent, felt the aching need to talk. As they curved to come alongside the gunner, he told Marshall: 'He was too young, you know – just a frightened boy.' Dripping and gasping, Giglhuber was hauled aboard. From his seat in the bows, Schumacher could see the shelving cliffs of Goulter's Gap, where the Marshalls' cottage lay, the cliff paths alive with scrambling troops and farm-workers. Eagle Day was five hours old, but for him the war was over. Looking at Giglhuber he said again, with no tinge of emotion: 'He was too young – too young.'

In one way, Kurt Schumacher was supremely lucky. Day by day, as the air battle mounted, the English Channel, its tides sometimes reaching a rate of seven knots, would claim victim after victim. Within days of Schumacher's rescue, Air Chief Marshal Dowding, pressed for accurate figures by Winston Churchill, reported the worst: 60 per cent of all air fatalities were taking place over the sea.

Despite soaring casualties – 220 killed or missing over the sea in three July weeks – the Air Ministry had provided only eighteen high-speed rescue launches to cover the entire British coastline, just two craft more than the 1936 establishment. Pilots like Flying Officer Guy Branch, 145 Squadron, drowned literally within sight of the Dorset shore; the only rescue craft on hand, the Poole lifeboat, just hadn't the turn of speed to reach him. At Warmwell airfield, nearby, Squadron Leader Peter Devitt's 152 Squadron counted every casualty except one in terms of death by drowning.

As he lay in a cool white room at Margate General Hospital, the fear of death by drowning still lingered in the mind of Pilot Officer Geoffrey Page. Twenty-four hours earlier, as he saw the dark rushing

33. The Operations Control Room at HQ, RAF Fighter Command, Bentley Priory, 1940.

34. Veterans. Spitfire pilots of 41 Sqn, commanded briefly by Sqn Ldr D. O. Finlay, DFC (centre), the pre-war Olympic hurdler. Second from left, standing is Norman Ryder; while second from right is E. P. 'Hawkeye' Wells; two stalwart squadron members throughout the Battle.

shape of the Hurricane vanish from beneath his legs, his chances of rescue seemed one in a million. The cool and blessed air had struck his livid face and, as the crazy kaleidoscope of sky and sea tumbled before him his brain had commanded: *Pull – pull the ripcord* – but each time the mutilated fingers touched the chromium ring, they jerked from the agony of contact.

Pain lanced from his fingers, but then his shoulders jerked violently as with a snapping crack the silk canopy opened. Now, swaying soberly at eleven miles an hour, the sensitive Page's nostrils wrinkled fastidiously – it was the smell of his own burnt flesh. With everything he knew, he fought back the desire to vomit. In the same instant Page felt another fear rack him. If he didn't get rid of his parachute within seconds, it would entrap him beneath the water, as surely as the tentacles of an octopus. But Page discovered that, try as he might, his blackened, blistered fingers just weren't equal to it. Still struggling, he hit the water feet first. Kicking out madly he came to the surface, arms fearsomely entwined in the parachute's wrapping shrouds.

Then Geoffrey Page battled literally for his life. Flesh was flaking from his fingers, blood poured from the raw tissues, but still, spewing mouthfuls of salt water, he fought on. If he didn't master the disc the water-logged chute would tug him inexorably towards the sea-bed. Suddenly, with a jerk, he felt the disc give; he was free. Sobbing with relief, he thrashed blindly away from that nightmare patch of water. Then he saw that fire had scorched a gaping hole through the rubber bladder of his 'Mae West' life jacket.

Now Page made a desperate decision: if air-sea rescue was non-existent, he could only keep swimming for the shore until his strength gave out. It was a brave resolution – brave because every measured stroke sent pain coursing like liquid fire through his body. The salt was fast drying on the weeping tissue of his face; the strap of his flying helmet, contracting too, cut like a thong into his chin. Flames had welded buckle and leather into one solid mass; he couldn't even wrench it off.

Then, close to his last gasp, he remembered the brandy – a slim silver flask, a present from his mother, conserved in his tunic's breast pocket. Again, as his fingers inched beneath the useless Mae West, he suffered the tortures of the damned, holding his breath to bursting-point to withstand each wave of pain, legs still paddling feebly. At last, when he found the flask, his fingers could take no more; gingerly, using his wrists as a clamp, he brought it to the water's surface.

Grasping the screw-stopper between his teeth, head tugging backwards, he felt it give, the hot tang of the spirit tormenting his nostrils.

Suddenly the flask slipped between his wet wrists, vanishing for ever beneath the water. And then Page wept, as uncontrollably as a child; he knew that everything was against him now; he didn't stand a chance. He was cold and exhausted, the flesh so swollen about his eyes he could no longer see the sun to steer by. When the black smoke-trail from a friendly merchant ship hove into view, Geoffrey Page had resigned himself to die.

All that followed seemed unreal, like a half-remembered dream. There'd been the merchant ship's motor launch, circling cautiously and asking if he was German. Dimly he recalled they had stripped off his sodden clothing, swaddling him in blankets; the skipper had fashioned fingerless gloves for his ravaged hands with large squares of pink lint. Then the Margate lifeboat had taken charge and, recumbent on the stretcher, Page had remembered an ambulance waiting at the quayside. Now, like any youngster on the threshold of life, Page was beset by one anxiety: what had the fire done to his face? Why wouldn't they tell him? Were they afraid? Was he so marked that all his life he'd be set apart from other men? Twice he'd asked to see a mirror, as casually, he hoped, as possible – and twice the doctors had hastily switched to other topics.

Geoffrey Page could hardly know it, but by noon on Eagle Day the eyes of the world were on this stretch of coastline. The broad sweep of Dover's Shakespeare Cliff, with its fluttering clouds of white chalk butterflies, was now an amphitheatre packed with newsmen, squatting amid ripening red-currant bushes, eyes straining upwards. Beyond the barrage balloons, tethered like flocks of grazing sheep, the newsmen saw thin streamers of smoke staining the sky, moving in deadly concert with the whirling, snarling ballet of planes.

At Detling airfield in Kent, shrieking from thick cloud cover soon after 4 pm, the Stukas had achieved the measure of surprise they needed: many airmen were taking tea in the canteen as the first bombs came tumbling down, wrecking every runway, firing the hangars and destroying twenty aircraft on the ground. As the Ops Room vanished in one nightmare detonation, the CO, Group Captain Edward Davis, a former Wimbledon tennis champion, fell dead, a dagger of concrete driving clean through his skull. Casualty Clearing Officer Wallace Beale, a Maidstone undertaker, sped to the shattered

aerodrome to find a death toll topping fifty – though many needed only the five-foot coffins reserved for unidentified remains.

But over Portland, with height in their favour, seventy Hurricanes and Spitfires came peeling from the sun – into a battle so frenzied that Pilot Officer Red Tobin, chafing back at Warmwell airfield, heard the details of the combat with something akin to despair. Until Red, Andy Mamedoff and Shorty Keough had mastered every technicality of the Spitfire, Squadron Leader Horace Darley, commanding 609 Squadron, was confining them to routine ferrying jobs – yet now, it seemed, they had missed out on one of the squadron's bloodiest actions.

As thirteen Spitfires touched down at Warmwell, it was plain that each man had seen hard fighting. On the wings of every plane, long black streaks showed where the fabric covering the gun ports had been blasted away by the first shots of the battle. Glumly the three Americans heard the lucky combatants excitedly gabbling out their

35. 'I gave him a two-second burst and his starboard engine blew up . . .' A Heinkel He 111 'buys it'.

66

6. Some got back – a
Heinkel crew survey the
damage from fighter
attacks after
belly-landing in France.

story: in thirteen minutes thirteen Spitfires had accounted for thirteen Stukas.

In fact, the Germans had lost only five Stukas, but in the flaring heat of combat such exaggerations were invariable. Flushed with victory, Flight Lieutenant David Crook announced excitedly that never again would he distrust number thirteen. Flying Officer Ostazewski, a Polish ace, had actually seen the cockpit door of a 109 hurtle into space like a giant tea-tray as the pilot baled out. Flying Officer Harry Goodwin, so carried away that he had forgotten he was out of ammunition, had chased a fighter thirty miles to Yeovil in Somerset – only to find it was a British Blenheim. Red Tobin and his friends exchanged rueful glances: maybe, some day, somebody would realize they had come to England seeking some action, too.

To the Stuka crews in the sky above the Kentish cliffs, air supremacy seemed as far away as the mountains of the moon. Dry-mouthed with horror, Major Paul Hozzel saw planes transformed into fantastic fiery rockets as they blew up with their bombs still on board. Breaking for base, he loosed his own bombs on any coastal target he could see, then skimmed back across the water of Dinard. As angry as Oberst Johannes Fink had been that morning, Major Walter Enneccerus, another wing commander, got back, too, to lay it on the line to the top brass: 'They ripped our backs open right up to the collar.'

And the men who had flown with him saw his anger as fully justified. Many planes in the fighter escort had been unwieldy Me 110s – Göring's beloved Zerstörer – and most had been too caught up in a free-for-all with three Spitfire squadrons to offer protection to the Stukas. Those 110s that got back did so by a hair's-breadth – Oberstleutnant Friedrich Vollbracht curving away so fast that the thrust of G blacked out his gunner; Oberleutnant Schafer calling in mounting agitation to a gunner so riddled with bullets he would never hear again. Feldwebel Johannes Lutter still recalls: 'If you survived three trips like that one, you were lucky.'

As the last skirmishes of Eagle Day drew to a close, one of the most formidable adversaries the British would ever know was over Dover with his wing, flying as escort to German rescue planes, and mentally giving the British their due. To Major Adolf Galland, one thing was plain: if this day's combat was any guide, no easy task lay ahead for his unit, the 26th Fighting Group's 3rd Wing. What he had seen only confirmed his opinion of the British ever since those first Channel battles of July. These men who would fight on with their engines smoking, often when their planes were too near the earth to risk baling out, won his unbounded admiration. Their courage and discipline were equal to anything he had ever seen.

And Adolf Galland, for the most part, was a man grudging with praise; a tall, moody twenty-eight-year-old, whose swarthy good looks bespoke his Huguenot descent, he'd seen action enough to justify his own high standards. As a veteran of 280 missions in the Spanish Civil War Galland had gone on to fly eighty-seven missions in Poland – and only three times had he seen the Polish fighters up. Twelve days earlier, on August 1, after seventeen confirmed victories, Galland's status as an ace had been confirmed, as Generalfeldmarschall Albert Kesselring pinned the coveted Knight's Cross to his breast at Cap Gris Nez.

The knowledge that he was something of a legend in the Luftwaffe did not displease Galland. Beyond a point, few men could probe his restless, complex mind – yet everything about the man somehow set

37. Return from combat. Plt Off A. G. Lewis, DFC, of 85 Sqn climbs out of his Hurricane. A South African by birth, Lewis survived the war with at least twenty-one victories and settled in England.

him apart. To the fury of the ascetic Hitler, Galland not only smoked twenty black Brazilian cigars a day; he had coolly installed a special ashtray and lighter in the cockpit of his Me 109. Up to 9,000 feet, when the oxygen mask went on, he could puff contentedly away.

A ruthless logician, Galland had seen one factor as plain: the Luftwaffe's recent attempts to attain air supremacy as a tactical fighter-force simply could not succeed. To set the fighter pilots a task beyond their strength could do nothing but discourage them. But as his plane winged its way towards Caffiers airfield at Calais, Galland saw fresh hope: the bomber attacks that were now building up could prove to be the answer they had sought. Now, at long last, the RAF would be forced to leave their airfields – and come up and fight to the last man.

4. 'So Much

Owed by So Many to So Few'

August 14–15

Pacing his office at 10 am on Tuesday, August 14, thumbs, as always, hooked in his tunic belt, Air Chief Marshal Dowding's normally pallid cheeks were flushed with excitement. To Lieutenant-General Sir Frederick Pile, Chief of Anti-Aircraft Command, who set this hour apart each morning to hear his old friend's troubles, the architect of Fighter Command was more animated than he'd ever known him. Now steering a waste-paper-basket with his foot, to simulate a German bomber formation, next swooping on it with his folded spectacles to demonstrate the fighter attacks of Eagle Day, Dowding burst out: 'Pile, it's a miracle.'

And for the RAF, Eagle Day had indeed proved a miracle. Though Fighter Command's initial claim – sixty-nine German planes shot down – was swiftly scaled down to thirty-four, the RAF had lost only thirteen Hurricanes and Spitfires, losses easily made good. Both Detling and Eastchurch had paid a heavy price – but these were bases of Coastal Command, whose prime function was look-out patrols against German naval raiders. The main aim of the Eagle Attacks was to vanquish Fighter Command – yet time and again German bomber units had been sent to blitz the wrong bases. Hence Dowding's jubilation, for if no worse attacks than these developed, the RAF had little to fear.

Only one factor nagged Fighter Command's chief: how would his pilots stand up to still harder pounding? But on August 14, at least, it seemed that the front would stay quiet: at 2,000 feet, cotton-wool clouds still blanketed the English Channel. Those Germans who attempted a sortie would have all their work cut out.

It was true – yet some were determined to try it. At 4.30 that afternoon, a lone Junkers 88 dive-bomber of Oberst Alfred Bulowius' *Lehrgeschwader* (Training Unit) 1 passed high over the Hampshire coastline, heading for the Army Co-op Command base at Upavon. By chance the crew sighted instead a plum target seventeen miles east: Middle Wallop airfield, sector control station and home

74

base for two-day fighter squadrons. One was 609 Squadron, of which Pilot Officer Eugene 'Red' Tobin was still a reluctantly non-combatant officer.

At 4.45 pm on August 14, death, for the first time, seemed to lay its hand upon Red Tobin. He was within eighty yards of Hangar Five, on his way to deliver a Spitfire to Hamble, when fear charged him like an electric current. Just 1,500 feet above the hangar he saw the blue-bellied Junkers 88 dive-bomber, its twin Jumo engines bulking enormously, gliding like a giant bat. As the first stick burst from its bomb bay, Red, moving faster than he'd ever done, dived headlong for the earth.

Whoever the pilot was, he didn't lack courage; he lived a bare thirty seconds to enjoy his triumph. For the Spitfires of 609 Squadron were airborne and as Red Tobin pressed his face to the dirt, debris and broken glass showering all round him, Sergeant Alan Feary, already on base patrol, was only 350 yards behind the steeply-climbing bomber, slugging tracer home at its belly. For one moment it hung like a torch in the sky, then smashed into the ground with unimaginable violence several miles away.

Shakily, his head ringing with concussion, Red Tobin clambered to his feet; his flying overalls, even his dark-red hair, were as white with dust as a miller's smock. Then he was pelting for Hangar Five with all the strength his legs could muster. The hangar entrance was like a charnel house, one airman's foot had been blown off, another's arm had been torn off at the shoulder, and three lay dead beneath the thirteen-ton steel hangar door they had been struggling to close when the bomb fell. Sickened to his stomach, Red Tobin thought, this is war at its worst – then, for the first time, the implacable calm of the British came home to him. There wasn't a trace of panic, scarcely a man in sight was even running; in the Ops Room, a democratic flight sergeant, picking himself from the floor, was just then remarking to the CO, Wing Commander David Roberts: 'This is where we're all on the same level, sir.' Limping back to dispersal, Red Tobin reminded himself that in Britain stiff upper lips were mandatory.

At Manston airfield, two squadrons of Hauptmann Walter Rubensdörffer's Test Group 210 had met with the same unexpected tenacity. As Oberleutnant Wilhelm Roessiger dived with his sixteen Me 110s in the second all-out attack launched on Manston, a withering curtain of fire from the site named Charlie Three came rising to meet them. Crouched on an improvised fire-step of trestles, Pilot

0. Much was expected
f the Junkers Ju87
Stuka', but their sorties
against southern
England proved
disastrous, with a heavy
oll of casualties.

1. (*Bottom left*) The
slightly improved Bf
09E-4b version, with
ate-style cockpit
canopy, which entered
rst-line service in July
940.

2. (*Below*) 'Off-duty' –
Spitfire pilots of 66
Squadron relax in their
Mess. Normal
peace-time Mess dress
regulations were
necessarily ignored on
front-line operational
tations.

Officer Henry Jacobs was one of six squadron air-gunners who were
out to show the Germans; as Roessiger's 110s shrank to slim pencils
in their sights, fire from their dismantled Brownings went hammering
up the sloping roof of 600 Squadron's crew room. At 600 feet, a
Bofors forty-millimetre shell blasted Unteroffizier Hans Steding's
tailplane clean away; its engines screaming in an uncontrolled dive,
the plane cartwheeled across the aerodrome, smashing into the
ground upside down.

As it struck, astonished onlookers realized that Steding's gunner,
Gefreiter Ewald Schank, had baled out at 500 feet, barely 100 feet
above the lowest safety height, for now his chute was dragging him
across the concrete outside 600 Squadron's hangar. Miraculously,
Schank was still alive; peeping from the sand-bagged slit trenches,
men of 600 Squadron saw him staggering in crazy circles, one hand
clapped to his head, while bombs from his own unit's planes tore the
ground about him like shellfire. Without hesitation, Flight Lieutenant

Charles Pritchard sprinted from the trench to his rescue, dragging him, shocked and bleeding, to safety.

But though Pritchard and the others tried gently to question him, it was useless. Half-delirious, the wounded gunner had only scant English: 'The big lick', he muttered, over and over like an incantation, 'very soon, the big lick'. The implication of the phrase seemed plain enough – but just how long before 'the big lick' came?

At mid-morning on Thursday, August 15, Oberst Paul Deichmann could scarcely believe his eyes. No major sorties against England were scheduled on this day – that much he knew. Angered by the reverses of August 13, Göring had summoned every top commander – Kesselring, Sperrle, even Deichmann's own chief, General Bruno Lörzer, the head of No. 2 Flying Corps – to justify their failures to him at Karinhall. It had seemed as good a day as any – again the weathermen had forecast only impenetrable cloud.

Yet now, staring from the rat-haunted farmhouse at Bonnigues, near Calais, which was 2nd Flying Corps HQ, Deichmann, the Chief of Staff, saw only blue sky and brilliant sunshine. The wind was zephyr-calm, directed west-north-west at little more than two miles

an hour and cloud was negligible, a scattered front around 3,000 feet. It was perfect weather for what Gunner Schank had styled 'the big lick'.

The abortive Eagle Day sorties had in fact been part of a complex blueprint, applicable for any time the weather held good – and on airfields all down the coast, Deichmann knew, more than 1,000 fighters and 800 bombers of the 2nd Flying Corps, which was scheduled to lead the attacks, were already fuelled up, alert for take-off once the signal was given. 'Well,' Deichmann recalls thinking, 'here we go'.

Reaching for the phone, Deichmann gave crisp orders. A dozen Stukas under Hauptmann von Brauchitsch, airborne from Tramecourt, were to form the spearhead of the attack, bound for Hawkinge; two dozen more under Hauptmann Keil, loaded with 500-kilo and 250-kilo bombs, would head for Lympne. Twenty-five Dorniers of Oberst Chamier-Glisczinski's 3rd Bomber Group should work over Eastchurch yet again. Another wing of the same group, over Rochester airfield, were to use both delayed-action and incendiaries, while Rubensdörffer's Test Group 210 were to try their skill against Martlesham Heath, on the Suffolk coast. In no time at all the planes roared overhead, wave after glinting wave; black, hump-winged Stukas, silver shark-nosed 109s. The sky was suddenly a sounding-board, giving back the thunder of their engines, and from their side of the Channel the Germans could see the tiny specks of bombs falling over Hawkinge airfield, the black smudges of ack-ack.

43. 'Scramble!' A Vic of three 66 Squadron Spitfires get away.

Robert Bailey, twenty-seven miles away, was among the winter oats at Densole Farm, Hawkinge, two miles south of his own farm, Ladwood. Months earlier, Bailey had managed to buy a second-hand self-binder, and since then requests from neighbours for a helping hand had flooded in from all over the district – requests that it just wasn't in Bailey to refuse. Bailey prized nothing in war more dearly than this heightened camaraderie, with neighbour gladly helping neighbour as the need arose.

This morning was no exception: Bailey and his tractor driver, Earl Knight, weren't the only two who'd come to help Harry Greenstreet, Densole Farm's owner, with his winter oats. Old Walt Fagg and Sid Wood were there, too – old-time tenant farmers of the kind who still used binder twine to hitch up their corduroys. Suddenly, from above in the sun, they heard a strange sharp-edged whining, followed by the

79

snarl of engines – and with no more warning the Stukas of Hauptmann von Brauchitsch's 4th Wing *Lehrgeschwader* 1 fell like falcons
from the sky.

The quiet, sunlit farms were suddenly a devil's chorus of sound –
the metallic panging of the airfield's Bofors guns, the high-pitched
scream of the diving Stukas, the pandemonium of exploding hangars
as the bombers made their mark. The farmers felt nakedly exposed,
marooned in the centre of the eight-acre field; as one they began
running, pell-mell, for the shelter of a distant elm grove. It was now
that Robert Bailey, bringing up the rear, became conscious of a
pulsating sense of excitement. He was under fire, and never before
having sought any greater stimulus than the changing seasons of the
year, he suspected he was secretly enjoying it.

Abruptly he was choking with laughter, because old Walt Fagg,
bent on warding off stray bullets, was running altogether blind, his
jacket sheathing his head. Somehow, by sheer instinct, the old man
found the five-barred gate at the far end of the field – then, a
countryman to the last, still navigating blind, he swung and slammed
the gate shut. It was one move Bailey wasn't expecting; with bone-
jarring force he cannoned head-on into it.

All unknowing, the farmers had just witnessed the first bombs of
Eagle Day proper. The time was 11.35 am, Thursday, August 15.
Between now and 8 pm, approximately 2,119 German planes of all
types would be unleashed in a pile-driving effort to bring the RAF
fighters into the air and smash Fighter Command once and for all.
Oberst Paul Deichmann's plans were to succeed beyond his wildest
dreams for, in the next crucial hours, fully twenty-six squadrons –
almost 300 fighters of Dowding's force – would be airborne to face
the worst the Luftwaffe could do.

Although Göring's plan committed less than half the Luftwaffe's
total bomber force to the battle, the targets allotted to them ranged
over 125 miles of the south coast of England alone. Kesselring's Air
Fleet Two, striking once more across the Straits of Dover, was
heading for the Short Brothers' aircraft factory at Rochester, Kent,
then again to the radar stations of Dover and Rye, while to the west
the units of Sperrle's Air Fleet Three were to launch feint attacks to
bring up the fighters over Portland naval base, the airfields of Odiham
and Middle Wallop.

One formation was doomed from the start: the sixty-three Heinkels of Oberstleutnant Fuchs' 26th Bomber Group, called 'The Lion

Geschwader', just then winging its way towards Newcastle-on-Tyne, 274 miles north. Their sole escort was twenty-one Me 110s of the 1st Wing, 76th Zerstörer Group, led by Hauptmann Werner Restemeyer. Pitifully vulnerable as they were, the 110 was the sole fighter with the range to do the job. In a daring attempt at a flank attack, only recently sanctioned, the Heinkels, part of Generaloberst Hans-Jürgen Stumpff's Air Fleet Five, flew over 400 miles from Stavanger, Norway – confident that Dowding's fighter squadrons in the south would be too tied up to oppose a northern thrust.

It was a vain hope. Already in Fighter Command's Filter Room, Dowding, steel-helmeted, was watching absorbed; forty minutes distant from the coastline, the radar stations had picked up tracks of a sortie approaching northern England. Unerringly the WAAF plotters showed the raid building up, the long-handled magnetic plotting rods indicating the track, the news passing to the Sector Ops Room at No. 13 Group at Newcastle-on-Tyne, to 12 Group at Watnall, near Nottingham. More to himself than aloud, the C-in-C's aide-de-camp, Pilot Officer Robert Wright, murmured, 'My God, they're plotting well' – and was startled when Dowding rejoined quietly, 'But they always do.'

Dowding now knew a moment of quiet triumph. His determina-

14. Captured Luftwaffe crews, heavily escorted, arrive at Waterloo Station during the battle; for them the war was over . . .

tion, despite all pressures, not to strip northern England of fighter squadrons was vindicated this morning. Thanks to him, at least nine squadrons would be ready to intercept – among them the Hurricanes of 605 Squadron, milling expectantly over the Tyne River. Fifteen miles north of them, from Acklington airfield, near Morpeth, the Spitfires of No. 72 Squadron were already airborne and closing in – forty miles out to sea off the Northumberland coast and 25,000 feet above the rocky blur of the Farne Islands.

What followed was stark slaughter. As fighter-leader, Werner Restemeyer had planned that his Me 110 should function as a kind of flying Ops Room from which he directed the battle – but barely had he seen the Spitfires, 4,000 feet above, than his radio-telephone crackled into chaos: 'Red Indians on the left', 'Red Indians from the sun' – a score of fighter pilots yelling the Luftwaffe's code-alert for British planes. Simultaneously, in 72 Squadron's formation, someone hailed Flight Lieutenant Ted Graham, the leader, 'Have you seen them?' and Graham, who stuttered badly, replied: 'Of course I've seen the b-b-b-b-astards – I'm t-t-t-rying to w-w-w-ork out what-to-d-do.'

But already the attack was on. As Graham hurtled in on the starboard flank, reefing through the gap between bombers and fighters, every man picked his own target. Awed, Pilot Officer Robert Deacon-Elliott saw the mass formation split, and the Heinkels were jettisoning their loads: the grey swell of the North Sea churned white with bombs, as if a colony of whales were spouting. Before he could even coordinate the defences, Restemeyer was dead; a soft, yellow gasp of flame and his Messerschmitt was lost to view.

At the tail-end of the fighters, Unteroffizier Karl Richter, out cold with a glancing head-wound, swooned forward over the control column; his 110 spun without check towards the sea. In the nick of time, Richter came groggily to; half-blinded by blood he still fought his plane back across the North Sea for a crash-landing at Esbjerg, Norway. Oberfeldwebel Lothar Linke made it, too, limping back to Jever, North Germany, with only the power of the port engine. Others, like Oberleutnant Gordon Gollob, fought like furies and somehow made it to base – at a fearsome cost of six fighters, eight bombers.

This one ill-planned sortie cost Air Fleet Five twenty of the 154 planes available. From this moment on, it was out of the day-fighting altogether – and the battle had barely started.

Three hundred miles south, between Dover and Southampton, it seemed to most observers that the battle had never stopped – the whole day was given over to the fearful martial music of the bombardment. To widowed Mrs Joanna Thompson, crouched inside her garden shelter with her small son, Roger, the sky seemed to rain blazing planes, parachutes, even flying boots; shrapnel was crashing and bouncing like thunderbolts on the shelter's tin roof. At St Mary Cray, near Biggin Hill airfield, Mrs Mary Simcox darted for her mother's shelter nearby, a dustbin lid serving as a steel helmet – but even underground, with three thick topcoats wound round her head, she couldn't shut out the noise.

The noise troubled others in the strangest ways. At Abbotsbury, Dorset, swanherd Fred Lexster, who had worked at the unique 1,200-strong swannery for twenty-five years, was perplexed and disturbed: the cacophony so outraged his birds they refused to hatch their eggs. Flight Lieutenant Geoffrey Hovenden, Hawkinge airfield medical officer, was puzzled, too – by an entire sick parade of station defence troops troubled by wax in their ears. With an auriscope, Hovenden corrected their diagnosis: the non-stop percussion of their pom-pom guns had blocked their ears with blood clots, rendering them temporarily stone deaf. To the *Daily Express*'s Hilde Marchant, watching from Dover's Shakespeare Cliff, the thundering phalanxes of planes seemed 'to make an aluminium ceiling to the sky'.

It was a heart-stopping sight – yet everywhere along the southern coast hundreds who had never been under fire resolutely summoned up their courage, almost as if conscious it was now the fashionable thing to be a front-liner. At Dover's Grand Hotel, one luncheon guest complained bitterly of shrapnel in his soup, but headwaiter George Garland coaxed him to rise above it, and greeted newcomers to the dining room: 'Good morning, sir! A nice table here, sir, away from the broken glass. . . .' A few miles down the coast, at Folkestone, it was the same. As Mrs Mary Castle queued outside a pastrycook's, shrapnel and machine-gun bullets spattered the pavement. At once, without more ado, two airmen queueing in the shop's doorway, ahead of her, stepped politely back, raising their forage caps, enabling her to pass inside. At Homefield, Kent, ancestral home of the wealthy Smithers family, William, the butler, did the rounds of the velvety lawn after each dog-fight, sweeping up spent machine-gun bullets as deftly as ever he had brushed crumbs from a damask tablecloth.

To Dowding's pilots, the score was still in doubt. By the early afternoon of August 15, British radar stations monitored track after confusing track over northern France. Minute by minute the numbers increased, 60-plus Ostend, 120-plus Calais, the range still constant though the heights escalated steadily . . . 8,000 feet . . . 10,000 feet . . . 18,000 feet . . . 20,000 feet. In the Receiver Block at Rye Radar Station, Corporal Daphne Griffiths heard one of the duty watch shatter the mounting tension: 'They're under starter's orders – they're off!' Rye's cathode ray tube, like every other, was indeed an amazing sight. So massive were the German formations this time that there was not even the ghost of a trace for forty miles – and as the planes broke and spread over the Channel, to plot or distinguish individual tracks was well-nigh impossible. Already eleven British fighter squadrons – 130 Spitfires and Hurricanes – were airborne, yet every Sector Controller, confused as to the ultimate target, was forced to improvise.

Unopposed, Raid 22, Rubensdörffer's top scoring Test Group 210, accepting Oberst Deichmann's challenge, swept down on Martlesham Heath airfield, loosing salvo after salvo for five long minutes. Though Rubensdörffer's subsequent report that Martlesham was 'a heap of smoking rubble' was optimistic, it took officers and men, working full pitch, one whole day to clear the debris.

On a score of airfields Air Chief Marshal Dowding's pilots were as hard-pressed as any men alive. At least 100 of them had been at their dispersal points, life-jackets already adjusted since dawn: others, more sorely tried, had been on stand-by – strapped in their cockpits, facing the wind, engines ready to turn over. Only the fortunate few had drawn available – in the mess and ready to take off within twenty minutes. Garbed in flying overalls or rolltop sweaters, with silk scarves for comfort, they had lolled on the grass or on canvas cots, the thump-thump of the petrol bowsers' delivery pumps dinning in their ears, lucky enough to breakfast off luke-warm baked beans and tepid tea.

And still, ten hours later, the pressure was stepping up: at North Weald, Essex, the pilots of 56 Squadron, starting lunch soon after noon, were scrambled so often they did not reach dessert until 3.30 pm. At Hawkinge, the station defence officer warned others clustered in the mess: 'Don't take too long over that sherry. I've only sounded the all-clear so that we can get some lunch.' For many, food, even a bed, became a luxury. At Rochford, 151 Squadron's pilots bedded down in their cockpits; the airfield's dew-soaked grass was the one

alternative. It was the same for 32 Squadron at Biggin Hill; on call since 3 am, Squadron Leader John Worrall's men had slept beneath their Hurricanes, using parachutes for pillows.

Grimly the pilots kept going, because they were the kind of men who would – freebooters who were often frightened sick, but men who lived for the moment. Men like the lean, handsome Robert Stanford Tuck, with his affected monogrammed silk handkerchiefs and long cigarette holders, who had shot down eleven planes already and could start up a Spitfire blindfolded; the explosive pipe-puffing Douglas Bader, whose tin legs, the result of a pre-war crash, were a legend even with the Luftwaffe, and Adolph 'Sailor' Malan, late Third Officer of the Union Castle Line, soon styled 'The Greatest Fighter Ace of all Time'.

Not all were aces, but the backgrounds they hailed from, the way they lived now, marked them down as different. Warrant Officer Edward Mayne, Royal Flying Corps veteran, at forty the oldest man to fly as a regular combatant in the battle, young Hugh Percy, an undergraduate from Cambridge University, who kept his log-book in Greek; New Zealander Mindy Blake, Doctor of Mathematics, who approached each combat like a quadratic equation, the Nizam of Hyderabad's former personal pilot, Derek Boitel-Gill, Randy Matheson, ex-Argentine gaucho; Johnny Bryson, a former Canadian Mountie; Squadron Leader Aeneas MacDonell, official head of the Glengarry clan; and Red Tobin from Los Angeles with the barnstormers, Andy and Shorty.

And to back the pilots at this critical hour, there were still station commanders who saw things their way – men who would turn the blindest of eyes to protocol and red tape. At Biggin Hill, Group Captain Richard Grice laid on crates of beer for all returning pilots, invited WAAFs hauled up for breaches of discipline to sit down and have a cigarette. Wing Commander Cecil Bouchier, Hornchurch's peppery CO, handed out candy as often as rebukes – and kept station morale at peak with non-stop running commentaries on the Ops Room's tannoy loudspeaker. At North Weald, Victor Beamish, a fire-eating Irishman, would leap clean through his open office window sooner than miss a scramble – and Northolt's Group Captain Stanley Vincent, World War I fighter ace, felt the same. His Station Defence Flight – one lone Hurricane – was formed to get him airborne whenever possible.

The pilots proved worthy of such backing. Outnumbered as they were on August 15, they were still suicidally valiant in their efforts. Canada's Flight Lieutenant Mark Brown, sighting Rubensdörffer's Test Group 210, twenty-four strong, returning from the attack on Martlesham, thought the east coast port of Harwich, lying below, might soon be in trouble. Single-handed, he climbed to divert them, then a 109 harassed him with fire; he had to bale out. Though Brown had drifted five miles out to sea before a trawler sighted him, Harwich was untouched.

Others were just as resolute. Over the Channel, Flight Sergeant 'Gilly' Gilbert felt a bullet fracture his radiator's coolant system; one rending explosion and his Spitfire was enveloped in clouds of blinding glycol steam. Still with 109s on his tail, Gilbert unfastened his safety straps, raised himself in the cockpit, then peering over the top of the windscreen like a fogbound motorist, steered his plane back to Hawkinge. Even in defeat, they did things in style; at the controls of a blazing Hurricane over Folkestone, New Zealand's Flying Officer John Axel Gibson saw no need for indecent hurry. Slipping off a brand-new pair of handmade shoes, he lobbed them into space; he didn't want them spoiled by seawater. Next he set course for the open sea – that way he couldn't endanger life or property. Finally, at 1,000 feet he baled out. A thoughtful civilian, retrieving his shoes later, posted them on the off-chance back to Hawkinge airfield.

Despite all such efforts, the bombers of *Kampfgeschwader* 3, forging westwards over Kent, with a strong fighter escort, reached their targets unscathed. As Hauptmann Rathmann's 3rd Wing showered Eastchurch airfield with bombs, thirty Dorniers of the 2nd Wing were over the Short Brothers' aircraft factory at Rochester, jubilantly reporting one direct hit after another – with ugly black palls of smoke burgeoning skywards.

To the German fighter pilots, high in the sun, it was something of a miracle to have got the bombers through at all. That afternoon, Major Martin Mettig, the 54th Fighter Group's commander, had adhered to all the precepts which to date had ensured him minimal losses – one fighter group flying as direct protection, covering the bombers on every flank, right through to the target, a second batch moving in to relieve them, escorting the bombers from the target back to the Channel, a third group on 'free hunt', combing the sky for British fighters, yet a fourth taking over at the Channel, shepherding the fighters back to France. Yet Mettig, as fighter-leader, had flown the whole length of this formation, and now he wondered, how long before the system breaks down, for how can 120 fighters protect a bomber formation forty miles long? The Me 109's tactical flying time was eight minutes and its operational radius 125 miles – which left just ten scant minutes, if the RAF were in the mood for combat, to fight and break away.

Oberst Deichmann's plan to bring the fighters up had succeeded triumphantly – but not quite as he had planned. Now came the worst part of this day's assault on southern England. To Hauptmann Joachim Helbig, leading the 1st Training Group's 4th Wing, it seemed he had barely sighted the coastline when eighty Spitfires were howling at him from 23,000 feet – a fire-power of 600-plus machine-guns matched against Helbig's one rear-gunner, Oberfeldwebel Franz Schlund. For Helbig, it was only Schlund's iron nerve that saved the day. In the moment the lone machine-gun erupted, dealing death to at least one Spitfire, Helbig heeled sharply to port, a turn so sheer the Spitfires over-shot, then jinked to a lower altitude. His Junkers 88 sieved with 130 bullets, he soared due south for Orléans airfield – with five of his wing already lost to the British fighters.

For every bomber that made the target, three more were in trouble; their leisurely run-up to the rendezvous had cost them dearly. Frantically they looked to the fighters for protection, but most were lost to view in the vast egg-shaped swarm wheeling and stalling above the Hampshire coast. And already every German fighter was watching his fuel gauge, knowing the moment to break for base must be reckoned in seconds now.

Typical were the last desperate moments of young Josef Birndorfer, an Me 110 pilot, seeking vainly to shake 609 Squadron's implacable Flying Officer Ostazewski off his tail. Diving steeply for the ground in a series of S-turns, Birndorfer found himself curving, at 300 miles an hour, round a church spire . . . snaking perilously through the steel cables of Southampton's balloon barrage, cheating the grey, motionless sixty-foot-long porpoise-shapes by a hair's breadth . . . now at hedgetop level, a dark speeding shadow across the lavender shadows of evening . . . onwards over the Solent's laden waters, with Ostazewski closing relentlessly from 300 yards. Then the Pole was down to 100 yards, still firing, and white stars were winking and dancing along the Zerstörer's fuselage. At Ashley Down, on the Isle of Wight, it struck a metalled road head-on, and suddenly it was a plane no longer but a fiery, skidding projectile ripping itself apart.

Still the Germans were coming: Oberst Deichmann's onslaught had reached juggernaut pitch by now. At 6.28 pm, the Spitfire pilots of 54 Squadron, slumped on the grass at Manston airfield, were dreaming wistfully of beer and supper at their home base, Hornchurch, when the telephone's jangle sent their hopes plunging. Another seventy-plus German aircraft were in mid-Channel, surging for a landfall between Dover and Dungeness.

In truth, with several of Dowding's squadron grounded after the hard day's fighting, this was the moment to have launched a saturation blitz. But on this day, known always to the Luftwaffe pilots as

47. Tigers' lair – pilots of 74 ('Tiger') Squadron at immediate 'readiness' state, Hornchurch.

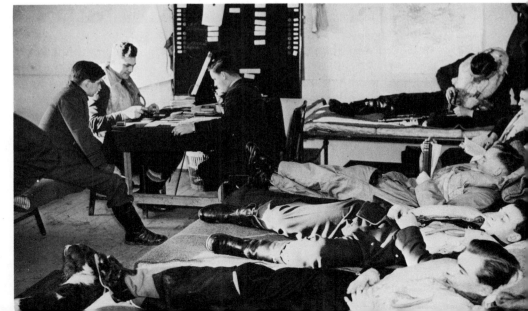

'Black Thursday', they had already lost close on fifty machines – and none of these, unlike the British planes, would be salvageable for further use.

Of all who had narrow squeaks this day, none came closer to bidding their comrades a long farewell than 54 Squadron's Flight Lieutenant Al Deere, who had so nearly missed forestalling Rubens-dörffer's first raid on Manston. Now, at 20,000 feet over Dungeness, Deere was in trouble once more; as 54 Squadron swept on towards the arrowhead German formation, one Me 109 broke from the chain, heading precipitately for France. At once Deere was away in pursuit, careful to stay just below the German's height, in the blind spot formed by the Messerschmitt's tail unit. If the 109 spotted him he knew he would lose it in the dive. Outfitted with fuel injector pumps, an Me 109, unlike a Spitfire or a Hurricane, could dive steeply without its engine cutting out.

At 5,000 feet, almost in range to fire, Deere cursed softly; the 109 was suddenly swallowed by a thin curtain of cloud. Then he was flying in clear sky once more, and his jaw dropped stupidly; no longer flying level, the 109 was steepening its dive towards an airfield lying to starboard. The stalk had so absorbed the stocky little pilot that he had never even realized they had crossed the Channel – or that the 109 was preparing to land on its home base, Calais-Marck airfield. There was no time to wait. Still out of range, Deere thumbed the firing button.

In that second, all hell broke loose. As if galvanized, the German fighter went for Calais-Marck like a rocket. But below the airfield circuit was a bee-hive of 109s, and two were now streaking for the water to cut Deere off. Throttle wide open, he broke for Dover's white cliffs at sea level, the 109s screaming in pursuit. Twice Deere swung the Spitfire's nose viciously outwards, forcing them to break away, but soon the violent manoeuvres tired him, and in this moment they struck. Bullets riddled the instrument panel and the perspex canopy, ripping the inner casing of his wrist watch from his left hand; the engine stuttered loudly. Thick heavy spurts of liquid bathed his cowling like rain – the oil tank had been hit.

At 1,500 feet over Ashford, Kent, with the 109s long departed, writhing flames took the Spitfire's engine, and Deere, releasing his Sutton harness, rolled the aircraft on its back, pushing hard on the stick. As the ground reared up to meet him, he broke loose, the blazing aircraft nearly vertical now, striking his wrist a savage welt against the tailplane. But the chute responded to the tug of the ripcord, and seconds later, with only a fractured wrist as souvenir, Deere was floating miraculously alive, over silent woods, landing only 100 yards from where his Spitfire was exploding in blast after blast.

Meanwhile the Observer Corps HQ at Bromley, Kent were puzzled. At 6.37 pm, the very moment that Deere's squadron had dived to intercept the incoming raid over Dungeness, the German formation had scattered and split. Within five minutes the seething mass had dissolved into eight distinct formations, and the last of these, tagged as Raid 8 by the reporting chain, had mysteriously altered course. First heading north over Orpington and Bexley Heath, fifty miles inland, it had suddenly swerved and was dodging south.

Craning from their sandbagged posts, binoculars sweeping the evening sky, the observers could not realize that these twenty-three planes of Test Group 210, led on the last sortie of the day by their chief, Hauptmann Walter Rubensdörffer, had lost not only their way but their escort, the 52nd Fighter Group. Oberleutnant Otto Hintze heard Walter Rubensdörffer ask quizzically: 'Are we over land or over sea?' No one could answer with certainty, so Rubensdörffer decided: 'I'm going down.'

So twenty-three planes were sweeping lower, down to 9,500 feet, with the mottled clouds still blocking their view. Then, in the same instant, two things happened. Rubensdörffer's voice shorn of reproach or bitterness, was quiet in their headphones: 'The fighter protection has withdrawn.' And they saw what they took to be Kenley: the sprawling, solid, red-brick huddle of a peacetime fighter station. So now it was too late. They fanned out for the attack.

Neither Rubensdörffer nor any of his detachment realized that this was not Kenley, but its satellite, four miles north, the old peacetime airport of Croydon, only ten miles from central London. On Hitler's express orders – for the Führer still hoped for a negotiated peace – Croydon and all London targets were forbidden, and any man attacking them was booked for a courtmartial if he came back alive.

On the ground there was no time to think, only to act. All over Croydon airfield the tannoy loudspeaker blurted into life, 'Attack Alarm!' 'Attack Alarm!' and Sergeant Frank Freeman, of the Middlesex Regiment, was doubling from pill-box to pill-box, checking that every crew stood by to man the aerodrome's sole defences, twelve Vickers machine-guns. Then, high in the sky, he saw the wings of Rubensdörffer's 110 waggle convulsively, the signal for attack. At the pitch of his lungs he roared, 'Look out, here they come!' Then the machine-guns' coughing chatter was blotted out, the screaming engines of Test Group 210 seemed to burst through the solid concrete of the pill-boxes, and all the earth trembled with the shock waves. Coughing and retching through a fine rain of chalk dust, Freeman thought the situation still called for a soldierly demeanour: crawling angrily towards one man, who was calling on all the saints to preserve him, he shook him into slack-jawed silence.

Curiously, though the airfield had been alerted by 6.29 pm, no air-raid warning had sounded for the general public. Not until 7.16 – seventeen minutes after the first bombs had dropped – did the cry of the siren rise and fall over Croydon's streets. In the red-brick streets radiating from the airfield, bystanders watched aghast – then reacted as their backgrounds prompted them. From the door of his Duppa's Hill Lane office, 600 yards away, Commandant John Robert Smith, an on-the-ball civil defence chief, saw the first bombs fall, and bellowed, 'One, one and one.' Within minutes a stretcher party, an ambulance and a sitting-case car for walking-wounded had ground away from the depot. At Headcorn Road, Thornton Heath, Miss Lillian Bride asked her father fearfully: 'Dad, what will it mean? You've seen through a few wars', and the eighty-four-year-old ex-soldier pondered: 'Well, we don't know, but we've got to keep a stout heart.' Roy Owen Barnes, a fifteen-year-old, at his third-storey bedroom window, riffled through his aircraft recognition booklets, trying clinically to identify the first Luftwaffe planes he had ever seen.

In the circular gallery of Fighter Command's Ops Room, Winston Churchill watched in silence as the WAAFs below him charted the raid, plying their long-handled plotting rods as deftly as croupiers. That very afternoon he had told Parliament that despite heavy attacks the Germans could not penetrate to London – yet now the blast of Rubensdörffer's bombs was rattling the House of Commons' windows. Beside him, Air Chief Marshal Dowding, General Sir Hastings (later Lord) Ismay, and Lord Beaverbrook, grave-faced in a crinkled blue serge suit, were silent, too. No man to shirk an issue, Churchill had taxed Dowding bluntly: 'You realize that serious doubts have been cast on your pilots' claims?' and Dowding had countered laconically: 'If the German claims were correct, they would be in England now.' But then Ismay saw Churchill freeze into total absorption: along the base of the wall display-panel, glowing red bulbs showed that every squadron in southern England was engaged or out of action. Ismay had to confess that at this instant he felt sick with fear.

Twenty-two miles south, above Croydon, Rubensdörffer's unit were fighting for their lives. To Oberleutnant Otto Hintze, in the last wave of all, the attack had suddenly assumed an unreal nightmare quality; planes zoomed and dived like spectres in the haze, then were lost to view. As he levelled out above the airfield's billowing dust, the RAF fighters seemed everywhere, looming in his windscreen. Hintze didn't know it but 111 Squadron had been reinforced now by Squadron Leader John Worrall's 32 Squadron from Biggin Hill. Overhead he saw Oberleutnant Martin Lutz's Me 110 rotating steadily in the circle of death: flying white-hot tracer criss-crossed the sky, as the RAF sought to penetrate their defences, and then Hintze was climbing steeply to join them, knowing that only an unbroken front against the British could hope to see them through. As he soared, orange flashes winking from the nose of his 109, he saw a 110 break from the circle, hotly pursued by a lone Hurricane. Hauptmann Walter Rubensdörffer had seen that his fuel was getting tight.

Below the combat, the airfield's surroundings were a scene of horror. To Sergeant Frank Freeman, of the Middlesex Regiment, one of the first on the scene at the shattered Bourjois scent factory, the mingled reek of blood and a perfume called 'Evening in Paris' seemed

48. (*Below*) Tiger Leader. Sqn Ldr Adolph 'Sailor' Malan, commander of 74 Sqn in 1940. Malan, a South African, was acknowledged as possibly the RAF's greatest fighter leader of World War Two.

49. (*Right*) Alan Deere, the tough New Zealander, whose various brushes with death earned him a reputation of having a cat's nine lives. Seen here after the Battle, as commander of 602 Squadron in 1941.

50. Charles Brian Fabri Kingcombe – invariably known as 'Kingpin' – the ebullient ex-Cranwell officer, who was the 'soul of 92 Squadron during the Battle. With only brief intervals, Kingcombe continued on operations throughout the war.

to lodge in his stomach. Commandant John Robert Smith, following up his light rescue units, was appalled to see soldiers grope through writhing smoke bowed down by white naked torsos. It was a moment before he recognized them for what they were: huge white lengths of Army shaving soap, still unprocessed. From an inferno of dust and licking flames, an incident officer's blue lantern glowed dimly; close by, a warden totting up the appalling casualty roll – sixty-two fatalities, 164 injured – stood calmly on one of the dead, a man stamped almost below ground level by hundreds of trampling feet.

At HQ Fighter Command, the wall display-panel showed more and more of Dowding's squadrons landing to refuel. But now the last waves of German raiders were receding towards the coast. With scarcely a word, Winston Churchill left the gallery, head bent in ferocious thought, shoulders squared, moving at speed. As his Humber staff car took the road for Chequers, Ismay made to comment, but Churchill almost savagely cut him short: 'Don't speak to me. I have never been so moved.' Five minutes passed, then Churchill, leaning forward, his voice shaken with emotion, said: 'Never in the field of human conflict was so much owed by so many to so few.' But Ismay could say nothing: he sat silent, the immortal words that were to echo round the world seeming to burn into his brain.

94

Far to the south, over Limpsfield in Surrey, Hauptmann Walter Rubensdörffer's 110 sank lower and lower towards the white corn, seeking a landing place; behind him his gunner, Feldwebel Richard Eherkecher, was still firing doggedly, but the Hurricane on their tail that had followed them all the way from Croydon would give them no peace. They veered south over Crockham Hill in Kent, the deadly Hurricane still closing, still firing. Edenbridge was past, and then Chiddingstone, and as Rubensdörffer raced south, blazing petrol from his punctured fuel tanks was rippling along his wings and fuselage. Only one of his unit, twenty-one-year-old Leutnant Horst Marx, was still valiantly keeping up; over the radio-telephone he'd heard his chief cry: 'I've been hit,' and he wouldn't break for home.

Then more Hurricanes were in view, singling out Marx's 109; over an apple orchard at Frant in Sussex, he baled out hastily, and Rubensdorffer was left alone, easing back his stick to gain height, needing all the 'courageous leadership' for which Kesselring had officially paid him tribute, for this last lap of the journey. Then, at 7.30 pm, Rubensdörffer's luck ran abruptly out: his starboard engine stopped dead. The tall, smiling Swiss, who had pioneered his unique fighter-bombing attacks as meticulously as he had left instructions for his own cremation, could hold up the plane no longer. As it passed over Denis Fishenden's smallholding, at Rotherfield, Sussex, molten fragments were already dripping from its wings.

A few hundred yards south, jobbing gardener Charles Wemban, stooping over the white waxy rows of his potato harvest, beheld a hair-raising sight: a blazing German plane, swooping clean over the roof of his tiny cottage, was coming for him head-on. As Wemban fell prostrate, Rubensdörffer, with one last effort, lifted the plane, and it fell, trailing a great banner of flame, into the valley beyond, where it smashed with awful force into a tree-studded bank. At once the pent-up fuel burst violently outwards, ammunition splintered and rained like fire-crackers, and pigs ran squealing through the blazing wreckage.

From 10,000 feet up, to the last men still airborne, the blaze was barely more noticeable than a farmer's bonfire. To the civilians on the sidelines of the combat, the lone, flickering fires, the yellow-green dye patches splodging the sea, and the contrails graven in the sky above the apple orchards remained to show that scores had fallen in a battle still undecided.

5. Island Assault

August 16–18

51. Ditched Luftwaffe crew in the Channel, August 1940.

Reichsmarschall Hermann Göring had just one resolve as his conference re-assembled soon after breakfast on Friday, August 16. Whatever happened his Luftwaffe would win the battle, or he'd know the reason why. Polished knee-length boots straddling his desk, arms folded, his face puckered in an unrelenting scowl, he told his staff bluntly: 'England's no island any more – remember that.'

Right from the start of the previous day's post-mortem, Göring had been in no mood to brook argument. To him, the lessons of the convoy attack and of the first abortive Eagle sortie were plain enough: if the Stukas had twice taken a beating over Portland, this was no good reason to abandon them. They'd fared so badly because they'd lacked fighter protection. From now on each Stuka wing should have three fighter wings – 120 planes, an entire group – to protect it. One wing to fly level with the Stukas – and dive with them in the same instant. A second to zoom at low level over the target, ahead of the rest, to intercept any RAF planes poised to catch the bombers after their dive. The third wing would oversee the whole operation from above. No technician, Göring ignored the one lesson the convoy attack had driven home – that since the Me 109 had no air-brakes it was bound to over-shoot the Stukas once it dived. And when the Stukas pulled out from their bombing attack, twice that many fighters would find themselves hard put to it to protect them.

Oberst Werner Junck, regional fighter commander for Air Fleet Three, jumped bravely in. If so many extra burdens were to be thrown on the 109, wouldn't the Reichsmarschall give serious thought to stepping up fighter production? Even in July, German aircraft factories had produced only 220 Me 109s – less than half Lord Beaverbrook's total output – and by the end of August, the figures would have slumped again, to 173. Mock-solicitous, Göring stretched out his hand: 'I must take your pulse to see if you are all right physically – it seems you have lost your senses.'

It wasn't the first time Göring had heard such an argument from his production experts – and as summarily rejected it. Others had stressed that at the present rate of attrition, theLuftwaffe would need to shoot down four British fighters for every one they lost – yet even so, the Me 109 factories at Regensburg and Augsburg often worked a minimum six-hour day against the ten or twelve needed.

As the meeting broke up, Göring hadn't a doubt in the world; the RAF couldn't have more than 300 serviceable planes left to them. Properly protected, the Stukas and Zerstörers would finish the job.

Gently, Pilot Officer Robert Wright closed the door leading from his outer office to Air Chief Marshal Dowding's high Georgian room – then sadly shook his head. A loyal aide-de-camp, he felt for Dowding deeply, and, this morning when Dowding had arrived as late as 9.30 am, it was plain to Wright he had overslept after another gruelling small-hours vigil at a night-fighter interceptor station. No sooner had Dowding entered his office than his buzzer had sounded again – and Wright, hastening in, had found his chief rooted to the floor, spectacles lodged on the bridge of his nose, staring trance-like into space. At length, rousing himself, he gestured: 'All right, Wright, I'll ring for you again' – and his aide-de-camp, gently closing the door, knew that whatever was on Dowding's mind had been anaesthetized by fatigue in the seconds it had taken to cross the threshold.

Contrary to Reichsmarschall Göring's belief, the shortage of fighter planes was the last thing on Dowding's mind this day. Within the week, Lord Beaverbrook's Ministry of Aircraft Production was to achieve its highest-ever total during the battle – a record 440 fighters. It was trained pilots to fly those planes that Dowding lacked above all – a need so dire that this day he was 209 pilots below strength. Although Dowding had time and again pressed the Air Ministry to divert Fairey Battle pilots to fill the gap, the Air Staff were still wavering. A large-scale withdrawal from the day-bomber squadrons could seriously jeopardize Britain's striking power come invasion day.

It was no idle concern. The mounting losses now decreed that a pilot's expectation of life was no more than eighty-seven flying hours – and many were so near collapse that their reactions were a long way off the medical board's touchstone: one-fifth of a second quicker than average. At Hawkinge, some pilots no sooner taxied in their planes than they slumped forward in the cockpit, as dead to the world as men under morphia, often close to coma for twenty-four hours. Young

Pilot Officer Peter Hairs, a Hurricane pilot operating from Hawk-inge, was typical of many. After the day's eighth sortie, he would stare at his log-book, unable to record a thing except the times of take-off and landing. His mind blurred and seemed to take hold on nothing, and all night long he writhed and moaned, dreaming of blazing planes.

Many cushioned their fear with liquor: 32 Squadron's CO, Squadron Leader John Worrall, still recalls: 'If you weren't in the air, you were plastered.' At Andover's Square Club, where Middle Wallop fliers thronged, near-lethal mixtures were commonplace – vodka and apricot brandy, even brandy and port. At Wallop's forward base, Warmwell, the canny station doctor, Flight Lieutenant Monty Bieber, was for ever fixing up 'harmless' pink drinks to quieten morning-after stomachs – in reality, near-neat alcohol which kept pilots grounded for safety's sake.

To every man in those razor-edged days, the sense of impending doom took on a different guise. At Tangmere airfield, it was the thin black line in the mess ledger recording each pilot's mealtimes, ruled beneath name after name. Mess Steward Joseph Lauderdale, at

52. Hurricane pilots of 43 Squadron. Sgt J. A. Buck; Fg Off Tony Woods-Scawen (killed September 2); Flt Lt Caesar Hull, DFC (killed September 8); Plt Off Wilkinson; Sgt G. W. Garton (later Wing Commander, DSO, DFC).

Middle Wallop, had his own yardstick: often his pilots died too soon to qualify for a change of sheets. Day by day, a North Weald flight mechanic, George Perry, saw boys come back men after one eighty-minute sortie, their faces grey, a yellow froth about their mouths.

The ground staffs showed infinite forethought. At mealtimes in Hornchurch officers' mess, Old Sam, the chef, with his tall white cap, kept up his soothing flow of patter: 'Don't say you can't touch a bite, sir . . . just a shaving of the roast beef now . . . some of the under-done.' For evening meals, Wing Commander Cecil Bouchier cut off the electricity altogether, importing candles from Harrod's department store. Few even realized Bouchier wasn't out to save fuel – or that the soft light was kind to the taut, strained boyish faces.

The more a squadron's losses mounted now, the more superstition held sway. At Tangmere at least two pilots wouldn't fly without their magic scarves – pink and blue checkered silk squares which South African Caesar Hull had brought to 43 Squadron. Pilot Officer Tony Woods-Scawen, of the same outfit, clung doggedly to his 'lucky' parachute. He knew it worked: he'd baled out four times already and come back to talk about it.

Known to all the novices coming on the scene was the unvarnished truth: they would learn the art of survival the hard way, and to live through your first three sorties was to achieve a tenuous hold on immortality. Few understood this better than Pilot Officer Red Tobin, Andy Mamedoff and Shorty Keough. On August 16, stretched out on the grass at Warmwell airfield, they were counted fully operational for the first time – each of them attached to a section of three as 'weavers'. As Squadron Leader Darley had explained: though the numbers one and two men flew absolutely straight, the weaver's job, as 'Arse End Charlie', was to fly on a twisting snake-like course behind them to protect their rear.

When the telephone shrilled, twelve men sprang as one for their parked Spitfires, and Red Tobin, elated, whooped to his four-strong ground crew: 'Saddle her up, I'm riding!' As the twenty-four cylinder Merlin engines roared into life, a sirocco of dust whirled about the tailplanes, and Red, eyes alert, saw his section leader, Frank Howell, taxi to his take-off point and turn into the wind. The squadron was airborne: twelve pilots, 15,000 horse-power, ninety-six machine guns with a total fire-power of 120,000 rounds a minute.

The radio telephone crackled into life; it was Squadron Leader Gavin Anderson, Middle Wallop's Sector Controller: 'Hullo, Sorbo

Leader, this is Bandy. Patrol Portland angels twenty. Many, many bandits.' Coolly, Red Tobin noted he still wasn't scared; there was too much to do. His mind was a catalogue of swiftly-posed queries: Is the manifold pressure too high? Will the guns work? Is the oil pressure dropping?

The squadron was at 18,000 feet now, levelled off, each man flying by throttle, opening and closing it to keep in correct formation position. Then Red heard his section leader, Flight Lieutenant Frank Howell: 'O.K. Charlie, weave.' Red Tobin was as alert for trouble as he'd ever been: an order to weave meant something was about to break. So as Frank Howell and young Geoffrey Gaunt, the number two, flew resolutely on, Red was rocking the Spitfire's three tons of streamlined metal back and forth at 300 miles an hour, his blue eyes probing the bright morning sky.

His headphones crackled again: 'Many, many bandits three o'clock'; momentarily he relaxed. Using the clock system to spot planes in the air, the pilot saw himself in the centre of an imaginary dial – and three o'clock meant directly to starboard. He could see them now – over fifty milling gnat-shapes – but he didn't worry. Time and again the veterans had told him, 'You don't worry about the ones you can see.' Then came a whispery voice, packing a jolt like a high-tension cable: 'Many many bandits at six o'clock and five thousand above.'

Now Red knew a moment of sweating horror, for his task was to protect the two men ahead, yet he had seen not one single German plane 5,000 feet above. And the thought struck him: in this rigid display formation the RAF still flew, made up of tight V-shaped formations of three, there was no one to protect 'Arse End Charlie' – except Charlie himself.

Eyes dilated, his neck muscles standing out like pencils, he craned frantically, then saw them, about a mile back, knowing he was safe for a second or two.

Everything happened so fast that later Red was hard put to it to sift his mind for the reasoned details a combat report needed. He saw Howell peel away, Gaunt followed, and he too was howling down behind them, but in seconds he had lost them and he saw no bomber, only an Me 110 that went into a tight climbing turn to shake him. Then Tobin fired, the glittering paper-chain of tracer telling him his shots were going as wide as the German rear-gunner's, and he told himself: 'Nose up, pull your nose up. Get him in front.'

But he jerked up the Spitfire's nose too fast, nearly blacking out; a grey veil swam before his eyes, and he had time only for one long burst before the 110 was gone. Momentarily he was lost; the air seemed to split apart with screaming, diving planes, but he had no idea where Howell or the others had gone. Then there was that strange loneliness which always seems to follow an air battle, when men who have seen the sky choked with planes find dazedly that all have gone and they set course eagerly for home, because between the earth and the stratosphere theirs seems the only plane.

Back at Warmwell, Red Tobin was dumbfounded to find that in

53. Flight Lieutenant E. J. B. Nicolson of 249 Squadron, the only fighter pilot to gain a Victoria Cross during World War Two. Awarded a DFC for operations in Burma later, Nicolson was killed in action on 2 May 1945.

little more than an hour he had used up eighty gallons of 100-octane fuel and fired 2,000 rounds, but the flurry of the morning's combat soon faded in the bleak news that greeted 609's return. Already Middle Wallop Sector Station was barely operational, alive with unexploded bombs – despite 609's efforts, the morning's raid had succeeded as never before. And smashing through the RAF's defences by sheer force, bombers of Air Fleet Three had struck the vital sector station at Tangmere, Sussex, with appalling accuracy. All lighting, power and water were cut off – and almost every building on the aerodrome had suffered crucial damage. Hangars and workshops had been gutted to the ground level – and fourteen planes destroyed or damaged on the field.

It wasn't the Luftwaffe's only triumph of the day. Across the Solent, on the Isle of Wight, five Stuka dive-bombers had worked over Ventnor Radar Station yet again for six merciless minutes, negating all the work that hard-pressed technicians had put in since August 12. At Gosport, across Portsmouth Harbour, Junkers 88s had struck a devastating blow at the anti-aircraft co-operation station. Eastwards, near Maidstone, Dorniers of the 76th Bomber Group had put West Malling airfield out of action for four long days. By mid-afternoon on August 16, it looked as if all Göring's faith had been justified, and that the Luftwaffe would triumph after all.

Dowding's pilots were doing their best, but it was bitter uphill work. Many had never flown a fighter sortie until this very day. Barely 10 per cent had undergone stringent gunnery practice. From first to last, their training had stressed disciplined air-display flying in the V-shaped formations that had so puzzled Red Tobin – so tight-packed that it was not uncommon for planes to return after mid-air collision with airscrews as snarled as metal tentacles.

Almost as frustrating were the four standard Fighter Command attacks on bomber formations. Based on the pre-war theory that German bombers would fly in a straight line, without rear gun-turrets, unescorted by hovering fighters, the attacks still, incredibly, won favour with the Air Staff. In the pre-battle lull, most pilots spent hours daily perfecting the No. 1 Attack, where fighters swung into line behind their leader, queued to deliver a three-second burst, then swung away – their under-bellies a sure target for a German gunner.

If Dowding's pilots lacked experience, however, they compensated, on August 16, with courage – and sometimes with sheer blind valour. At 1.45 pm, while the shroud of brick-dust was still rising over

Tangmere, Flight Lieutenant James Nicolson, 249 Squadron, was at 17,000 feet over Romsey, Hampshire, the enamelled blue of Southampton Water glinting nine miles off his Hurricane's port wing. A toothy, mop-headed, twenty-three-year-old, six feet four inches tall, his thoughts lay mostly with the baby his wife Muriel was expecting back in Yorkshire. But when three Junkers 88 dive-bombers crossed his section's bows Nicolson, who had never come within shooting range of a German, did not hesitate. Promptly he dived to investigate – then, cursing, swung back to rejoin the squadron. Twelve Spitfires, conjured from nowhere, were already attacking the bombers.

But Nicolson wasn't destined to make it. Unsuspected, an Me 110 was on his tail, and suddenly with shattering echoes, his entire Hurricane seemed to fall apart. A cannon shell tore through the perspex hood, and splinters peppered his left eye, blinding him with blood. A second shell struck his reserve petrol tank; in one searing moment the plane took fire. More shots sledgehammered – tearing away his trouser leg, disabling his left heel. As Nicolson reefed his plane blindly to starboard, away from the deadly shells, he saw that the 110 had over-shot and was now 200 yards ahead, diving at 400 miles an

54. Hauptmann Kaminski, 'Last of the Prussians' (*left*), and his gunner, Unteroffizier Strauch.

hour. Beneath the blowtorch assault of the flames, his instrument panel was 'dripping like treacle', but a deadly resolution took hold of him: the man who had subjected him to these terrors should be his first victim. The 110 was steady in his gunsights, and as he streaked in pursuit, the pent-up anger burst in him and he screamed: 'I'll teach you manners, you Hun.' His right thumb on the firing button, his left hand on the throttle, were boiling into white blisters in the furnace of heat.

Nicolson fired until the pain passed all tolerance level, his feet bundled up on his seat beneath the parachute, and he saw the 110 fall smoking for the sea. Lurching, he struck his head on the closed hood, then fought with his mutilated fingers to disentangle the harness straps, before diving head first, flames lapping at his overalls. For 5,000 feet he fell sheer, and when he found strength to pull the ripcord he saw blood was dripping from the lace-holes of his boots.

Through his one good eye, he saw that heat had melted the glass of his wrist watch, the strap hanging by a charred thread, but the watch was ticking merrily. It was still ticking three months later, when Nicolson, for an action that typified the whole last-ditch endeavour of the battle, became the first fighter pilot of World War II to win the VC.

The uniformed driver let in the clutch and the Horch staff car slid smoothly away from the ramp of Staaken airport, Berlin. From the back seat, Major Adolf Galland, erect bearing belying the bloodshot fatigue in his eyes, moodily surveyed the crowded sidewalks as the car purred steadily through the city towards Göring's Karinhall head-quarters. To his pilots, Galland was a man who'd pull no punches putting their point of view to the top brass – and this afternoon, as the Horch purred through Karinhall's high gateways, surmounted by marble lions, this was what Galland intended. Why Göring had summoned him he didn't know – but as always he felt out of place here, away from fighting men, jostled by natty staff officers with their white-and-raspberry-striped trousers.

As Göring stomped across the entrance hall to pump his hand, Galland knew the Reichsmarschall didn't really like him. He spoke out too forcibly for that. But today, Galland was a guest of honour. He and Werner Mölders, who had received a similar summons, were to be formally invested with the Gold Pilot Medal with Jewels as a token of their prowess. Major Adolf Galland half suspected more was to follow – and too soon events proved him right. The ceremony over, Göring led him and Mölders to his vast library, and the mood changed as abruptly as the setting. Both pilots had earned their decorations, Göring granted that – but as a whole the fighter effort just wasn't good enough. There wasn't enough effort, enough aggression – and their co-ordination with the bomber units was shameful.

And Göring went further: this farce of rendezvous going awry had got to stop. From now on, a single aircraft from the bomber formation would circle the fighter escort's airfield, to signal they were ready to go. Then the fighters must get airborne, follow the bomber to its main formation, and stay with that formation all the way. Clearing the sky ahead of the raiders would be the task of special fighter units – but the bulk of the fighters would cling to the bombers, no matter how the RAF tried to deflect them.

Before Galland could lose his temper, Göring forestalled him: the true solution to the problem had eluded him, but he had it now. Much of the faulty leadership was due to the present group commanders – they were all too old. From now on, no group commander would be older than thirty-two, no wing leader older than thirty, no squadron commander older than twenty-seven. In this way they would mount a really vigorous offensive against the British. Then beaming, Göring offered his pièce-de-résistance: in four days' time Mölders would take over the 51st Fighter Group at Wissant. Galland would relinquish his 3rd Wing at Caffiers and succeed Major Gotthard Handrick, 1936 Olympics champion, as group leader at Audembert.

Galland protested hotly. His wing was all he asked for – already they were responsibility enough, and the last thing he wanted was to be tied to the ground. Surely it wasn't the fighter leaders who were lacking in aggression – the whole concept of the battle was against them. And he instanced: with the Me 109's operational range pinned to 125 miles at most, every fighter battle was confined to southern England. Perhaps one-tenth of the British Isles – and in the other nine-tenths, the RAF could build and repair aircraft, train their pilots, well out of fighter range. He wound up: 'All I ask is combat, combat with my wing' – but Göring reassured him. He'd see all the combat he wanted, and more: this was the whole beauty of the scheme. The eight group commanders and seventeen wing leaders then operational would all be young thrusting pilots, men like himself and Mölders who'd personally lead their units in action.

Angry and suspicious, Galland still smouldered as Göring hashed

Frank Carey –
ıota' – the
ckney-born ace who
ved with 43 Squadron
ring the Battle, and
nt on to become one of
RAF's
hest-scoring fighter
ots of the war.

over final points, then as Göring wound up the meeting – 'Any last requests?' – he stubbornly resumed his old stand. 'Yes, Herr Reichsmarschall – to remain a wing leader.' Göring went purple: 'Request refused.'

South of Canterbury, Oberleutnant Gerhard Schöpfel, leading the 3rd Wing in Galland's absence, knew his luck was in. Not one but nine Hurricanes were flying unsuspectingly 1,000 metres below him, in the strange tight formation the British flew – 'the bunch of bananas', the Luftwaffe dubbed it. Schöpfel also glimpsed the squadron's two weavers, quite alone, to the rear of the formation. As they veered north-west, away from Canterbury, he dived.

His two cannons, each loaded with sixty rounds, blasted out, and two rear Hurricanes of No. 501 Squadron fell flaming. Now Schöpfel was hard on the tail of a third, and he watched almost incredulous, as this, too, spiralled burning from the sky. Still the squadron flew serenely on, and Schöpfel's confidence grew. Too close for safety, he jerked the firing button again and the Hurricane blew up almost across the nose of his 109. Debris jarred his airscrew; a viscous niagara of oil swamped his windshield. Hastily, unable to see any longer, Schöpfel broke upwards. The battle had lasted just four minutes – and still he'd fifteen bullets left, enough for another victory.

Two outstanding
hter leaders were
ter Townsend (left)
d the South African,
esar Hull; both of 43
uadron in 1940.

This morning, Sunday, August 18, a confident feeling had gripped all the pilots of Air Fleet Two. For twenty-four hours their morale had been at lowest ebb: low-lying cloud had closed in on England and four bomber units between them had failed to locate the priority fighter airfields at Debden, Duxford and Hornchurch. Now, with the ceiling lifting, their spirits soared too; even if the first sorties had gone less well than they had hoped, the top brass could be expected to iron out the wrinkles.

The confidence wasn't misplaced – yet every Luftwaffe success this day was achieved at a fearful toll of human lives. At 1 pm soon after the people of southern England had filed from morning service, thirty-one Dorniers of Oberstleutnant Frohlich's 76th Bomber Group were churning inexorably from Cormeilles-en-Vexin airfield in Normandy towards the English Channel, along with twelve Junkers 88 dive-bombers. Their targets, though the crews did not fully appreciate it, were two of Fighter Command's most vital sector stations, covering the southern approaches to London – Kenley, which the unlucky Hauptmann Rubensdörffer hadn't located, and

109

Biggin Hill. Contrary to the RAF's belief, the Luftwaffe never once suspected these for what they were – the nerve-centres of Dowding's command. From first to last they assumed that priority command posts would be sited underground away from the centre of operations – not in unprotected buildings plumb in the airfield's centre, lacking sandbags or blast walls, locations which had served well enough until the Luftwaffe had reached the Channel. Like every other sortie, these raids were aimed solely at putting Kenley and Biggin Hill airfields out of action – though with a novel difference. To fox the radar stations, a spearhead of nine Dorniers would fly at wavetop height, creating maximum confusion by homing in on Kenley and Biggin Hill at nought feet, in concert with the high-level raids.

Farther west, on the Cherbourg peninsula, Sperrle's Air Fleet Three planned no surprises – merely the mixture as before. Twenty-eight planes of Stuka Group 77, escorted, under Göring's new decree, by no less than three fighter wings, would fly in decoy attacks on a broad thirty-mile front against the airfields at Thorney Island, Gosport and Ford – all of them Coastal Command or Fleet Air Arm stations.

At Uxbridge, Middlesex, headquarters of No. 11 Group Fighter Command, the duty controller, Lord Willoughby de Broke, hardly knew where to turn. On him lay the responsibility of planning the first steps of the battle like a gigantic game of chess, before relinquishing on-the-spot control to the sector stations – but already more than 600 plots swamped the situation map. Now Lord Willoughby begged Fighter Command's Filter Room, which sifted incoming details from the radar stations: 'Is there a lot of mush building up behind?' To the Filter Room, the request made sense – how many formations might be mustering just outside radar range? But at 1 pm no one could be certain – and suddenly it was every Sector Controller for himself.

In Kenley's Ops Room, Squadron Leader Anthony Norman, the duty controller, was on the horns of a dilemma: the Observer Corps had spotted those low-level Dorniers before any warning from No. 11 Group. By rights, 11 Group should make the final decision – but though the Dorniers were only ten minutes flying time away, no word came. So Norman acted fast. Across the airfield Spitfire pilots of Squadron Leader Aeneas MacDonell's 64 Squadron got the call: 'Freema Squadron, scramble. Patrol base, angels twenty.' At the same time, Squadron Leader John Thompson's 111 Squadron at Croydon had wind of their role: their Hurricanes were to make for

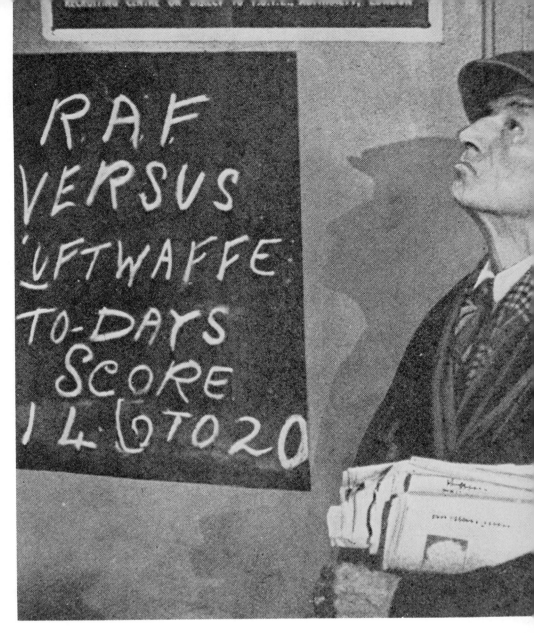

Kenley and circle the airfield at 100 feet, poised for a head-on
intercept of the low-level raiders. At Biggin Hill, Group Captain
Richard Grice, the station commander, came to the same decision:
still he had heard nothing from 11 Group, and if the raiders were
flying with fighter escort, his planes needed fully twenty minutes to
reach a 109's operational height. On his own initiative he ordered the

controller to scramble the two squadrons available – No. 32 and No. 610.

Over Kenley, the pilots of No. 64 Squadron were completely in the dark, even when Squadron Leader MacDonell's voice came high-pitched with urgency: 'Freema Squadron, going down.' Sergeant-Pilot Peter Hawke was one of several who thought, Why down? – we need all the height we can get. Then he knew: a black pillar of smoke shot skywards like a gusher from Kenley's hangars.

Fifty feet above the airfield, Squadron Leader Thompson's Hurricanes, racing for their head-on attack, got the shock of their lives: ack-ack fire burst above them and the air seemed full of whirling wires. No one had warned them that the station defences were firing PAC (parachute and cable) rockets at the raiders – electrically fired rockets whooshing upwards at forty feet a second, mounting to 700 feet to grapple their wings with four hundredweight of steel wire. Anguished, Thompson thought: my God, if one of those hits us we're finished.

At Biggin Hill, the damage was minimal; in the confusion caused by the high-level raid's late arrival, the bulk of 500 bombs landed wide, on the airfield's eastern periphery. But at Kenley the Dorniers did their work too well. With deadly accuracy, the bombers destroyed six Hurricanes on the ground, shattering ten hangars and damaging six more, putting the vital Ops Room out of action, reducing buildings to trembling shells. Only one factor saved the station from total destruction: many bombs were released so low they landed horizontally and didn't explode.

Yet the 76th Bomber Group had paid a heavy price: four Junkers 88 dive-bombers, six Dorniers, and all their crews. Sixty miles west, the losses were appalling; of the twenty-eight Stukas that attacked the coastal targets around Portsmouth, in one more endeavour to draw up the British fighters, eighteen were lost or severely damaged. Again the bombers made their mark – pounding hangars and workshops at Gosport, Thorney Island, and the Fleet Air Arm station at Ford – but at a cost no air force in the world could have counted. When the news reached Karinhall, Göring's reaction was decisive: no further low-level raids would be launched from this day forward.

Those Stuka pilots who did get back made it by a hair's-breadth. Oberleutnant Karl Hentze saw the powdery black spirals of smoke as his bombs struck Ford airfield, but somehow, try as he might, he couldn't retract his diving-brakes: the first onslaught by British

112

fighters had shot away most of his hydraulic system. The Stuka seemed top-heavy and jolting violently – 'like riding over cobbles' – and he knew that whatever had him in their sights could hardly fail to score.

Nor did they. Suddenly two Spitfires were on his tail, circling and feinting like vicious birds; a bullet struck his radio telephone then ricocheted back, furrowing through the skin at the base of his skull. Momentarily, he blacked out, then a roar from the gunner awoke him to life; the plane was skimming the water like an albatross and in one second of stark terror he felt the wheels dip beneath the waves.

North-west of Bayeux in Normandy, he landed almost blind in a meadow, his wheels skidding and scarring the soft turf, then blacked out again; somehow his gunner hauled him out and when Hentze came to he found a party of French peasants pressing perfumed handkerchiefs to his nose to revive him. One, not realizing he was concussed, pressed a flask of brandy on him and within minutes Hentze was doubled up, vomiting painfully. Then a jolting, horse-drawn cart took him to a field hospital where a case-hardened doctor, probing the bullet from his skull, chaffed him: 'You'll pay duty for importing English metal.'

From this moment on, the Stukas – 280 planes – were virtually out of the battle: the first casualty in Göring's thrust.

At Air Fleet Two's advance headquarters, the losses totalled up were in no way comparable, yet Oberst Theo Osterkamp, regional fighter commander, whose office was at Le Touquet close by, was at his wits' end. Since the afternoon's sortie began, Generalfeldmarschall Albert Kesselring had barely given him a moment's peace, first hastening from the fetid underground dug-out to his private look-out post, feverishly enumerating every returning plane he could see, then returning to the dug-out to telephone Osterkamp afresh. 'What has happened? Where are the planes? At least thirty flew out a while back, but I've only counted seven returned.' Bridling his temper, Osterkamp assured him: 'I'm dealing with the problem now. They haven't been signalled in yet.' Unappeased, Kesselring roared: 'Well, they're long overdue. And you should know where they are already. It's your job.'

One man who was given up for lost certainly wasn't going to die if he could help it. Ten days after the battle had begun Hauptmann Herbert Kaminski's 'throat-ache' – his ambition to win the Knight's Cross – was keener than ever, but that afternoon, twelve miles east of

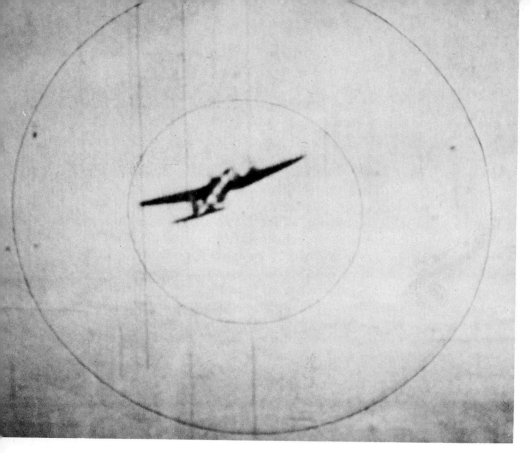

58. 'First, arrange your Heinkel . . .' – Heinkel He 111 at dead-centre of a Hurricane's reflector gun-sight ring, prior to its destruction.

Foulness Point, he fleetingly bade this ambition farewell. Spitfires had shattered his port and starboard engines; there was nothing for it now but to ditch the Me 110 in the choppy sea. To his long-suffering gunner, Unteroffizier Strauch, he cried: 'We're landing – so pay attention and get the dinghy ready. And remember – don't ditch your hood until I've ditched mine.' As he released the canopy, it spiralled away into the wind, and in that instant Kaminski saw with horror that the 110's nose was head-on to the waves.

Still flying without harness straps, because of the unhealed wound in his right shoulder, 'The Last of the Prussians' knew the impact would be hard indeed. The engulfing sea swept up to meet them, and though Kaminski vainly threw his arm before his face, he was hurled forward with such force against the instrument panel that he broke his nose. He swooned downwards in pain and oblivion; but as the world grew cold and dark and wet and Kaminski came to, his first thought was one of unrelieved joy: It's wet. Hell is not wet. I'm alive.

114

He struggled upwards to the water's surface, his nose pouring blood, calling: 'Strauch, Strauch, where are you?' Then he saw Strauch, too, come thrashing to the surface, spitting water, bleeding from a head wound. Swimming steadily, they sought to inflate the dinghy, and Kaminski grew rapidly furious: Strauch hadn't even connected up the oxygen flask in advance, and there was the angry hiss of escaping air. Still swimming, Kaminski roared: 'I sentence you to ten days' close arrest. Do you realise we are going to die because of your foolishness?'

Then, to their joy, a plane was circling them, and both men ripped off the yellow scarves all Luftwaffe pilots wore for recognition purposes and waved them wildly. But Kaminski noticed that it was flying on one engine, perhaps crippled from the same sortie, and whether it would even make the French coast to alert the rescue services was doubtful. The enormous weight of their water-soaked clothing seemed to tug them deeper into the sea, and soon they had recklessly stripped off their flying overalls and boots and helmets and swam on in their underwear. They ripped their fluorescine packets open, and the yellow-green patch of marker dye swirled outwards from them.

It was twilight before the rescue plane zoomed low over the water, and the navigator came perilously down the collapsible ladder, inflating a yellow rubber dinghy, and launching it onto the waves. But it fell fifty yards away from them, and the waves were head high. It was ten icy minutes before Kaminski reached the second dinghy that was dropped and, in the gathering darkness, he'd quite lost sight of Strauch. It was the navigator, craning from the escape hatch, who guided him back again – but it was a further half-hour before Kaminski, puffing and cursing, had paddled the dinghy back. Clumsily the gunner tried to clamber in, swamping his chief with icy water. Each time Strauch manoeuvred afresh, the dinghy bobbed like a balloon, tipping Kaminski back into the water. Splashing and floundering like men sporting with a porpoise, they made it finally – but now the bulky Kaminski was lodged in such a way that every fresh wave swamped his rear, while the lightweight Strauch sat snugly in the dry.

Past all patience, forgetting it couldn't hear, Kaminski shook his fist again after the retreating rescue plane: 'And don't forget to come back in the morning!'

In southern England it was like a resurgence of hope. As news of this day's fighting spread, the people, for the first time since Dunkirk, showed more than passing interest in the news; the battle seemed almost won. Travelling the south coast, Ben Robertson noted that newspaper sellers already chalked up the day's results in terms of a cricket match: 'RAF v Germans, 61 for 26 – Close of Play Today, 12 for 0.' A cocky farmer put a novel proposition to Kent County Council: he'd rope off a meadow, charge sixpence admission for the Spitfire Fund, and bill it as 'The Only Field in East Kent in which No German Aircraft Has Yet Fallen.'

At Bembridge, Isle of Wight, youngsters whooped through the streets, clips of live 303 ammunition festooning their belts – but on many battlefields, the adults were just as avid. At Kenley airfield, smoke still plumed from gutted hangars as airmen toiled to haul away every unexploded bomb in sight, pursued by burly sergeants bawling: 'Put them down, you fools – they may be delayed-action!' Outside Tangmere airfield, one man, inside a shattered Stuka, calmly toiled with a work-bench and tools until he'd dismantled its electric wiring. Near Poling in Sussex, RAF salvage crews, arriving to fly a German aircraft away, found that souvenir hunters had removed the entire tailplane. At Portisham, Dorset, hearing a Stuka had force-landed, garage proprietor William Duck set off at a trot; its tail-wheel would be just right for his old wheel-barrow.

Some wanted grimmer keepsakes. Two schoolboys from Smallfield, Surrey, chancing on a German flying helmet weren't one whit perturbed to find a chunk of the pilot's skull adhering to it; threading it on a length of string, they hung it in their father's cowshed. At Braishfield in Hampshire, pub regulars spent all that evening passing round a crony's memento of the day: a bloody flying boot with the foot still in it.

Few had as yet grasped that the future they cherished was at stake, and that all civilization depended on the outcome of this battle, and that the vain glory was premature. But many were learning: one brief dog-fight could impose indelible sights on the memory. At Five Ashes in Sussex, a direct hit on his cowshed from a bomb jettisoned in flight cost one farmer, James Berry, thirteen cows and his two sons James and Alfred. Boat-builder Herbert Merrett, returning to his bungalow workshop, near Bosham, Sussex, after a peaceful Sunday afternoon outing, was riveted to the ground: a Stuka had crashed in his willow-bed, the gunner baling out 100 feet above the marshy ground had

59. War is a young man's game; exemplified here by members of a captured Dornier crew, August 1940.

60. Last sortie – a crew member of one St.G2 Junkers Ju 87 who fell, without parachute, from his crippled aircraft during the August 16 raid on Tangmere.

dashed his brains out on Merrett's old car, and now an RAF salvage team had commandeered the boat-builder's gate to carry the body away. Sightseers swarmed everywhere, oblivious to two 50-kilo bombs still attached to the Stuka's smouldering wings.

The war struck mercilessly and indiscriminately. At 2 pm, though the air-raid warning had sounded, there was nothing to warn Mrs Doris Addison, a coalman's wife and mother of two, that the tiny cottage called 'The Warren', close by the millstream at Hurst Green in Surrey, stood in imminent danger. She was just dishing up the Sunday joint to her children when they heard the droning of an engine, louder and louder, until the drone gave place to a high-pitched scream. Even Bob, their two-year-old liver-and-white springer spaniel, huddled uneasily beneath the table. Though the Addisons didn't know it, one of Kenley's retreating Dorniers, hotly pursued by the pilots of 111 Squadron, was in dire distress.

Just south of 'The Warren', the Dornier struck the ground, with the inhuman screech of tortured metal, already disintegrating in a sweeping sheet of flame, ripping through a hedge, shedding its bomb-load everywhere, bouncing partly over 'The Warren' and spraying everything in its path with blazing fuel. From the Fire Service post up the lane, from where he had seen everything, Auxiliary Fireman Dick Addison was racing furiously to protect his family.

Inside the cottage, Doris Addison and the children were taken unawares: one appalling explosion and then the open kitchen door was a shaking yellow curtain of flame. Resourceful Mrs Addison bustled the children into the downstairs bathroom and out through the window, then turned back once more for Bob. For a second her heart failed her; the spaniel had bolted panic-stricken through the open door, into the leaping heart of the flames.

Tumbling through his garden gate, Dick Addison was numb with outrage; his little cottage and garden seemed somehow desecrated. An unexploded bomb, one of eighteen thrown clear, lay beneath the kitchen table, Delma's new doll's pram had been gutted to its frame, the ravaging fury of the flames had stewed the fruit on his plum trees, roasted his chickens in their run.

Somehow, though they never forgot this day, the Addisons managed to come through. At first, the children were inconsolable, lamenting the loss of Bob; it had been Delma's whim to dress him up in a bonnet and shawl and wheel him round in her new doll's pram.

61. The high tension of incessant combat brought swift exhaustion, and sleep was snatched where and when ever possible between sorties; as exemplified here by Fg Off W. P. Clyde of 601 Squadron, AAF.

But when the dog was found, a few fields away, badly burned but alive, McConnachie Ingram, the local vet, took Bob into his care and six weeks later delivered him alive and well – his black nose scorched pink, four bootees protecting his damaged pads.

And the Addisons, after only one night spent with neighbours, moved back into 'The Warren'; the damage had been superficial after all. Opening the larder door, the first thing Doris Addison saw was the blancmange, still untouched, and she told Dick triumphantly: 'I think if I dust if off we can eat it after all.'

At Manston, on the Kent coast, the morale of many was now at its lowest ebb, their officers' example notwithstanding; for six days many airmen had not ventured forth from the deep chalk shelters, Some were close to breaking point; in the nick of time Squadron Leader James Leathart, 54 Squadron, stopped an overwrought technial officer firing blind down the shelters to flush the scrimshankers out. Manston's chaplain, the Reverend Cecil King, acted as promptly. Near-berserk, another officer had burst wild-eyed into the mess, a

revolver trembling in his hand, threatening to finish off himself and every man present. Gently, King led him from the room, talking of God's infinite mercy, until the man broke down and surrendered his gun.

In Manston's smoke-filled horror and confusion, the thirty-four-year-old chaplain was an inspiration to all who saw him. Armed for safety's sake with his uncle's Webley revolver – which he later found would have blown up after one round – King had helped to organize every detail of the shattered station's routine. He had noticed that the Germans zoomed in from Cap Gris Nez at mealtimes, when many airmen were queueing outside their dining halls; his suggestion that all mealtimes be put back an hour kept casualties low. Even burial services needed careful planning; for German airmen he had thoughtfully procured a German flag, captured at Narvik, to drape the coffins. And few would forget King's dispersal-hut services, his text from Psalm 63 hand-picked for pilots: 'In the shadow of Thy wings will I rejoice.'

At 3.30 pm on August 18, Manston was again, without warning, under fire. The Spitfires of 266 Squadron were still on the ground, being serviced by the flight crews, when sixteen Me 109s burst from the sun, machine-guns hammering. Planes took fire with a white incandescent flame, and everywhere men fell wounded. There was no time for anything but evasive action. Spitfire pilot Dick Trousdale, a canny New Zealander, too weighed down by flying kit to run for it, presented his rear-end to the raiders like a Moslem at prayer; obligingly, his low slung parachute stopped three bullets. Sergeant Don Kingaby, hitting the deck saw the earth spout ahead of him and marked the line of fire; rolling rhythmically back and forth for five minutes, gauging the spouts, he escaped with a nicked thumb.

Others sought shelter as and where they could. Pilot Officer Henry Jacobs, at the base of an apple tree while Squadron Leader Graham Deverley tossed down fruit to him, dived without hesitation for a bed of stinging-nettles; when Deverley fell clean on top of him he judged himself amply screened. Flying Officer David Clackson and six others lay prone beneath the mess billiard table – while raking shots sheared the baize from the slate as cleanly as a knife might have done. Crawling from beneath the table they stared, unbelieving: it was as if the Germans had meant to do that. They felt a sudden unutterable sense of helplessness.

120

At HQ Fighter Command, the hour was late. Though the RAF had claimed 140 German planes – swiftly amended to seventy-one, including thirty ill-fated Stukas – it was his own command's casualties that held Dowding spellbound now. Twenty-seven planes had been written off altogether, as many were badly damaged. Ten fighter pilots were dead; eighteen were severely enough wounded to need hospital treatment. Small wonder Dowding looked grave. On the previous day, the Air Ministry had at last acceded to his long-standing request: the thinning ranks of Fighter Command would be stiffened now by many Fairey Battle pilots, Army Co-operation Command pilots, and by Allied pilots like Squadron Leader Ernest McNab's No. 1 RCAF Squadron. But again the training period had been slashed – from one month to two short weeks. Many of these pilots, like those now serving, would never have fired the guns on a fighter, were unable to use a reflector sight, and would have done exactly twenty hours on Spitfires and Hurricanes. These were the men who would bear the brunt of the battle that lay ahead.

To Robert Wright, it seemed a long time before Dowding, with a superhuman effort, aroused himself. Almost it seemed as if he found difficulty in arising from his chair. Then, shrugging slowly into his greatcoat, the Air Officer Commanding-in-Chief contrived to put a brave face on things: 'Must be on parade in the morning, Wright, must be on parade in the morning.'

62. (*Over the page*) German bomb exploding on the parade ground of RAF Hemswell, Lincs, on 27 August 1940

6. The German Bombers

August 18–28

At Kirton-in-Lindsey, 100 miles from the battle-line, on the Lincoln-shire fens, the pilots of No. 264 Defiant Squadron were agog with excitement. For weeks now their sole link with the war had been the BBC's nightly news bulletins; never had the shepherding of convoys along England's peaceful East Coast seemed more irksome. But soon after breakfast on August 20, Squadron Leader Philip Hunter, the dark dapper CO, had warned that tomorrow they would be moving out.

And by noon on August 21, his pilots were past all worry. Airborne from Kirton, Hunter had set a southerly course from the first, and soon the grey ribbon of the Thames curved beneath their wings. As they touched down, however, at Hornchurch airfield, Essex, har-dened veterans shook their heads. If 264 Squadron was part of the battle, it showed the desperate straits Dowding had reached. A two-seater fighter with an unwieldy power-operated gun-turret, the Defiant had a maximum speed of 304 miles an hour. And since the pilots relied solely on their gunners' verbal instructions to manoeuvre into a firing position, they were almost powerless against frontal attack.

Yet Dowding saw no other choice. By the end of August, 181 fighter pilots had been killed in combat or on training flights, another 145 wounded. Some 426 aircraft had been written off, with fully 222 undergoing repairs. Already, by August 20, six squadrons had been pulled from the unblooded outfits affording fighter cover to the north and midlands. Those who fought in the south must find strength to fight on.

On every airfield, there was hourly proof of how tough things were. If tools and spares were lacking to keep planes airborne, maintenance men improvised. Faced with an eighteen-inch gash in a Spitfire wing at Biggin Hill, Aircraftman Harold Mead cut a slice from a petrol can and tacked it into place with four rivets. At Duxford, Leading Air-craftman William Eslick and his mates saved precious minutes by

124

switching the access point to the compressed-air bottles powering the guns – from an inaccessible trap in the cockpit floor to a point behind the pilot's seat, with ingress through the sliding hood.

To the squadron commanders it made no sense at all. Why go on sending up units twelve strong when the bulk of that strength was made up by novices who were downed on their first flight? A small cadre of veterans who knew the ropes would be twice as effective. At Biggin Hill, where he often spent an hour each night wrestling with letters to next-of-kin, Squadron Leader John Ellis, commanding 610 Spitfire Squadron, bravely broached this very point with Air Chief Marshal Dowding. As Ellis saw it, it was a futile waste of planes and personnel. Replying, Dowding was stony: if twelve planes were serviceable, twelve planes would at all times be airborne.

Other commanders were just as baffled. At Tangmere, 601 Squadron's commander, Flight Lieutenant Sir Archibald Hope, put a personal request to Air Vice-Marshal Keith Park, commander of No. 11 Group. If 601 withdrew to Scotland for one week's rest and training they would return like giants refreshed. For answer, Park switched the squadron to the sector station of Debden in Essex, covering the hotly-contested Thames Estuary approach to London, then back to Tangmere. In one sortie, the weary Hurricane unit lost four men; by early September, below strength, they had been pulled out altogether.

At Kenley, this same problem faced Flight Lieutenant Denys Gillam, moving spirit of the newly-arrived 616 Auxiliary Squadron. Forcefully he put his case to Air Vice-Marshal Park: he had no time to train the green replacements sent him and the older hands were too weary to give of their best. He, too, sought brief respite – one short week to teach the new boys the tricks of survival. Park's reaction was as violent as if Gillam had preached sedition. Under no circumstances could he agree to front-line squadrons being released to study tactics.

Still Gillam failed to see how this thin-red-line outlook made any sense. If the RAF withdrew to the airfields north of London, they would be out of the 109s range – and the pilots would have time to gain operational height before speeding south. True, airfields would be within bomber range – but shorn of fighter protection, the bombers were easy meat. At Hawkinge and Manston, the RAF invariably climbed beneath hovering fighters, knowing they'd be jumped at 18,000 feet before they'd ever had time to gain height.

It was hard for any pilot to grasp that Dowding and Park saw a show of front-line strength as paramount. As yet, with large scale daylight raids on British cities an unknown bogey, the morale of the people was in doubt – and even retaining advance bases like Manston, tactically wrong, was as politically expedient as the Navy's attempts to force the Channel passage. To keep morale at peak, every plane available must be up there in the sky.

It wasn't surprising that few saw themselves as heroes: press eulogies and parliamentary oratory alike left them unmoved. At Kenley, the pilots of No. 64 Squadron, ranged beside their planes, could scarcely contain their laughter as Under Secretary of State for Air Archibald Sinclair paid warm tribute to these Hurricane pilots of No. 12 Group; until then, to the best of their belief, they had been Spitfire pilots of No. 11 Group. On August 20, when Churchill, before a packed House of Commons, paid his immortal homage to 'The Few', the reactions of most aviators were affectionately ribald. At North Weald, Pilot Officer Michael Constable-Maxwell chuckled: 'He must be thinking of our liquor bills.' Flying Officer Michael Appleby thought instead of the meagre fourteen shillings and six-pence a day at which the country valued his services. Irreverently he capped the speech: '. . . and for so little.' Most saw themselves as expendable and Red Tobin's wisecrack, as he tapped the wings on his tunic, summed it up for all of them: 'I reckon these are on a one-way ticket, pal.'

Both Red and Andy Mamedoff had good reason to know. Until their first August 16 combat they, too, had had a bare twenty hours on Spitfires – and now, within five days of Churchill's speech, both had looked death squarely in the face. At 6 pm on August 24, there was nothing to alert Red and the others that the Germans were planning a daring 100-plus dive-bombing attack – Junkers 88s escorted by Zer-störers and Me 109s – on this Dorset forward base. One moment the pilots were sprawled on the dusty grass at dispersal, swapping stories – the next they were staring, unbelieving, at scores of German planes flying in perfect, stepped-up box formation. It was all so orderly that Aircraftman Laurence James, peeping from a slit trench, applauded aloud: 'Have you ever seen anything so damned cool?'

Airborne so swiftly that the raiders had no time to scatter more than a score of bombs, 609 Squadron were soon blazing across the four-mile channel of the Solent, between Portsmouth and the Isle of Wight. At 19,000 feet Red Tobin saw an Me 110 drifting in a gentle bank ahead of him, enormous, seemingly impregnable with its fifty-

63. Spitfire pilots of 610 Squadron at immediate readiness, next to their aircraft, Biggin Hill.

foot wing span. Before the rear-gunner could swing his long barrel round, Tobin thumbed the firing button, holding the gunsight steady just to starboard of the gunner's goggled face. Tracer sparkled along the whole length of the fuselage, and then the Me 110 was climbing, almost vertically, as if the pilot was trying to loop. For a moment it seemed to hang like that, motionless, a giant silver projectile aimed at the evening sun. Then it veered steeply to starboard, vanishing from sight.

Barely had Red broken, jinking through a lethal latticework of curving, glowing tracer, than another Messerschmitt swam into his sights. As if by reflex, Red jerked the firing button; the 110 see-sawed and a thin straight ribbon of black trailed from its engine. Then the German was losing height in a giddy succession of spins and turns, and Red, on fire with the chase, followed after him, banking steeply at more than 370 miles an hour. In that instant, 18,000 feet above the water, he blacked out. The thrust of G pushed him deep against the bucket aluminium seat, bending his backbone like a bow, pushing his chin downwards onto his chest. The inexorable centrifugal force was driving the blood from his head towards his feet, turning it to the weight of molten iron, and for a second his brain was no longer working; his jaw sagged like an idiot's and a yellow-grey curtain swam before his eyes. And at this moment he had a dream so terrifying that no man could ever persuade him to reveal it, until suddenly a gentle insistent voice was urging him: 'You are in an airplane and you are fighting. You'd better come to.'

Then drowsily, Red found his brain clearing, and he was flying absolutely level, only 1,000 feet above the water. Back at Warmwell airfield, he excused himself shakily to Squadron Leader Darley: 'I blacked out colder than a clam,' but the squadron were all solicitude. Sick at heart, they had watched him spin all the way, fearing the worst. From this moment on, Red felt less lighthearted – and even the veterans were the same.

At Northolt airfield, outside London, Squadron Leader Ernest McNab, leading No. 1 Squadron, Royal Canadian Air Force, had reached 'the lowest point in my life' – though the pilot shortage decreed that McNab's Canadians should be operational from August 17, he knew his men were not ready for combat. Like most outfits, they had fired at a moving target in the air only once. But word had come that German bombers were heading north across the Isle of Wight and at HQ 11 Group, Park's controller feared the worst: the raiders must be once more bound for Tangmere Sector Station. The Canadians' orders were explicit: intercept the Germans over Selsey Bill, the southernmost part of the West Sussex coastline.

Nine miles north-west, at RAF Station, Thorney Island, three slow-paced Blenheim patrol planes of No. 235 Squadron, Coastal Command, were ordered up on the same mission.

It wasn't until the German bombers pressed steadily on that the controllers spotted their intention: a mass strike against Portsmouth Harbour. Over Selsey, Squadron Leader McNab's Canadians realized this, too; black oily puffs of smoke hung motionless in the sky to the west. At 4.40 pm, flying at 10,000 feet, the Canadians swung towards Portsmouth.

Ahead of McNab at 6,000 feet, north and east of Thorney Island, three aircraft were flying in line astern, heading away from Portsmouth. Through the dark curtain of ack-ack puffs, McNab saw them as Junkers 88s, though smoke and sunlight didn't make for easy identification. Flight Lieutenant Gordon McGregor still recalls with fascinated dread: 'Those planes were black – black against the sun.'

In the fearful instant before the attack, McNab, leading his section of three, called: 'Echelon, starboard – go!' and then they were diving at 300 miles an hour, faster and faster; but too fast, however, to hear McNab's next electrifying scream in their earphones: 'Break, break, break! Don't attack!' For at 3,000 feet above the dark silhouettes, McNab had seen the gun turrets which Junkers 88s conspicuously lacked and the white flash on the aircraft's fins, marking them as British. He and his section broke violently to port and did not attack. But the following planes saw what they took to be long, yellow spears of tracer curving towards them, and opened fire – not realizing the Blenheims' gunners were firing yellow and red Very pistol flares, the colours of the day, which were the recognition signal.

Tyres holed, undercarriage wrecked, Blenheim pilot Sergeant Naish was within an ace of disaster; he escaped the Hurricanes' point-blank fire only by crashlanding on Thorney Island airfield. Starboard engine holed, his windscreen starred with thick opaque blotches, the second pilot, Flight Lieutenant Flood, was lucky to follow suit. It was the purest tragedy that the third Blenheim, Pilot Officer David Woodger's, never made it. Smoke was streaming from its tailplane, its starboard engine was already on fire. East of Thorney Island, over Bracklesham Bay, it fell apart, blazing like a petrol-soaked brand, in the second before it struck the water.

Back at Northolt, the Canadians' home base, it was the station commander, Group Captain Stanley Vincent, who broke the news as gently as might be, to the shaken Squadron Leader McNab. When McNab, appalled, cried: 'My God, what have we done? What can I do?' Vincent was compassionate. 'There's nothing you can do, these things happen in war – the one thing you must do is to fly down and see them and explain.'

It was war indeed – and now the Luftwaffe's revised tactics were working triumphantly. From August 19, Sperrle's Air Fleet Three, on the Cherbourg peninsula, had been stripped of every single-engined fighter; by August 24, all were transferred to the Pas de Calais, operating under Oberst Theo Osterkamp, regional fighter commander for Air Fleet Two. Now the main onus of the battle lay with Generalfeldmarschall Kesselring: the main concentration of effort was in the east, and the bombers that droned in over Kent would be escorted by almost every single-engined fighter the Luftwaffe had.

No. 264 Defiant Squadron felt the full impact of this new tempo. Not long after 5 am on August 24, they had been ordered by their

home base, Hornchurch, to furnish Manston's fighter cover – a near insuperable task for an aircraft whose rate of climb barely exceeded 2,000 feet a minute. Yet in the first shattering attack, only one section, under Flight Lieutenant John Banham, even had time to climb. As Banham's section circled on sentry-go, three other sections were on the ground refuelling. Then, as seven Defiants prepared to take off anew, came the emergency Fighter Command dreaded the most: twenty Ju 88 dive bombers, with a powerful fighter escort, hurtled from the early morning mist, their bombs falling in black ugly salvoes amongst the taxi-ing planes.

Aloft the confusion was as great. At a converging speed of 600 miles an hour, the fighters flew clean through the Defiant formation, neither side firing a shot. To his eternal surprise, Flight Lieutenant Banham found himself diving with the bombers, hauling both feet onto the control column to keep level. Pilot Officer Eric Barwell, trying for a nose-shot, turned so steeply he blacked out his gunner. Caught up in his first sortie, Pilot Officer Desmond Hughes saw the looming black crosses and thought: This is it, they really do come over here. The five-minute skirmish cost 264 Squadron six men, and three machines – and soon they must face the Germans yet again.

Manston airfield was also suffering cruelly. In 600 Squadron's Ops Room, Pilot Officer Henry Jacobs was relaying a blow-by-blow commentary to HQ 11 Group when a hollow note like a gong echoed up the wire and then the line went silent. A bomb had struck the telephone and teleprinter lines, severing 248 circuits at one blow. Dashing from the Ops room, he saw the East Camp guardhouse next door had vanished – nothing but chalk dust mushrooming above a crater forty feet deep.

In a savage frenzy of impotence, 600 Squadron hit back with everything they had, rifles, Very pistols, the pole-mounted Vickers called 'The Armadillo'. Corporal Francis De Vroome hurled stones and clods of chalk skywards. Close by, dashing from a slit trench, the Reverend Cecil King stooped among the ruins of the guardhouse, beside himself with grief as he uncovered fragments of human flesh, passionately shaking his fist at the raiders. Later, told by eye-witnesses that he had cursed like a trooper, he couldn't remember a word of it.

Defiant gunner Freddie Sutton couldn't believe his eyes; as the bombs tore up the airstrip, men ducked beneath petrol bowsers, seemingly too dazed with shock to realize the danger. Leading Fire-

131

man Herbert Evans, Margate Fire Brigade, tut-tutting through the airfield's main gates on a motor cycle, as spearhead of the main fire force, felt he had hit a ghost airfield. Hangars, the armoury, aircraft at dispersal, all were burning with a yellow flickering flame – yet the grass acres were as deserted as a prairie.

Margate's Chief Officer Albert Twyman arrived on the scene; though unexploded bomb craters pitted the ground all round them, there was work for his firemen to do. Dashing into the blazing armoury, Twyman's men time and again stumbled forth with armfuls of precious Browning machine-guns, while a blazing Very light store next door spangled the afternoon sky with whooshing red and white lights. Only when the roof-timbers sagged ominously inwards did Twyman lead his smoke-grimed shock-troops to safety – his feat was to earn him the George Medal for bravery.

Although many squadrons were due to withdraw, making way for new blood, the irony was that the veterans, dog-tired though they were, were still scoring. All too often men fresh to the battle could contribute little more than bravery, the ability to face death with disdain.

Take the case of Sergeant Ronnie Hamlyn, a dashing twenty-three-year-old of 610 Squadron, veteran of Dunkirk. Soon after 8 am on August 24, Hamlyn's Spitfire, off Ramsgate, was diving from 12,000 feet onto a Junkers 88, hosing it with fire, watching it rip like a hydrofoil along the water's surface. Banking, he fastened on the tail of an Me 109, firing until this, too, fell, trailing a red garland of flame. By 9 am, Hamlyn was back at his home-base, Biggin Hill – preparing to face a different kind of ordeal.

A few days earlier, the young sergeant had made a careless wheels-up landing at Gravesend – and now he must face his station commander, Group Captain Richard Grice, on a charge of negligence. But at 10.35 am, as he lined up outside Grice's office door, the tannoy loudspeaker blared into life: 610 Squadron was to scramble. Politely, Hamlyn excused himself to Warrant Officer George Merron, his escort: trouble threatened, but he'd be back.

Vectored first to Gravesend, then over Dover, 610 Squadron had patrolled for a full hour before they swept into six Me 110s – all of which swung abruptly for France. The Messerschmitts had a head-start; even flying at full throttle, Hamlyn couldn't open fire until he had crossed the French coast. Then, closing to 150 yards, he sent six three-second bursts blasting into the centre of the fuselage, aiming

6. (*Above left*) Two from 74. Flight Lieutenants H. M. Stephen, DSO (*left*) and C. Mungo-Park, DFC, of 74 ('Tiger') Squadron, 1940. Mungo-Park became commander of 74 in April 1941, but was killed in action over France on June 27 that year.

7. (*Right*) Sergeant Ronald Hamlyn, DFM of 610 Squadron. He later rose to Wing Commander rank and was awarded an AFC.

from beneath and astern. Black smoke vomited from the stricken port engine as the Me nose-dived beyond control into a field. Hamlyn saw no one walk away.

Around 4 pm bare-headed, braced to attention, Hamlyn was back in Group Captain Grice's office. As Grice pondered his offence, the loudspeaker rasped again, calling 610 Squadron, and Hamlyn, blushing to the roots of his hair, apologized profusely: there was man's work to be done. Then he was away, haring for his plane, and the swift flight towards the intercept at Gravesend.

North of the Isle of Sheppey, the Spitfires roared into battle with twenty 109s, and Hamlyn, holding his machine in the tightest turn ever, hauling with both hands on the control column, flayed fire at two more 109s until both fell flaming for the water. Homing for Biggin Hill, he pondered: it had been a busy day, but somehow no busier than most. Hamlyn did not know then that an unprecedented toll of five victories would earn him the DFM; he thought only that today, as never before, everything had seemed to click.

133

As he touched down at Biggin Hill, Group Captain Grice, poker-faced, came forward to meet his aircraft: 'As it seems impossible to meet you in my office, Hamlyn, I hereby officially admonish you.'

In the dinghy, in the English Channel, still light-headed, Hauptmann Herbert Kaminski had temporarily forgotten rescue: he was out to save Strauch from himself. All night the gunner had been fiddling at intervals with an unidentified object, but now daylight revealed it for what it was – a small pearl-handled revolver. Convinced Strauch was about to do away with himself, he ordered: 'Throw that pistol overboard. We will have no suicides here.' Strauch protested: he had no such intentions. It was a present from his fiancée and he was trying to keep it dry. Incensed, Kaminski roared: 'Throw the God damn thing overboard,' but the gunner shook a mutinous head. Kaminski sighed. There was nothing for it: Strauch would have to stay in close arrest another ten days.

Just then, far to the east, they saw four Me 110s sweeping over the water, until one pilot spotted the eddying green marker dye. The Zerstörers roared above them in ever-decreasing circles and gleefully Kaminski and Strauch brandished their yellow scarves. But when a minesweeper at last hove to, Kaminski hadn't even the strength to take the line they cast him; he fell top-heavily into the water. They had to rig a bowline and haul him on board, and as he sprawled on the minesweeper's deck he was palsied alternately with cold and laughter. For as Strauch, in turn, was hauled aboard, the gunner's pistol plopped into the water after all.

Oberstleutnant Huth and his pilots were so elated to see Kaminski alive they prevailed on Dunkirk's hospital authorities to let them spirit him back to Lille. They soon regretted it. Above all, Kaminski needed heat to thaw the ice from his stocky frame, and the fire they had to build in the billet was a roasting torment in mid-August. Sweat-soaked, and swooning, the pilots fed the blaze with logs, but Kaminski, sipping iced champagne in bed, felt life was just fine.

Then Kaminski, his 'throat-ache' still unappeased, flew to Düsseldorf; he and Strauch would be shot down and wounded five times more before he won his coveted Knight's Cross, but first a plastic surgeon must fix his broken nose. To celebrate, he rang up Grete Sima, the famous film-star, and invited her to supper at the Rauchpass, Düsseldorf's toniest restaurant. The headwaiter was at his haughtiest but 'The Last of the Prussians' quelled him with a glance:

'Give us the best damn table in the place and bring champagne. I've come from the English Channel.'

One squadron that certainly wasn't giving up without a fight was 264 Defiant Squadron – though by later afternoon on August 26, two days after entering the battle, it seemed more akin to gallantry than commonsense. Only that morning, orbiting between Deal and Herne Bay, the Defiants had slammed resolutely into a dozen Dorniers. Hard as they fought the squadron was outnumbered and out-gunned. As Flight Lieutenant John Banham saw a Dornier leap like a landed salmon under his gunner's fire, an explosive shell struck his own plane amidships. His greatest fear was for his gunner, Sergeant Baker: cramped in their turrets, their heads within inches of the gunsights, Defiant gunners, of necessity, wore their parachutes high on their shoulders. Until the pilot turned the plane on its back, his gunner had no freedom to bale out – and even then the chute harness almost always snagged on a projecting lever.

Now, with seconds to spare, Banham swung the blazing plane clean upside down, yelling urgently over the intercom: 'For God's sake get out.' They were over the Channel, ten miles off Margate, and as he jumped he wasn't even sure whether Baker had heard. After a chilly ninety minutes, Banham was picked up by an air-sea rescue launch, but Baker was never found.

Still the losses were rising. On August 24, twenty-two fighters had been written off, and two days later the toll was steeper – thirty-one aircraft lost, four pilots killed, twelve wounded. At HQ 11 Group, Air Vice-Marshal Keith Park was in despair: compared with the sorties flown, the RAF's interceptions were negligible, and thanks to low-lying cloud, the height and strength of many German formations were being imperfectly assessed.

At 8.30 am on August 28, under their new CO, Squadron Leader Desmond Garvin, the Defiants clashed with a mixed bomber formation, heading for Rochford and Eastchurch airfields – a task force escorted by the ace some feared more than death itself, Major Adolf Galland.

Galland knew his men were under heavy stress. Often they couldn't touch a bite before 10 pm; one jangle of the alarm bell set them vomiting. Galland himself kept going, but warm milk mixed with a little red wine was all he could choke down at breakfast. The

68. (*Over the page*) Boulton Paul Defiants of the ill-starred 264 Squadron.

135

strain of adjusting their cruising speed – 298 miles an hour – to a Dornier's snail-paced 265 was an endless frustration. So great a howl for protection had the bomber men set up that the fighters were all the time throttling back to screen them. Now, most humiliating of all, Göring had forbidden fighters to do the very job they were designed for – to range free and fight. Hugging the bombers – 'furniture vans' to the embittered fighter pilots – they must wait tamely until the RAF came and blasted at them. Droning across the Channel, astern of the glinting bombers, Galland knew the kind of combat he sought today – if combat was joined. Always he prayed for what he called a 'You or Me' fight – a relentless kill-or-be-killed duel which only the best man could win.

It was now 8.30 am. At heights ranging from 16,000 to 21,000 feet, 159 German planes slid unopposed across the coastline of North Kent: 120 of Galland's fighters escorting thirty-nine bombers. The two formations parted: the Dorniers of the 3rd Bomber Group swung north-west for Rochford airfield, the Heinkels turned west for East-church. Over Ashford, Kent, Galland's eyes narrowed behind his goggles. It was a second before he spotted them for what they were: eleven British two-seater Defiants, flying in close formation just below the Heinkels, closing in to attack from astern. At any moment the four Browning machine-guns in their power-operated turrets would be raking the Heinkel's bellies.

It was now or never. Slamming his throttle forward, Galland hauled back on the control column. Momentarily G clamped him to his seat, then he was blazing upwards, followed by his staff flight of three, and the tight Defiant formation, at the Messerschmitts' mercy, scattered and broke. Galland became caught up in a duel to the death with Flight Lieutenant Clifford Ash, the gunner in the Defiant piloted by Squadron Leader Garvin. Although the plane was already on fire Ash wasn't giving up. Four times his bullets holed Galland's 109, but even as he fired, Galland wondered what right had they to put such tragically outmoded planes into the firing line? Chunks rained from the Defiant's fuselage; white flames blossomed from the wing tanks. As Galland broke away, he didn't see Ash, baling out, swing mortally against the Defiant's tailplane. Garvin, too, baled out, badly shaken, his eyebrows singed clean away.

Five crewmen were dead, and now only three planes remained serviceable: the massacre of the Defiants was complete. Four days in action had cost them eleven aircraft, fourteen lives. Bitterly, Major

138

Adolf Galland set course for Audembert; it had been no 'You or Me' combat that, merely slaughter. But within seconds Galland himself was in trouble: the circuitous route the bombers had taken, the combat itself, had taken up precious minutes. Galland wondered whether he could get his group home. Already his earphones exploded with anxious voices: 'Red light showing! Red light up!' That meant that pilot after pilot had seen a red warning bulb glow on his instrument panel: very few litres of petrol left from the initial 400. Fifteen minutes' more flying time – twenty at the most.

Below loomed Manston, strangely deserted, dotted with the charred shells of hangars, and the realization struck Galland: in the last resort he might have to force-land and surrender on the airfield he had so often strafed. Then responsibility drove all thoughts of self from his mind: for better, for worse, the 26th Fighter Wing was his and he must survive to lead them. Sweating minutes of tension followed – but somehow he nursed his 109 across the Channel, roaring along the hard packed sand of the beach below Cap Gris Nez at 130 miles an hour. He was lucky: at least seven of his pilots, ditching in mid-Channel, were only just fished from the sea in time.

Had Galland hit Manston he would in all probability have been brought face to face with Winston Churchill who was just then, as part of a two-day coastal visit, trudging its cratered acres. Not surprisingly Churchill was both angry and perplexed. For thousands of civilians and servicemen now, the war was coming home with a violence they had never experienced or expected – and even the bravest could only wonder what lay ahead. Six days earlier, on August 22, Dover had come under fire from the giant guns at Cap Gris Nez; for eighty minutes shells had fallen like cabers among the grey winding streets. On August 24, during the heavy attack on Manston, 500 bombs had hit nearby Ramsgate, damaging 1,000 houses in three minutes. So Churchill worried: how would his people stand up to it?

None knew better than Churchill the faith they needed. With Lieutenant-General Alan Brooke, Commander-in-Chief, Home forces, he had toured almost every mile of Britain's threatened coastline, striding briskly out wherever crowds gathered, despite his weariness, to boost morale, creating chaos each time he flung away a cigar butt as onlookers scuffled for a souvenir. And on all sides, the moral was plain: if 'Operation Sea-Lion' was not to become a grim reality, everything depended on the RAF.

69. Just one of the many graveyards of Luftwaffe aircraft during the summer of 1940.

For all along the coast, the weird barricades showed the shape of the war to come, a guerrilla war with the people caught up in its midst. At Chilham in Kent, tree trunks from the sawmill, at Tonbridge, tar barrels from the distillery, at Goring-by-Sea in Sussex, a flimsy latticework of old iron bedsteads. Inland, at Sidcup crossroads, the police had dumped 100 tons of glass, as for a medieval siege. At Deal, an agricultural contractor, Reginald Blunt, each night waited until 11 pm, when the last bus had gone, then dutifully blocked the road with his three traction engines and a steamroller.

Yet strangely, Churchill had no cause for alarm: with blind faith that the RAF would win through, his people were preparing to stick it out. At Ramsgate, 60,000 of them had settled in for a long war – in caves seventy feet below the chalk cliffs, known locally as 'The Persian Market'. Together with beds, tables and chairs made from barrels, most had brought their own alarm clocks, ears attuned to sleep through every clangour save their own. Even groceries were no

140

70. Production of Hurricanes throughout 1940 reached a monthly average of 250 machines by October; far in excess of the vital replacements of trained pilots to fly them.

problem; at week-ends, local tradesmen lowered provisions down the bluff with a rope and pulley.

Those who didn't fancy shelter life clung doggedly on in their houses – scrubbing their doorsteps as white as a bleached bone after each air raid. Outside Ramsgate's blitzed Assembly Hall, a notice loomed: 'Cheer up – the best part of history is still to be written.' Even the errand boys carried on, wearing tin hats to deliver their goods. Under shellfire on the broad cliffs which rimmed St Margaret's Bay, Reginald Blunt and his minder Bill Harris were at work threshing several thousand quarters of corn, labouring from dawn to dusk. Some used danger to their own advantage. At a Chilham poultry auction, one man who stood resolutely fast as bombers zoomed low and the bidders scattered, got his lot dirt cheap.

Though Churchill only half suspected it, the Germans' day-by-day attacks were stiffening British resolution: a slow inoculation of danger in the blood. Each day that the battle raged further inland brought

141

the people closer to war. All over southern England, people prepared to meet the Germans with all the *sangfroid* they could muster. At Hadlow Down in Kent, Alan Henderson, a sharp-eyed ten-year-old, noted that men kept their pitchforks at the ready, the girls their lipsticks: Luftwaffe aces could be very devastating. In Mercery Lane, Canterbury, a puzzled Home Guard hastened into George Woods' high-class cigar store: was there a brand of cigarettes called State Express 555? When Woods obliged, the man explained: 'We've bagged a German pilot and he's sent me to get them.' At Buckhurst, Earl De La Warr's Sussex estate, the butler with flawless composure announced: 'An officer of the German armed forces is waiting to see you in the drawing-room, my lord.'

At 5 pm on August 28, the war, as never before, at last found Farmer Robert Bailey. Until recently, he had not for a second regretted his decision to stay on at Ladwood Farm. That deep shelter he had dug behind the house had been finished days back – but to date not one of the family had needed to set foot in it. His thoughts were far from the war: weighed down by buckets of swill he was in the farmyard, with ninety plump, grunting pigs clamouring for their feed. Five hundred yards away, on the crest of the hill by Ladwood Copse, old Rodney, the horse, was grazing peaceably, along with the cows and heifers.

Then, high above him in the sky, too far away to hear the roar of the engines, Bailey saw a formation of three Hurricanes flying from the direction of Canterbury. Suddenly, though he had seen no German plane, one of the pilots baled out. As far as Bailey could judge, the pilot would land some three miles from Hawkinge airfield – but though his eyes scanned the hazy blue, he couldn't see the abandoned Hurricane. Next instant he glimpsed it and his blood ran cold. It was spiralling to earth at 450 miles an hour, coming straight for Ladwood Farmhouse.

So petrified he couldn't even run or shout, Bailey watched, arms bowed like hoops under the weight of the swill buckets. He could hear the Hurricane now, the harsh, shrill screech of an engine out of control, the plane coming straight for the farmhouse as if it planned a perfect three-point landing. Then a breeze teased gently at one wing, and Bailey saw that the plane would miss the farmhouse, but hit the copse instead. Now, 500 yards from where he stood, the Hurricane struck the wood's topmost branches, the tall trees ripped open like matchwood and the plane ploughed on, cutting a swathe like a sickle

142

for 100 yards, shattering against the great stock of an ash tree. Then it blew up.

For Bailey 'the whole wood suddenly seemed to take on leaves of fire' – a blaze so fearful that Folkestone fisherman, trawling for mackerel eighteen miles away off Dungeness, saw the red shifting skyline. Above the crackling roar of the flames, running feet were audible: it was Bailey's neighbour, Mr Tobit of Standard Hill Farm. Dazedly, the two men exchanged news: three planes had crashed within seconds of one another, the Me 109 coming down in Garden Wood.

As Bailey hurried back to Ladwood, a car packed with RAF officers tore through the farmyard gate; a tall officer, cursing like a trooper, leapt out and hastened up to him. What had happened to the pilot? Had Bailey seen anything? When Bailey reassured him: 'He's safe enough, I saw him bale out, but there wasn't anything we could do for the plane,' the officer seemed content. 'We can get another plane,' he said. 'We can't get another pilot.'

Robert Bailey said nothing. Moments earlier, the war had reached out to destroy everything that was most dear to him, then, unpredictably, had stayed its hand. He needed time to think, to readjust.

71. (*Over the page*) Squadron Leader Ian 'Widge' Gleed, DFC, of 87 Squadron, in his usual Hurricane, P2798, LK-A, 'Figaro' (the Walt Disney cartoon cat insigne which decorated all his aircraft); leading the unit from Exeter to Bibury in September 1940.

7. Biggin Hill

August 28–September 3

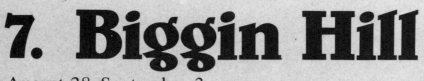

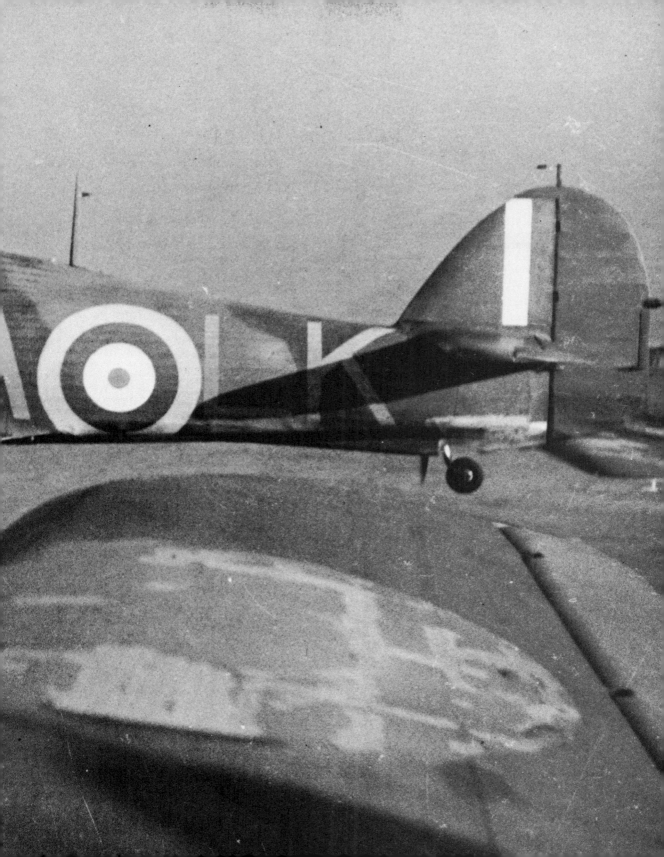

Pilot Officer Geoffrey Page lay in the Royal Masonic Hospital, Hammersmith, West London, sobbing helplessly. For the first time, the staff nurse looking after him, who had fed him and tended him ever since his transfer from Margate General Hospital, had brought a Red Cross trainee to help with the dressings. To Page, she was one of the loveliest girls he had ever seen – but what went through him was the uncontrolled horror in her eyes.

Hypnotized, Page saw, as if for the first time, the solid slough of boils covering his forearms from elbow to wrist. From wrist to finger tips his hands were blacker than ebony, smaller than he had ever remembered them. Then the staff nurse's voice came drily: 'That black stuff's tannic acid. It's not the colour of your skin.' As Page felt relief flow through him, the trainee, her face working, ran headlong from the room.

The silence seemed to stretch for ever, and the fear that had obsessed Page ever since Margate was surging uncontrollably: What had the fire done to his face? Why wouldn't they tell him? His voice icy, he commanded: 'Get me a mirror, please, nurse.' The nurse's voice was as cold as his own. 'You'll be allowed to look in a mirror, Pilot Officer Page, when I see fit to permit it and not before.' For ten silent minutes Page lay there hating her, until at last, dropping the tweezers with a clank into a kidney dish, she propelled the trolley from the room, without one parting word. With a twenty-year-old's stubbornness, Page vowed: 'Right, you miserable bitch – I'll look in the bloody mirror if it kills me.'

In fact, the mirror hung over the washbasin, only two steps distant from his bed – but how to dislodge the bedclothes which were tucked with hospital efficiency beneath the mattress? Five minutes of painful heaving with his elbows, sobbing for breath, had moved them as far as the cradle which kept the sheets from his injured leg. Now he had only to sit up and swing his legs over the edge of the bed – no easy task when he couldn't even use his hands for support. A wave of dizziness swept over him, teetering high on the edge of the bed, above the polished floor.

Gingerly, straightening his back, Page slid feet first to the ground. But the movement jolted his elbow painfully; his leg muscles were growing weaker by the second. As he took the first tentative step forward, icy sweat bathed him; he felt his knees buckle. One lurching pace further, squeezing the moisture from his eyes, he reached the mirror.

Then two things happened as one: the door swung suddenly open behind him and he saw the staff nurse's face, shocked and drawn, loom beyond his left shoulder. For one hideous second the black swollen mass that had been his face swam and bobbed in the mirror glass. Then mercifully, the room reeled and he smashed unconscious against the washbasin.

The battle to be a fighter pilot was over; for Page another, greater, battle was just beginning.

But for scores of Dowding's pilots, the shooting war had only now begun – and with little concept of what lay ahead, they greeted the news with gold-rush fervour.

As 603 Squadron flew south from Turnhouse, Scotland, one pilot, Richard Hillary, recalled a moving moment: the children of the Tarfside valley, hands raised in silent farewell as the squadron dived in salute, immobile on the sunlit grass beside the white boulders they had arranged to spell: 'Good Luck'. On August 27, 603 landed at Hornchurch airfield, Essex – and 222 Squadron landed soon after, parking their Spitfires wing-tip to wing-tip as neatly as in peacetime. Promptly the fiery Wing Commander Bouchier hailed Squadron Leader Johnnie Hill: 'What the hell do you think you're doing, lining up planes like that? Get them staggered and dispersed – don't you know there's a war on?'

The Battle had now reached the point where, despite their two weeks' crash-course, pilot losses were fast outstripping the training units' yield; in the whole of August they had turned out only 260 pilots, and casualties had totalled 300. Now the pilot wastage was approaching 120 men a week; from May right through August, losses had averaged 476 pilots a month – 346 killed or missing, 130 wounded. And aircraft production was falling, too – in the thirteen days following August 24, 466 fighters had been destroyed or damaged as against a total of 269 new or repaired. From July onwards, aircraft

production had fallen by 19 per cent; aero-engines by 26 per cent. As the losses mounted, the men close to Dowding knew that only a miracle could save the RAF now.

Some men, however, were in the mood for miracles. At Northolt airfield, Squadron Leader Zdzislaw Krasnodebski had seen his pilots' spirits sink daily lower – and their hatred for Group Captain Stanley Vincent grow daily more intense. Though over 100 Poles serving with British squadrons had played their part in the Battle's first three weeks, the all-Polish 303 Squadron was still grounded – for Vincent felt their grasp of English was still too rudimentary to risk their lives in the air.

But at 4.35 pm on August 30, at the hour of Air Chief Marshal Dowding's deepest despair, No. 303 Squadron, by blindest chance, became operational. As they took off from Northolt at 4.15 pm, gaining height to 10,000 feet, their training flight was as routine as

148

could be: north of St Albans in Hertfordshire they were to rendez-vous with six Blenheims and execute dummy attacks on them. Twenty minutes later, at 4.35 pm, young Ludwig Paszkiewicz, glancing down, stared, perplexed. Below, the tiny cathedral town slept in the August sun, but smoke furled steadily from a cluster of roofs like the prelude to an Indian attack.

At that moment Paszkiewicz saw another smoke trail, plunging downwards to meet the first: a Hurricane much like his own. A thousand feet above them, to port, sixty German bombers, as many 109s and a handful of British fighters were caught up in a running battle. At once he alerted Squadron Leader Ronald Kellett: 'Hullo, Apany Leader, bandits ten o'clock.' But if Kellett had heard he made no rejoinder. Pressing the emergency control which sent his supercharger to a maximum twelve boosts, Paszkiewicz broke for the battle.

In fact, the phlegmatic Kellett had heard the warning clearly, grunting: 'If you want to be a hero, be one' – but though it was too late to restrain Paszkiewicz, he wouldn't allow the others to follow. There was still an exercise in progress – and with 109s on the warpath they must now scrap the dummy attacks and escort the Blenheims safely to Northolt.

72. Sheep among the wolves. A Gotha Go 145 which landed on Lewes race-course on 28 August 1940. Its pilot was delivering mail to German forces in the Channel Isles but lost his way – to be painfully surprised on landing when greeted by a party of Home Guards.

But Krasnodebski saw it differently: this was his beloved squadron's turning point. For now, as Paszkiewicz winged towards the formation, the young Pole saw a strange plane turning towards him, then banking into a steep dive; following in a half-roll he saw the black cross marking its wing – a Dornier. From 100 yards dead astern, Paszkiewicz fired 303 Squadron's first symbolic burst, firing until the starboard engine gouted flame. He was still firing when a crewman baled out, then the bomber dived, more steeply still, lurching for the ground.

It was the forerunner of many victories to come. Air Staff officers might explode that the Poles were incapable of observing discipline, but Kellett, seeing their morale at fever-pitch, knew it was time to act. Later, phoning Fighter Command, he urged: 'Under the circumstances, I do think we might call them operational.' Without hesitation, Dowding had agreed. The Poles were needed now, as never before.

For the first time since the battle began, the German raiders were getting through with steadily diminishing losses: small compact bomber units, no more than twenty strong, shielded by three times as many fighters, probing for – and finding – their targets. And time and again, the newcomer squadrons ignored Air Vice-Marshal Park's edict: Strike for the bombers that will do the damage; whenever possible, leave the fighters alone. On August 28 their disregard of this order had cost the RAF twenty Hurricanes and Spitfires for thirty-one German planes – and twelve of those had been bombers. Next day, with 564 Me 109s and 159 Me 110s in a massive fighter sweep over Kent, Park kept his squadrons on a tight rein – but it was plain now that, unhampered by the Stukas, the Germans could get through.

To Reichsmarschall Hermann Göring, it was vital that they should. Plans for 'Operation Sea-Lion' had reached a crisis point: on August 23, the German Army and Navy had clashed decisively. Gross-Admiral Erich Raeder, the Navy's Commander-in-Chief, had urged that landings must be confined to the narrow Straits of Dover; naval strength just wasn't adequate to win command of any larger area. To the Army, a landing on so cramped a front was plain suicide. As Generaloberst Franz Halder, Chief of the Army General Staff, had put it: 'I might as well put the troops that have landed straight through a sausage machine.'

Then, on August 27, Hitler stepped in with a compromise. Why not confine the landings to four main areas – between Folkestone and Dungeness, Dungeness and Cliff's End, Bexhill and Beachy Head and Brighton to Selsey Bill? Still the Navy were dubious. To land eleven divisions between the North Foreland and the Isle of Wight might call for two million tons of shipping. In the last resort, it was plain, everything must depend on the Luftwaffe's vanquishing the RAF.

Although few Luftwaffe pilots had much belief in the invasion as such they were faring better in the air than they knew. All that week they had punched home their attacks: the successful Eastchurch–Rochford raid that Major Galland had escorted, a punishing strike against the 300-acre sector station at Debden in Essex, a strategic fifty-bomb sortie on Detling airfield which cut the mains cable and fired the oil tanks.

Then by sheer mischance, a mains supply failure along the eighty miles of coastline between Whitstable and Beachy Head put the radar stations out of action. At 6 pm on August 30, there was nothing to warn Squadron Leader Roger Frankland, the duty controller at Biggin Hill Sector Station, that nine Junkers 88 dive-bombers, loaded with 1,000 pounds, feinting towards the Thames Estuary, had now

73. Sergeant Josef Frantisek, a Czech who flew with Polish units in France, and then with 303 Squadron in England. After shooting down at least seventeen German aircraft during the Battle, he died in a simple landing accident on October 8.

turned south, driving for Biggin Hill. With the cloud layer at 7,000 feet, the Observer Corps were plotting by ear alone.

At Biggin Hill, there were only minutes of warning before the bombers were upon them. Biggin's Spitfire Squadron, No. 610, was too high and too far away from base to tackle the raiders: only one unit, No. 79 Hurricane Squadron, remained as defence. Distractedly, Squadron Leader Frankland tried to raise 501 Squadron, then patrolling from Hawkinge, but the first bombs severed the radio telephone link-up. Frankland then called the look-out on the officers' mess roof: 'Identify aircraft making low-level attack.' Back came the look-out's anguished cry. 'Hullo, Control, have no time to identify – am being attacked by a swarm of bees.'

In the shelter at the far end of the WAAF quarters, Corporal Elspeth Henderson, at this moment off-duty from the Ops Room, felt the walls transmit every salvo like a depth charge through water, yet strangely she knew no fear. A steel helmet on her trim red hair, Elspeth sat determinedly on.

It was a quaking nightmare to come. Flat on his face near the main guardhouse, Leading Fireman Patrick Duffy saw an old hydrant-

plate leap like a jack-in-the-box from the solid earth. In a slit trench close by, Section Officer Pamela Beecroft noticed that few were talking: the sharp crack of lightweight bombs followed by the deep vibrant roar of the 1,000 pounders ruled out speech. Soundlessly, in the thick darkness, a WAAF repeated the Lord's Prayer. In another trench, a WAAF who still had her voice had just remarked: 'I think we're being dive-bombed,' when the concrete walls caved in, smothering more than forty girls with tons of chalky earth and stones. Suddenly, from the choking darkness they heard the WAAF Flight Sergeant Gartside exclaim: 'My God, they've broken my neck' – then, incongruously: 'And they've broken my false teeth too!' Pinned there in the darkness, waiting to be dug out, there wasn't a girl who could help laughing. There was no panic, no hysteria.

Some saved their lives by sheer chance. Corporal John Tapp and his mate Amos Collins had just emerged from the airmen's mess when the first bombs came tumbling; at once they joined the throng of running men, carrying their mess tins, streaming across the tennis courts for the nearest shelter. On an impulse, both men decided to stay in the open, ducking round the side of the building. Behind them, machine-gun bullets ripped through a line of dustbins as if they were tinplate. When next they looked the shelter was gone – nothing but a

74. Formed on 10 July 1940, No. 310 (Czech) Squadron first saw action on August 26, based at Duxford. Seated centre, holding map, is an English Flight commander, Flt Lt J. Jeffries, DFC.

monstrous jagged crater, strewn with blue shreds of uniform cloth and the butchered bodies of airmen.

Others survived narrowly. WAAF driver Jackie Day was piloting two officers in her Humber station waggon when the raid began; ten seconds after they piled out into Elspeth Henderson's shelter, a bomb fell twenty-five feet away. Airborne above the aerodrome, Pilot Officer George Nelson-Edwards saw the Humber whoosh skywards, landing sixty feet up on a hangar roof before plunging through to the concrete floor. In the sergeants' mess, the NCOs, ignoring the bombing, were clustered round the radio, turned into Sergeant Ronnie Hamlyn's broadcast on his bag of five German planes. As Hamlyn finished speaking, their appointed slit trench close by was wiped out.

On all sides, the devastation was appalling. Ninety per cent of Biggin Hill's transport had been damaged or destroyed, one hangar had taken a direct hit, two aircraft had been burned out, the workshop and many barracks made uninhabitable, all electricity, water and gas mains cut, a staggering death-roll of thirty-nine dead, with twenty-six injured.

As the fury of the bombing passed, an eerie silence fell: slowly, dazedly, people began to emerge from their shelters. In the distance, Elspeth Henderson heard a faint droning: with empty magazines, the Hurricanes of No. 79 Squadron were returning. A panting messenger, thrusting into Section Officer Pamela Beecroft's trench, begged the chaplain, the Reverend A. J. Gillespie: 'Could you come at once, sir? A trench has been hit.'

The blind fury of the raid had one result: every man and woman on the station was seized by the urge to help. Already airmen, helped by an old countryman who tended the officers' mess garden, were digging in tight-lipped silence to reach all those entombed inside their shelters. Pilots came running from their cockpits to lend a hand; ambulance and stretcher parties stood by, along with a Salvation Army canteen, the first on the spot. Clawing with bare hands at the rubble, Corporal John Tapp winced: the black, burned face of one of his own airmen was staring vacantly up at him.

Everyone weighed in as and where they could. Leading Fireman Patrick Duffy joined Sergeant Joan Mortimer from the Armoury in marking every unexploded bomb on the airfield with a red flag; the hangars were too well ablaze now to need a fireman's attentions, but when the fighters took off at first light, they would need a flight path charted for them. Elspeth Henderson's place was normally in the Ops

Room, but it wasn't her shift and there was work to be done freeing the WAAFs still trapped in their shelter. One by one the bodies were brought out, their faces barely recognizable under a sticky paste of chalk and blood, but all, save one, were alive.

At the height of the raid, the main London–Westerham cable connecting Biggin Hill with the outside world was severed north of the airfield. Now the hard-pressed Hornchurch Sector Station, covering the Thames Estuary, must assume control of the squadrons and satellites of Biggin, Gravesend and Redhill, as well as its own, Rochford – six squadrons to manoeuvre in combat over 5,000 square miles of sky. The key to Dowding's whole system was constantly open telephone lines – but with Biggin Hill's lines out, how would the RAF intercept the bombers if they chose the direct southern route to London lying within Biggin's orbit? As the hours crawled by, Headquarters Fighter Command didn't know.

But the Post Office had taken Biggin Hill's troubles to heart. Inspector Abraham Thomson, a brawny Scottish maintenance engineer, was at home in Tonbridge, sixteen miles away, when word came through of the severed cable: though the airfield's Post Office maintenance officer had been blown clean out of a shelter trench, he still stumbled to the nearest Telephone Exchange to report the damage. The operators had evacuated – but with the aid of a lone workman the engineer manned the switchboard to alert Maintenance Control at Tunbridge Wells.

Around 9 pm – three hours after the bombing – Thomson, his foreman, Mossy Adams, and their six-strong working party set out for Biggin Hill, Thomson and Adams in the Inspector's Ford Prefect, the working party following by truck. The true urgency of their mission struck home to them; the night was inky black; somewhere above the clouds a German bomber droned; beyond Westerham the Home Guard refused them even parking lights to steer by. Towards 10 pm, after hitting a bank with bone-jarring impact, Thomson and Adams had scaled the long gradient that led to Biggin Hill.

By now the airfield was as quiet as a plague city. In the silence Thomson heard the hiss of gas, a broken water main gurgling like a brook. Until first light, at least, there was nothing the engineers could do. Cramped in a rat-infested shelter, they settled to a game of cribbage. It was not until dawn on Saturday, August 31, that Thomson and his crew set to work, slithering down the shingly sides of the six-feet-deep fissure by the officers' mess, where the main cable was severed. Jointer Sid Sharvill and his mates were armed with blow-lamp, lead cutters, wire brushes, crowbars, lead sleeves to seal the repaired wires. The cable, made up of seventy-four pairs of wires, with a gauge of forty pounds to the mile, was ruptured in three places; it would be a three-hour job, at best, before they could hope to effect repairs. But this morning, luck wasn't with the engineers. After half an hour below ground, Thomson's limbs were heavy as lead, he gulped thickly for air – carbon monoxide from a leaking gas main was making them all sick and dizzy. As they clawed their way up from the crater, the first siren of the day whined over the Kentish valleys. It was 8.30 am.

Only at mid-day, groggy from the foul air, could Thomson report to Flight Lieutenant Osmond, Biggin Hill's signals officer, that the main cable was restored. The telephone links with HQ 11 Group, the Observer Corps, the radio telephone transmitting and receiving links

75. The traditional British 'phlegm' was never better illustrated than during 1940; as witnessed by this calm notice.

RICHMOND GOLF CLUB

TEMPORARY RULES. 1940

1. Players are asked to collect Bomb and Shrapnel splinters to save these causing damage to the Mowing Machines.

2. In Competitions, during gunfire or while bombs are falling, players may take cover without penalty for ceasing play.

3. The positions of known delayed action bombs are marked by red flags at a reasonably, but not guaranteed, safe distance therefrom.

4. Shrapnel and/or bomb splinters on the Fairways, or in Bunkers within a club's length of a ball, may be moved without penalty, and no penalty shall be incurred if a ball is thereby caused to move accidentally.

5. A ball moved by enemy action may be replaced, or if lost or destroyed, a ball may be dropped not nearer the hole without penalty.

6. A ball lying in a crater may be lifted and dropped not nearer the hole, preserving the line to the hole, without penalty.

7. A player whose stroke is affected by the simultaneous explosion of a bomb may play another ball from the same place. Penalty one stroke.

155

with the squadrons were intact again – and Biggin Hill was back on the air.

For everyone at Biggin Hill it was a disastrous Saturday. Just before 4 pm, showing her pass to the armed sentry, Elspeth Henderson entered the main Ops Room – sited directly opposite the airfield's main gates, across the London Road. A few moments earlier, a passing housewife had pressed a bag of apples on her – they would help to stave off hunger pangs on the six-hour shift that lay ahead. Already, as the outgoing crew, thirty strong, handed over, the small oblong room facing north towards the officers' mess was alive with murmuring figures, shuffling papers, consulting scribbling pads. Swiftly Elspeth took up her station on the long wooden daïs, raised five feet above the main room where plotters, connected by head-and-breast sets to the Observer Corps centres and Fighter Command's Filter Room, were huddled round a huge glass wall-map of the sector. Fitting on her own headset, Elspeth now checked her own permanent line to HQ 11 Group, who would be controlling the first moves of the battle. This afternoon, two duty controllers had slipped into the seats on her left – Senior Controller Roger Frankland and 32 Squadron's former CO, John Worrall. To her right, Pilot Officer Arthur Bennett manned the keyboard linking him with 11 Group and with Biggin's squadron dispersals.

For more than an hour, there was only subdued activity. Then at 5.37 pm the Observer Corps were on the line: twenty miles east in the Maidstone area, the air-raid warning had sounded. The crew around the Ops Room wall-map were plotting furiously now: an unknown number of raiders was approaching from the south-west, making for the line of the Ashford–Redhill railway. Eight minutes later, Elspeth was scribbling frantically: in her earphones, 11 Group Control were ordering Biggin's squadrons airborne. The message passed to Pilot Officer Bennett, then swiftly to Frankland and Worrall.

Worrall seized the microphone; all over Biggin Hill's 500 acres his voice echoed, metallic, weirdly impersonal: 'Tennis Squadron, scramble. Tennis Squadron scramble. Patrol base.' Twenty-plus Spitfires of 72 Squadron were airborne within minutes, heading for Maidstone. A pause, then the unemotional voice again: 'Pansy Squadron, scramble. Pansy Squadron scramble. Protect base.' With only six machines serviceable, it was doubtful whether 79 Squadron could put up more than token resistance – but they were more vulnerable still on the ground. Simultaneously Frankland ordered the

156

flight supervisor: 'Sergeant Greave. Steel helmets!' And he added a rider: the old Ops Block had no reinforced concrete roof; everybody not urgently required on duty should take shelter.

Aching silence now; the ticking of the synchronized wall clock fretted the nerves like water on stone. On this sultry evening, the temperature was in the eighties; like the other girls in the room, Elspeth was working in blouse and skirt. As if mesmerised she watched the plotter's coloured counters, bringing the raid closer second by second. Worrall spoke again, his voice measured: 'This is an air-raid warning. This is an air-raid warning. All personnel except those employed on essential services are to take cover immediately. Switching off.' Then Frankland spoke to the squadrons: 'Hullo, Tennis leader, this is Rastus. Enemy approaching base, angels ten. Attack imminent. Attack on Rastus imminent. Do what you can.'

Split seconds later, Pilot Officer Bennett and all of them heard the excited voice of the look-out, from the officers' mess roof: 'Twenty Dorniers, sir, coming from the sun – they're coming straight at us.' At once Group Captain Grice, who'd just then entered, ordered: 'Now, all you girls, under the table.'

As fast as a falling curtain, chaos descended. With a thin, high whistling, a 500-pounder loosed by one of Oberst Johannes Fink's Dorniers tore through the Ops Room roof, bouncing violently from a steel safe, exploding in the Defence Teleprinter Network room next door. Simultaneously, as the lights went out, the glass plotting screen burst from its frame, shattering on the steel helments of the crouching WAAFs, spraying slivers of glass everywhere. Peering from the table where she had hastily taken shelter, Sergeant Helen Turner saw knife-edged steel fragments slice her switchboard in two.

Strangely, nobody seemed unnerved; despite the whirling blizzard of plaster dust, they acted as if danger was their heritage. One of the first men on his feet, Aircraftman Townsend, the Ops Room runner, had already hit on a way out – through the window and along a narrow crevice between the Ops Room and the outer blast wall. He exhorted Elspeth Henderson: 'Come along, Miss, you can get through here, show them how to squeeze through.' Peppered in the face and elbows by flying glass, Group Captain Grice was groping on hands and knees for his pipe, cursing strenuously: not until he had located it, undamaged, would he follow on. Pilot Officer Bennett, checking a girl who moved back to the wreckage, was told: 'If you please, sir, I forgot my knitting.'

Courage or not, it seemed as if the end was near. By 6.30 pm. the Observer Corps at Bromley had warned Fighter Command: 'Biggin Hill Operations Room on fire. They cannot take any more.' Nine minutes later Kenley Sector Station pressed Bromley: in this emergency they would have to handle Biggin's squadrons, but they had no note of either call signs or radio frequencies. One hour later, with still no word from Biggin, Kenley's CO, Wing Commander Tom Prickman, sent a motor cycle despatch rider speeding for Biggin. Sickened, the courier reported back: 'The place is like a slaughter-house.' In fact there had been few deaths – only devastation. Inspector Abraham Thomson's temporary lash-up of lines and power cables had been severed yet again – within six hours of completion.

Still Elspeth Henderson found it hard to take in; the plaster dust had lodged deep in her lungs and she couldn't stop coughing. At intervals she explained, almost fiercely, that the blood on her shirt-front had been spilt by someone else, and she didn't need first aid at all. The road outside was so cratered she couldn't even get back to see if her quarters were still intact. Then the question was decided for her, because word came through that the Emergency Ops Room would be functioning within the hour in a commandeered butcher's shop in Biggin Hill village, and the duty watch, bloody, dusty, and still in their shirtsleeves, would repair there to carry on.

It was better that way, Elspeth decided; there was less time to think of what had happened. She could not then know that this day's endeavour was to win her the Military Medal, one of only six awarded to WAAFs through the entire war. To herself, she said, with no sense of drama or occasion: 'All right, then, let's get on with it.'

At Fighter Command the news of Biggin Hill's ordeal was heard with consternation – did the Germans plan to concentrate the might of their bombers against the sector stations? Just five hours earlier, at 1.15 pm, the Dorniers of Oberst Fink's *Kampfgeschwader* 2 had broken through to Hornchurch, just then holding the torch for Biggin, with alarming ease. In the Ops Room, Wing Commander Cecil Bouchier, the airfield's CO, was standing on the daïs as the look-out, on top of a hangar, signalled the first of sixty bombers; in the gloom the white faces of the WAAFs seemed upturned as if in supplication. At that instant, Squadron Leader Ronald Adam, Duty Controller, was scrambling No. 54 Squadron.

Eight planes, led by Squadron Leader James Leathart, made it

76. Trio from 242 Squadron, Coltishall, 1940. From left, Flt Lt W. L. McKnight, DFC; Sqn Ldr D. R. S. Bader, DSO (OC); Flt Lt E. Ball, DFC. McKnight, a Canadian, and Ball were both killed in action the following year; while the legendary 'Tin-Legs' Bader became a prisoner of war.

77. P. S. 'Stan' Turner of Bader's 242 Squadron at Coltishall, 1940. English-born, Turner emigrated to Canada, but joined the RAF pre-1939, fought throughout the war, rising to Group Captain, DSO, DFC, and remained in the RAF post-1945.

narrowly, but now as the raid swept like a cyclone across the Hornchurch aerodrome, a stick of bombs followed the last three Spitfires up the runway. Again the look-out's voice came, all dispassion gone: 'Three aircraft Rabbit Squadron being bombed as they take off – three aircraft Rabbit Squadron crashed.' From their slit trenches, scores of people now saw a sight they would never forget. One moment the Spitfires were twenty feet up, in close formation; the next they catapulted apart 'as though on elastic' – one screaming down the runway on its back, the second plunging on its airscrew, the third spinning wingless into a field. Within seconds, Squadron Leader Adam had word through his look-out: 'The chap on the runway – it's Al Deere.'

At this moment the young New Zealander needed every one of his nine lives. Clamped in his cockpit like an astronaut in a capsule, he was skidding at 100 miles an hour, upside down along the tarmac for more than 100 yards, the thundering friction of the earth bludgeoning through his leather flying helmet, scoring an awful wound in his scalp. Then the plane came to a grinding halt, and Deere, trapped and helpless, heard the bombs still reverberating across the airfield and smelt with fear the rich, sweet reek of petrol.

The second man to crash, Pilot Officer Eric Edsall, was luckier; his Spitfire landed right way up. Despite a dislocated hip, he crawled painfully across the tarmac to Deere's plane, wrenching at the cockpit door while Deere pushed from inside. Concussed and shaken, Deere tumbled to the earth – only to find that Edsall, who couldn't even walk, was bent on carrying him. Cursing, Deere rejected any such indignity; along with Flying Officer Robert Lucy, 54's engineer officer, they helped Edsall to hobble to station sick quarters.

160

The third pilot, Sergeant Davies, blown clean off the airfield into marshy ground, scrambled out unharmed and made for the nearest garage. To his fury, the accountant officer wouldn't refund his taxi-fare: Air Ministry regulations offered no provision for downed pilots to charge up hire-cars.

An early arrival on the scene was Wing Commander Cecil Bouchier – as irate at the 100 craters pitting his airfield as a groundsman plagued by moles. Promptly all leave passes were cancelled, and Bouchier himself led the working parties, filling in the holes with pick and shovel, placing yellow cardboard cones to mark the sites of unexploded bombs. Pilot Officer Henry Jacobs, whose squadron, No. 600, had been transferred from Manston, recorded: 'Whatever your rank you were in there pitching.' By 8 pm, Hornchurch was operational again.

It was hard to believe that anyone but Deere could have lived through it – yet as the battle gathered force, man after man was surviving by the skin of his teeth. On this day, August 31, Fighter Command had suffered the heaviest losses yet – thirty-nine fighters shot down, fourteen dead – and as the hours raced by, it was amazing they had not lost more.

Sheer ingenuity saved some pilots. Airborne from Fowlmere airfield in Cambridgeshire, on his first sortie of the battle, Flying Officer Jimmie Coward was at the controls of one of the few cannon-equipped Spitfires in the RAF when disaster struck. As he took his section shearing in on a flight of Dorniers, his cannons jammed – and simultaneously, the Spitfire shuddered all over. Briefly Coward felt a dull pain 'like a kick on the shin in a Rugby football scrum', then saw his bare left foot lying on the cockpit floor, severed from the leg by all save a few ligaments.

As the Spitfire tilted uncontrollably forward, Coward baled out with ease – but the agony of his foot spinning crazily by its ligaments drove him to desperate action. Pulling the ripcord, he was floating for earth from 20,000 feet, but already blood was jetting from his tibial artery, vanishing in thin swirls far away below. Worse, the slipstream had sucked away his gloves – and his hands, blue with cold, couldn't budge the clamping parachute harness to reach the first-aid kit in his breast pocket. Yet if he was to survive at all, he must improvise a tourniquet, and fast.

Frantically, fumbling with numbed fingers, he picked open the

161

strap and buckle of his flying helmet – to which his radio telephone lead was still attached. Then, raising his left leg almost to his chin, he bound the lead tightly round his thigh, choking the flow of blood, and drifted slowly across Duxford airfield where the rest of his squadron were now landing. Within the hour, Coward was in a Cambridge hospital where a doctor amputated his leg below the knee.

He wasn't the only one to fall in good hands. Near Lympne airfield, Pilot Officer Richard Hillary, force-landed alongside a brigadier's cocktail party, relaxed while the Army plied him with double whiskies 'for shock'. Flight Lieutenant Robert Stanford Tuck, covered in hot black oil from his Spitfire's ruptured tanks, baled out at Plovers, the old-world estate of Lord Cornwallis, Kent's future Lord Lieutenant. As he soaked in a scalding tub, His Lordship encouraged him: 'Drop in for a bath any time, my boy.'

But many men, unable to master their machines, lived sweating moments of terror. Spitfire pilot Desmond Sheen, swooning over his control column from a painful leg wound, awoke to find the fighter streaking for the ground at 500 miles an hour – a speed so sheer he couldn't level out. Sucked from the cockpit through the open hood, he fell straddled along the fuselage, his feet trapped by the top of windscreen. He kicked free with only seconds to spare.

Some held on to the last, fearful of the danger to others. Pilot Officer Jeff Millington, a lively, fair-headed youngster, made to abandon his blazing Hurricane, then risked it for three more minutes; it might easily have hit Tenterden in Kent, one of the prettiest places he knew. Hurricane pilot, William 'Ace' Hodgson, had the same motives; ablaze over the Shell Oil Company's tanks at Thameshaven, on the estuary, he foresaw the havoc a blazing Hurricane could cause below. Switching off his engine and side-slipping violently, he kept the flames in check until he had made a rocky wheels-up landing in an Essex field.

For others, the luck was running out like sand from an hour-glass. All along, Pilot Officer Tony Woods-Scawen, 43 Squadron, had sworn by his lucky parachute; four times he had baled out and four times it hadn't let him down. The fifth time he left it too late; he was within 1,000 feet of the ground when he left his Hurricane. Before the parachute could snap open, the plane exploded above him. His elder brother Patrick, of 85 Squadron, had been shot down and killed a day earlier; the only two brothers to serve from the start of the battle had died within hours of one another.

162

Lucky or not, the wounded put a brave face on it – as if courtesy was as great a requisite as courage. Swaying towards the earth, his left toe smashed by a cannon shell, Squadron Leader Peter Townsend saw two housemaids standing in a garden, staring open-mouthed. With the urbanity that was later to serve him as equerry to King George VI, Townsend called: 'I say! Do you mind giving me a hand when I come down?' Pilot Officer Robert Rutter, wounded in the right foot, baled out in a ploughed field and hobbled into a lane, bathed in blood and oil, to accost a passing civilian: 'Do you know anything about pressure points?' Squadron Leader Tom Gleave of 253 Squadron took the palm for understatement: baling out from a blazing Hurricane 'like the centre of a blow lamp nozzle', the skin drooping in folds from his body, he was already on the dangerously ill list when his wife arrived at Orpington Hospital, Kent. When Beryl Gleave asked, 'What on earth have you been doing with yourself, darling?' her husband shrugged it off, 'Had a row with a German.'

A few came back to earth to meet with a mixed reception. One sergeant baled out in the grounds of a girls' school, roosting uncomfortably in a tree above a horde of giggling pupils until firemen arrived to cut him down. Near Canterbury, a pilot officer ran the length of a village street pursued by housewives armed with rolling pins, convinced he was a German. An ambulance picked him up in the nick of time. George Gilroy of the 603 Squadron, pounded almost insensible by Local Defence Volunteers, received a £10 whip-round in his hospital bed when the shamefaced locals realized their mistake.

As the battle continued, however, not every man on English soil was in the mood for mercy. At Tandridge in Surrey, blood-crazed troops did a tribal dance round a hayrick, parading a German's head on a pitchfork. On the beach at East Wittering in Sussex, a local gardener, Ernest Collier, saw a Heinkel bellyland at the high watermark; as the first crewman, unhurt, clambered out on the wing, a soldier raised his rifle and shot him dead. Local Defence Volunteer Richard May, hastening towards Coulsdon Golf Course in Surrey, where a German had baled out, met two soldiers who had got there first. One of them, carrying a pilot's gauntlet glove, announced tersely: 'We've fixed him.' In the field, May found a tall man wearing the Iron Cross, his head smashed to pulp.

There were flashes of the same ugly mood in the air, too. Above Crowhurst, Sussex, as Oberleutnant Hasse von Perthes, 52nd Fighter Group, swung like a tiny black pendulum on the end of his parachute,

79. (*Top*) John Kent, DFC, AFC (*centre*), when a Flight commander in 303 Squadron, Northolt, September 1940. Two other members of this famous Polish unit were Z. Henneberg (*left*) and M. Feric. 80. (*Bottom*) Quartet of 87 Squadron Hurricanes in September 1940, over Exeter.

81. September 1940 over Westminster.

RAF fighters filed past, opening fire at point-blank range. Miraculously von Perthes lived through it, landing with bullet-riddled legs in a tangle of telephone wires at Hurst Green in Surrey. And Pilot Officer James Caister, airborne on one of his first sorties from Hornchurch, wondered what kind of battle he had come into: as a German pilot baled out, a Spitfire was circling him watchfully, flying lower and lower until the German reached the ground. From the air, Caister watched in fascination as an ever-narrowing circle of troops converged on the German, it was like a slow-motion film. Suddenly, as the Spitfire swooped for the last time, its pilot opened fire. For an instant the wings were barbed with blue and orange flame, then the German crumpled dead.

But there was also compassion on both sides. As a former naval chaplain, the Reverend Edward Bredin, Vicar of Ulcombe in Sussex, had lost an arm in the Battle of Jutland, but when the badly-burned Leutnant Werner Kluge landed in a nearby field it was the one-armed vicar who carried him to safety. At Stourmouth in Kent, the Reverend Harry Whitehouse's parishioners were furious: the vicar had not only taken a captured German to the vicarage but entertained him to tea. Unrepentant, the vicar, as the text for next day's sermon, chose the parable of the Good Samaritan.

Even in the heat of battle chivalry often won the day. It was the sudden knowledge of a life in the balance that seemed to turn the scale. Hauptmann Erich Dobe was heading back over the Channel, escorting a returning Dornier formation, when Spitfires bounced the Me 110s beneath him. Vainly, the Zerstörers milled to form a circle of death; but before the manoeuvres were complete, two were plummeting from the circle, engines smoking. In his earphones, Dobe heard one of the Zerstörer's gunners cry: 'I'm hit, I'm wounded'; not even knowing who it was, he yelled urgently: 'Bale out, bale out.' Then, with a bull-roar of '*Scheisse*', Dobe's adjutant, furious, broke from the formation, blazing into battle with the Spitfires.

Now Dobe's earphones came alive with the wounded gunner's screams and he put his 109's nose down, flying close to the Zerstörer, shouting: 'Keep calm, stay close to the bombers, we'll see you home.' It was too late; the plane had broken from the circle and at that moment a Spitfire dived for the kill. Somewhere beyond Margate, the 110 went down in flames.

The shock of it made Dobe reel in his safety harness. He wanted nothing now but to kill, to empty his magazines into a British plane until the perspex canopy was a seething mass of yellow flame. Six thousand feet below, he saw a Spitfire break from the battle, trailing a thin white stream of glycol like blood from a wounded animal, and he set off in pursuit, closing slowly as he stalked it . . . 800 yards . . . 700 . . . 650. His body was rigid with hatred against the harness, and at 200 yards he would open fire. Then his eyes dropped from the shining graticule of the gunsight, swiftly checking his turn-and-bank indicator. The black needle quivered at dead-centre – his reading was true and he couldn't miss. The 109 was hovering like a hawk, and still the Spitfire suspected nothing. Abruptly, Dobe cursed; in his blind hate, he had forgotten to turn the safety ring surrounding the gunsight from safe to fire.

But at this moment, looking down, Dobe saw the British pilot's face craning up at him – the eyes dilated behind the goggles, in mindless imploring terror, like an animal at bay. Suddenly the hatred drained from him and he felt shabby and ashamed; you couldn't kill a man when you'd looked in his eyes. You couldn't even fire. Abruptly he swung his 109 away, heading east for Marquise airfield, but the battle seemed cleaner now.

At Fighter Command, Air Chief Marshal Dowding paced his room slowly, back and forth, like an automaton. His calls on Pilot Officer Bob Wright were increasing now, yet as often as not, Wright had no sooner entered than he found himself dismissed. The Old Man had momentarily forgotten why he had issued the summons. And Wright knew there were reasons. On August 31, Fighter Command was 166 pilots below strength – and seven days later the figure had soared to 209. If the losses for September 1 were lighter – fifteen aircraft, six pilots – the next day they had risen alarmingly: thirty-one aircraft lost, eight pilots killed, seven wounded.

And still the Germans pounded the airfields with the deadly precision of a hammer driving home nails. Eastchurch, Hawkinge, Detling, Lympne, Biggin Hill again – all were priority targets on September 1. Next day Eastchurch was raided again, an eighteen-bomber attack that destroyed an ammunition dump and five planes. Now, like Manston, the main camp was evacuated. Then Detling again, Debden, Biggin Hill, North Weald, Rochford . . . it seemed as if the bombers would never stop. Even seasoned pilots looked askance at the lengthening odds. Flight Lieutenant Johnnie Kent, losing sight of 303 Squadron's main formation, was leading his flight of six Poles when Northolt's controller hailed him: 'Garter calling Apany Red Leader, vector one-four-zero, angels one-five, one hundred and fifty-plus twenty miles ahead of you.' When Kent, aghast, pointed out his force was just six strong, Northolt replied: 'Understand you are only six – be very careful.'

On September 3, Dowding cut official squadron strength from twenty-two aircraft to eighteen – though, as things stood, it was little more than a gesture. At Croydon, 111 Squadron were down to seven pilots; at North Weald two Hurricane squadrons between them often mustered only two serviceable aircraft. From 1,438 men available, pilot strength had slumped to 840 – a casualty rate which would give the Germans victory in just three weeks. Few conceded this more readily than Dowding. Already, in the long hours of pacing, he had made a bold decision: 'I'll lose no more fighters until the Germans cross the Channel.' To withdraw his fighting line beyond the range of the 109s was now the one trump left to Dowding – though fearing Air Staff intervention, he told no one what was in his mind.

Many pilots were nearing the end of their tether. At Croydon, Squadron Leader Thompson's pilots averaged four hours unrefreshing sleep a night – then crawled from their beds to fight again. Sergeant James Lacey, a young Hurricane ace from Hawkinge, had to fly with his right foot tucked in the loop of the rudder bar in order to combat the twitching. At Stapleford, Essex, the pilots of the incoming 46 Hurricane Squadron found the seven surviving pilots of the departing 151 Squadron taking lunch at 11 am. When a breathless telephone orderly reported, 'Controller says one fifty-one scramble,' the jaded flight commander threw back: 'Tell him we're finishing our bloody lunch first.'

Around 2 pm on September 4, Dowding returned from lunch at 'Montrose' to hear the worst news yet. Not only had Eastchurch and Lympne been attacked yet again, but from a whirling confusion of 300 German planes, fourteen Junkers 88s had broken through to the vital Vickers Armstrong aircraft factory at Weybridge, Surrey, bringing all production to a standstill, killing eighty-eight and injuring 600. Now every flight squadron Dowding could spare must be diverted to give cover to four top-priority Hurricane and Spitfire factories – while all reports stressed that the invasion of England was only days away.

8. Invasion from the Air

September 4–14

General Kurt Student, commanding all airborne troops for 'Operation Sea-Lion', never forgot taking tea with Göring at Karinhall on the afternoon of September 2; rarely had he seen *Der Dicke* so depressed. Without ceremony, Göring cut into Student's monologue, 'The Führer doesn't want to invade Britain.' Shocked, unbelieving, Student pressed him, 'Why not?' Göring gave a shrug: 'I don't know. There'll be nothing doing this year, at any rate.'

Later Student nourished the intriguing theory that, from now on, Göring was engaged in an all-out bid to force Hitler's hand. On September 3, the Reichsmarschall, along with Kesselring, Sperrle, Oberstleutnant Josef Schmid, Luftwaffe intelligence chief, and the heads of each Flying Corps, was involved in an angry no-holds-barred conference at The Hague. Now Göring was putting the pressure on his Air Fleet Commanders; the time had come to alter tactics and switch their forces to an all-out, pile-driving attack on London. Just one problem remained: had Fighter Command been sufficiently depleted, or would the bombers be running too great a risk?

Kesselring, who saw it as his duty to infuse every man in his command with optimism, jumped in at once. Of course the RAF was finished; a study of combat reports made that plain. All along he had urged this mass attack on one key objective, rather than against so many diversified targets – now ports, next airfields, then factories. In fact, Kesselring, who had sounded out No. 2 Flying Corps' Oberst Paul Deichmann on this topic, had received only qualified assurance, but this wasn't going to deter him.

Next Generalfeldmarschall Hugo Sperrle took the floor. A sceptic who loved disagreeing with Kesselring whenever possible, he found it all too easy now. So the RAF were finished, were they? This was just playing up the need for optimism; he didn't believe a word of it. He would wager a good dinner that the RAF had every one of 1,000 fighters left. (The truth: they had only 746 serviceable.)

Tempers rose dangerously; fists pounded the long polished table.

82. Heinkel He 111 over the Surrey and West India Docks area of London on September 7.

168

Hotly, Kesselring reiterated his credo: the RAF were done for, figures proved it. Coldly, Sperrle sneered his disbelief – and his regional fighter commander, Oberst Werner Junck, lent strong support. A finished force couldn't inflict such losses. Junck wound up: 'This is a Verdun of the air.' Goaded, Kesselring rounded on Oberstleutnant Schmid, the intelligence chief: 'Well, are they finished, or aren't they?' Caught between the crossfire of two Air Fleet commanders in fighting mood, the unhappy Schmid temporized. Perhaps the RAF had between 100 and 350 planes left – no one could be sure.

At once Sperrle cut in: a London attack would have his support, provided target selection had top priority. As he saw it, the whole object of the battle was the destruction of British ports and shipping – not the loss of German bombers. The priority target should be the London docks, handling the greatest bulk of Britain's sea-borne traffic, and to cut down bomber losses they should be raided by night. He summed up: 'Raid the docks by night, their airfields by day.'

Kesselring would have none of it. The object of the battle was to defeat the RAF, but airfield attacks were not the answer. Shrewdly he anticipated Dowding's secret resolve: the RAF didn't need airfields like Manston when they could withdraw to fields north of London, out of fighter range. Why they had not done so weeks ago, God alone knew. He urged: 'We haven't a chance of destroying the British fighters on the ground – they're always in the sky. We must force them to fight with their last reserves of Spitfires and Hurricanes.' The 2nd Flying Corps' General Bruno Lörzer saw this as sound sense. A heavy London raid might produce useful results, political as well as military – either forcing the RAF to come up and fight, or the Government to sue for peace.

Right from the start of the battle, in fact, Kesselring and Lörzer had urged this all-out London attack – yet stubbornly, all through August, Hitler, still hopeful of peace, had refused. Nothing in the battle had made him so angry as Rubensdörffer's Croydon attack: only narrowly had Oberst Paul Deichmann, as the officer who had triggered off the raid, escaped a court-martial. Then, on the night of August 24, the navigational error of a few bomber crews had started a chain reaction. Probing for the oil tanks at Thameshaven on the estuary, they drifted over central London – and for the first time in twenty-two years bombs were scattered across the City and the East End. Angrily, Winston Churchill had ordered immediate reprisals – and eighty-one twin-engined Wellington, Whitley and Hampden bombers

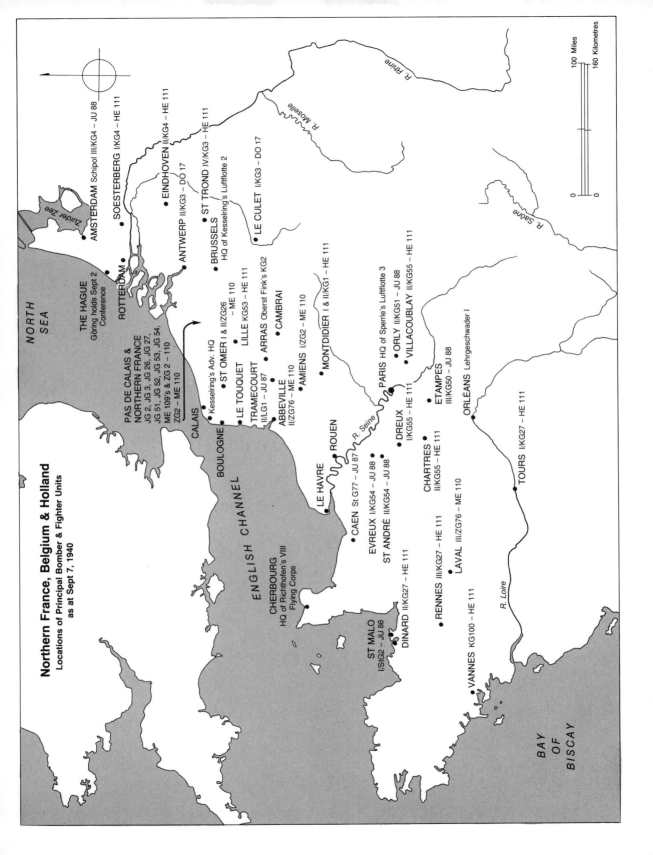

Northern France, Belgium & Holland
Locations of Principal Bomber & Fighter Units
as at Sept 7, 1940

100 Miles
160 Kilometres

NORTH SEA

Zuider Zee

AMSTERDAM Schipol III/KG4 – JU 88

SOESTERBERG I/KG4 – HE 111

EINDHOVEN II/KG4 – HE 111

ST TROND IV/KG3 – HE 111

ANTWERP II/KG3 – DO 17

BRUSSELS
HQ of Kesselring's Luftflotte 2

LE CULET I/KG3 – DO 17

R. Rhine

R. Moselle

R. Saône

THE HAGUE
Göring holds Sept 2
Conference

ROTTERDAM

PAS DE CALAIS &
NORTHERN FRANCE
JG 2, JG 3, JG 26, JG 27,
JG 51, JG 52, JG 53, JG 54,
ME 109's & ZG 2 – 110
ZG2 – ME 110

ST OMER I & II/ZG26
– ME 110

LILLE KG53 – HE 111

ARRAS Oberst Fink's KG2

CAMBRAI

CALAIS
Kesselring's Adv. HQ

LE TOUQUET

ETRAMECOURT
II/LG1 – JU 87

ABBEVILLE
II/ZG76 – ME 110

AMIENS I/ZG2 – ME 110

MONTDIDIER I & II/KG1 – HE 111

PARIS HQ of Sperrie's Luftflotte 3

ORLY II/KG51 – JU 88

VILLACOUBLAY II/KG55 – HE 111

ETAMPES
III/KG50 – JU 88

ORLÉANS Lehrgeschwader I

TOURS II/KG27 – HE 111

BOULOGNE

LE HAVRE

ROUEN

R. Seine

DREUX
I/KG55 – HE 111

CHARTRES
I/KG55 – HE 111

CAEN St G77 – JU 87

EVREUX I/KG54 – JU 88

ST ANDRÉ II/KG54 – JU 88

LAVAL III/ZG76 – ME 110

ENGLISH CHANNEL

CHERBOURG
HQ of Richthofen's VIII
Flying Corps

ST MALO
I/StG2 – JU 88

DINARD II/KG27 – HE 111

RENNES III/KG27 – HE 111

VANNES KG100 – HE 111

R. Loire

BAY
OF
BISCAY

set out for Berlin. In fact, less than ten found the target – but four times in the next ten days the British tried again. Finally, on September 4, at Berlin's Sportpalast, came Hitler's angry decision: 'If they attack our cities, then we will raze *theirs* to the ground. We will stop the handiwork of these air pirates, so help us God.'

As the Hague conference broke up, Kesselring, jubilant, noted that his optimism had carried the day: in four days' time, soon after 4 pm, 625 bombers and 648 fighters would cross the coast, striving to embroil the last of the few in a battle to the death over London.

On the Channel coast, Göring's pilots as yet had no knowledge of the Reichsmarschall's plans. They were waging their own private battle with fatigue. The business of escorting the bombers back and forth to Kent was taking its toll – up to five sorties a day, and each time the fear: will I get back? Leutnant Erich Hohagen put it starkly: 'The Channel's a blood-pump – all the time draining away our strength.'

Every pilot felt the stress. In Leutnant Eduard Neumann's unit the red warning bulb glowed so often now, that they had evolved a code-cry: '*Trübsal*' (Distress). From Colembert, Oberleutnant Hans von Hahn, leading the 1st Wing, 3rd Fighter Group, reported home: 'There aren't many of us who haven't made a forced landing in the Channel in a badly shot up plane, or without a propeller.' Leutnant Hellmuth Ostermann noted the same at Guines – a tension so marked that pilots, for the first time, talked of a posting to a quieter base.

It wasn't surprising; daily their tasks were stepped up. With Sperrle's Air Fleet Three given over to night bombing, his single-engined fighters were detached to Air Fleet Two – and Kesselring found work for them to do. The August 31 raids against Hornchurch and Biggin Hill had seen 1,301 fighters escorting 150 bombers; in twenty-three days, the Luftwaffe had lost 467 fighters.

The truth was that Göring and his commanders were now less and less in touch with the realities of the air war, and the pilots sensed it and were angry. At Samer, near Boulogne, Hauptmann Erich von Selle was beside himself. Today his fighter wing was only eighteen machines strong, and the weatherman's forecast was so far out they had the lost the bombers they were escorting in cloud. By the time they had sighted the French coast they were less than 250 feet above the earth, every man's red bulb was glowing, and there wasn't even time for a circuit. The eighteen machines somehow touched down, eight of them without one drop of fuel left.

172

Two hours later, with the cloud worsening, von Selle had Kesselring's advanced headquarters on the line: the 2nd Wing, Fighter Group Three, would take off on another protection flight. Bluntly, von Selle refused; his wing was twenty-two aircraft below strength. Only blind chance had preserved those planes he had brought back. When Kesselring's office grew steely – 'This is an order, not a request' – von Selle dug in his toes. 'If it is an order, we'll fly it – but if I see no land again at a thousand feet, I'll take the wing up to thirty-five hundred feet and order every man to bale out.' No more orders were forthcoming.

Other commanders beside Adolf Galland noted how tired men were – and the errors that fatigue engendered. One Zerstörer pilot, Oberleutnant Schäfer, circled so long before touching down that the three 110s on his tail narrowly escaped a crash landing. Profusely, he apologized: forgetting he wore sunglasses, he thought night had fallen and was searching for a flare path. Unteroffizier Delfs, not even realizing he was duelling with another Me 109, baled out over a railway siding near Calais, snagging his parachute harness in the points. Only the swift thinking of Oberleutnant Josef 'Pip' Priller saved him from death beneath an oncoming train; after firing Very lights that the train driver ignored, Priller had to swoop again, a head-on-attack with cannon, until it ground to a halt.

As the tension mounted and men made it back only by a hair's-breadth, a few went to pieces. South of Gravesend, en route to London, the pilots of No. 1 Wing, 27th Fighter Group, saw their red bulbs already aglow; despite all Göring's caveats, the bombers had arrived half an hour late, then picked the most circuitous route ever. As the shouts of 'Red lamp! Red lamp!' crackled in his earphones, Oberleutnant Gert Framm was one of several squadron commanders who ordered: 'It's hopeless – forget the bombers, we turn back.' Machine after machine banked steeply as the pilots flew for their lives towards Guines airfield, Calais. Even before it loomed in sight, Framm ordered: 'Down at once when you see the field, no circling' – but to his horror, one pilot, a callow eighteen-year-old, dived for the airfield like a bullet, without even throttling back. As Framm breathed, 'My God, this can only end in disaster,' the boy's fuel gave out forty feet above the ground. The Messerschmitt 'fell like a piano', strewing wings and engine parts across the field, and already Framm could see the fire tender rocketing towards the wreckage.

Then, as the planes touched down, the pilots were unbuckling their

harness, vaulting onto the wings of their planes, racing to free the boy still trapped with his cockpit crushed about him. To Framm's relief he saw him move, and suddenly the youngster had freed himself and jumped to the ground, blood pouring from his face, his eyes as vacant as an imbecile's. When he saw Framm, his head jerked furiously like an epileptic's and he began to shout hysterically: 'I'm a bloody fool, I did the one thing I was told not to do. I did the one thing my squadron leader told me not to.'

Stricken, Framm tried to calm him, but it was useless; the boy raved on in shock. Fatherly Major Max Ibel, their Bavarian CO, was as gentle as could be: 'My dear, dear boy, calm down'; the lad didn't even hear him. Again he screamed, 'I'm a bloody fool – the one thing I was told not to,' and now Framm saw the tears streaming down his face and recognized that hysteria was taking hold of him. Muttering, 'Leave it to me,' he stepped forward, and suddenly, at the pitch of his lungs, he shouted, 'Be quiet, you swine, in the presence of a senior officer – and stand to attention.' Abruptly the boy snapped to attention like a marionette and the raving stopped. Instead he began to whimper like a child, and very gently they led him, shivering and shuddering, away from the airfield and away from the battle.

174

83. Generaloberst Ernst Udet, chief of the Luftwaffe's technical department, and a 62-victory fighter ace of 1914–18 (centre), visiting the Channel Front on 4 September 1940. With him here, from left: Wilhelm Balthasar, Walter Oesau, Adolf Galland, Werner Mölders, Joachim Muncheberg, and Hartmann Grasser. Of these, only Galland and Grasser survived the war.

Pilot Officer Robert Oxspring was one of many who received the shock of his life at this time. Two days earlier he had been enjoying a blissful leave in the Lake District; now, urgently recalled to No. 66 Spitfire Squadron, he arrived at Kenley airfield, Surrey, to find his comrades in a sorry plight. Two days of fighting in the south had cost his squadron two men dead, six others badly shot up. He thought only: Why 66 Squadron? What's the matter with us? He had no way of knowing that it was the same on airfield after airfield – and that in this first week of September, with the massed German onslaught on London only days away, Headquarters Fighter Command faced a grave crisis.

As Air Chief Marshal Dowding saw it, the truth was hideously simple. Of the fifty-plus men who had commanded squadrons since Eagle Day, ten were dead, nine were in hospital, almost twenty more had been withdrawn from the battle. And many now taking command, accomplished enough as aviators, had not so much as one hour's combat flying. Time and again it was only the flight commanders who were seeing the neophytes through – though not all gave advice as salutary as Oxspring's own, Ken Gillies: 'When you go up tomorrow morning, you'll see all the black crosses in the world – but don't get too excited about shooting them down. There'll be someone a lot more experienced waiting to play the same dirty trick on you.'

It was advice worth heeding. Dowding's decision on August 19, not lightly taken, to cut training time to two weeks, meant that most newcomers had just ten hours' experience on Spitfires or Hurricanes – many could barely land a Spitfire, let alone fly it. Some, after one night's cockpit drill by torchlight, did their first training flight at dawn. And the reserve squadrons still held in the north were often as unpolished.

To the veterans just quitting the fray, the newcomers were often as cocky as could be. Squadron Leader Joseph Kayll's 615 Squadron had moved north to Prestwick, but Kayll himself lingered on at Kenley, anxious to save the relieving 253 Squadron from their own folly. Flying in tight air-parade formation, lacking even weavers, the squadron seemed unable to grasp that German fighters hovered in the sun – swooping once the RAF tackled their bombers. In vain Kayll stressed: 'You must keep your eyes peeled for fighters – only take on the bombers if there's a good chance.' To his chagrin, the pilots of 253 found him the funniest man alive: 'Nuts to caution –

we've come south to see some action.' When Kayll next heard, they had lost thirteen planes, nine pilots, in seven days.

At Northolt, Squadron Leader Ronald Kellett put it harshly to Squadron Leader Zdzislaw Krasnodebski: 'The squadrons they're bringing in now are as near valueless as makes no odds.' To Krasnodebski, it was undeniable truth. Certainly his Poles were so eager for action, they already seemed to be doing the work of two squadrons. At the moment that Elspeth Henderson and the duty watch were groping from Biggin Hill's shattered Ops Room, 303's Poles, now fully operational, were east of the airfield, diving from the sun on three 109s – an attack so audacious that at seventy-yards range they couldn't miss. But Biggin Hill was too close to home for Krasnodebski's men; two days later, after a running battle over Dover, Flying Officer Zdzislaw Henneberg was eight miles inside France, down to 3,000 feet, and still attacking before he broke for base. Alarmed, Air Vice-Marshal Keith Park cautioned from 11 Group: 'There *is* good shooting . . . within sight of London.'

Though Krasnodebski did not then suspect it, the Poles' action on September 5 had set the seal on things. At Northolt, Group Captain

84. Air Chief Marshal Dowding (*rt*) receives HM King George VI and HM Queen Elizabeth at RAF Fighter Command HQ, Bentley Priory on 6 September 1940, at the height of the Battle.

Stanley Vincent, noting 303's spiralling victories, told his intelligence officer: 'Treat these claims with a lot of reserve – go through them with a fine-tooth comb.' When the officer, despairing, complained that each man corroborated the other, Vincent was resolved. Northolt's Station Defence Flight would be airborne: he would go up and see for himself.

What Vincent saw, at 21,000 feet over Thameshaven, astern of the Poles and 1,000 feet below, was a sight he would remember till he died – tier upon tier of glinting, well-drilled Dorniers, two Hurricanes, poised 1,000 feet above, suddenly crash diving into space with near-suicidal impetus, a sudden ripple of agitation running through the mighty horde as the leading Dorniers, foreseeing head-on collision, turned and broke. This was the spearhead. As the bombers scattered, Pole after Pole was diving – holding their fire until twenty yards distant, accepting the awful risk that the last great explosion would destroy them, too. Amazed, Vincent saw planes and parachutes fluttering like charred paper through the sky. Kellett, an Me 109 and Sergeant Kazimierz Wunsche fought only 100 yards apart, the sergeant closing to sixty yards to save Kellett's life. Flying Officer Waclaw Lapkowski baled out with a broken arm. Polish fighters angrily nosed Vincent's Hurricane aside, grudging him so much as one chance shot at a crippled bomber. Back at Northolt, fevered with excitement, Vincent sent for the intelligence officer: 'My God, they *are* doing it; it isn't just imagination.'

Then, soon after 9 am on September 6, more trouble broke. West of Biggin Hill, the Poles sighted the mightiest German formation they had ever seen: a solid air-bridge of fighters and bombers blackening the sky for twenty miles. Worse, every course they had been given to steer was the wrong one. The sun dazzled from a milky haze, blinding their eyes; above them, the vapour trails seemed as if a sinister invisible spider was weaving a gigantic web across the sky. They would have to attack on the climb, Krasnodebski knew – and at a sluggish 140 miles an hour.

Few got so far. From the spider's web above, Messerschmitts came spinning; with height, speed, sun and numbers, they overwhelmed the climbing Poles. Flying Officer Miroslaw Féric, a 109 in his sights, saw the black crosses on the plane actually take fire under his bullets; his luck was rare. Sergeant Stanislaw Karubin, hit by a Heinkel's cannon shell, force-landed near Pembury in Kent, his thigh laid wide open. Kellett, the ammunition boxes in his wings exploding under cannon, saw fabric drifting in strands from his tailplane; his starboard aileron was shot away. Holes a man could have leapt through were torn in his wing surface. At 160 miles an hour, he landed on Biggin Hill's cratered airfield, narrowly dodging a German bomber, its port engine ablaze, yawing helplessly above the aerodrome in a left-hand circuit.

One burst of fire, and flying glass had sprayed from Krasnodebski's instrument panel, peppering his face and hands. Petrol slopped from the bullet-holed tank into his Hurricane's cockpit, and fire was lapping greedily. Somewhere over Farnborough in Kent, Krasnodebski baled out. He fell free for 10,000 feet before pulling his ripcord; above him 100 planes were milling tightly in the sky, and it was politic not to drift gently while there was a chance of stopping a bullet. With 10,000 feet still to go, Krasnodebski pulled his ripcord – and once more he had saved his life. His trouser legs were smouldering ominously; yellow flames licked at the tough overall cloth. As he hit the earth, barely conscious, the fire had already reached his knees – for all the world it seemed as if he was wearing ragged shorts. Had he pulled the ripcord at 20,000 feet, the fire would have clawed up his body to the rigging lines of the chute, and nothing could have saved him. At Northolt, Group Captain Stanley Vincent heard with dismay of Krasnodebski's injuries; barely conscious, under morphia, it would be a full year before he flew again.

Towards 6 pm on September 7, as the last Hurricanes of 303 Squadron were touching down at Northolt, they knew they were the one squadron to have scored triumphantly. To the east, the livid, shifting skyline of London showed how staggeringly successful the Germans had been. At a score of dispersals in southern England, the fires of dockland glittered ruddily on aluminium wings. From Bermondsey to West Ham, mile after mile of London was ablaze – and 247 bombers of Sperrle's Air Fleet Three, operating under cover of darkness, would stoke up those fires until 4.50 am on Sunday, September 8. But the long testing-time of Krasnodebski's Poles was over at last. Before three weeks was out, their score had mounted to 11 Group's highest total – 44 German planes in five days' fighting over London alone. Today, the height, the luck and the skill had been all theirs.

It was, however, one of the few bright spots at this moment. On this calm, sultry Saturday, Fighter Command's controllers had nothing so urgent on their minds as the safety of the sector stations: above

Northolt, Biggin Hill, Kenley and Hornchurch circled weaving networks of planes, alerted to stave off the attacks that might soon put the command's control system out for good and all. No one realized, until too late, that the Germans had switched from the sector stations – or that the way to London lay clear.

It was a cruel necessity – yet Dowding and his commanders knew it was a godsend. Twisting above the inky pall of smoke swathing the Thames in his Hurricane, OK1, Air Vice-Marshal Keith Park saw 75,000 tons of food supplies burning, and breathed, 'Thank God for that.' As Park saw it, the Germans' focus on London meant precious breathing time for his sector stations – now so devastated that London might soon lack any fighter defence.

For the RAF it had been a bitter, frustrating day: the sky so crowded you could scarcely single out friend from foe. Sergeant Cyril Babbage, seeing his friend Andy McDowall with six 109s on his tail, had yelled: 'Hang on, I'm coming', and Andy still hadn't quite forgiven him: the quixotry had brought another dozen Messerschmitts down on top of them. Canada's Keith Ogilvie found the 109s, 'zooming and diving . . . like masses of ping-pong balls', disconcertingly swift; aiming at the first he was mortified to find he had hit the second. His friend Flight Lieutenant James MacArthur felt worse; back at Middle Wallop airfield, Mess Steward Joseph Lauderdale couldn't even tempt him to the pink, flaky Scotch salmon on the cold buffet. Bitterly, MacArthur told him: 'I couldn't face a bite of it, Mr. Lauderdale. We've been up there all afternoon and done nothing – there wasn't a British plane in the sky.' Though MacArthur wasn't strictly accurate, he had come uncomfortably close. For forty-one German planes, the bulk of them bombers, the RAF had lost twenty-eight fighters. Nineteen of their pilots were dead – and only one German plane in thirty had been harmed at all.

Across the Channel, Reichsmarschall Hermann Göring, at Cap Blanc Nez, had decided that, at this eleventh hour, all the magic formulas of the past weeks – Stukas, Zerstörers, radar attacks, closer fighter escort – boiled down to this: *he* must infuse the Luftwaffe's fighter arm with the belly-fire they so sorely lacked. To a wireless reporter with a recording van, he announced: 'I personally have taken over the leadership of the attacks against England . . . and for the first time we have struck at England's heart . . . this is an historic hour.'

But what Göring saw at the Channel coast didn't entirely please

him. Despite the mighty air armada of 1,200 shining planes, the attitude here, in the front-line, seemed all too light-hearted. Only recently Göring had ordered his regional fighter commanders to shift their quarters to overlook the Channel itself and now, binoculars levelled on the Cap Blanc Nez, he heard the irrepressible Oberst Werner Junck, Sperrle's fighter chief, announce: 'I'm going to build a new headquarters right in the Channel. When the tide's in I'll be up to my neck, when it's out I'll be up to my waist – but I shall be looking the enemy squarely in the face.' Grunting, Göring pretended not to hear. He wanted only to hear of plain, unadulterated victories. What cheered his heart most was to meet four of Adolf Galland's pilots – Gerhard Schöpfel, Joachim Müncheberg, 'Micky' Sprick and Hans Ebeling – with seventeen victories apiece. Beaming, Göring shook hands with every one – if only every pilot showed this spirit!

But as a teleprinter clacked out the day's results at Kesselring's advanced HQ, Göring's gloom deepened: fighter losses had been few enough, but a loss of forty bombers was insupportable. It bore out what Göring had all along felt – even given brand-new commanders, the fighters had no stomach for the battle. On impulse, he barked orders: each fighter group and wing commander was to report to his private train. It was poor psychology – the fighter leaders found themselves marshalled, like errant schoolboys before a headmaster, in a windy field, near the Pas de Calais, while Göring harshly rebuked their lack of courage.

Standing in line between his friend Helmut Wick and Werner Mölders, Adolf Galland just had to speak up: he thought of brave fliers he'd known, their wings for ever folded, and to see Göring shrug aside their tenacity gave him a sick feeling in his throat. Galland strove to stick to facts: the Me 109 was a plane built for attack, not for protection. The Spitfire, though a slower plane, was yet more manoeuvrable. On escort flights the 109s were for ever throttling back – it was like chaining a yard-dog and then asking it to fight. Impatiently Göring brushed him aside: this was defeatist talk.

Göring then addressed himself to group commanders only: what were their immediate needs? Werner Mölders was prompt: more powerful engines for 109s. Göring swung on Galland: 'And you?' Poker-faced, his voice modulated, knowing full well the sensation he'd cause, Galland replied: 'A squadron of Spitfires.' In truth, though the Spitfire was more agile for escort duties, Galland preferred the 109, but the stubborn incomprehension of the High

Command drove out all thoughts of caution. Göring went purple, flashed him one long look of hate, then stamped off, growling. Galland wasn't sure, but it looked as if he had reached the point of no return.

As the bombers forged on above southern England, en route for London, thousands of eyes followed their progress – some frankly curious, some in silent awe: were the RAF powerless to stop the Germans getting through? Nobody saw it as a raid to preface peace terms or to draw the RAF up into combat; the non-stop air armada convinced them of just one thing. The invasion fleet was coming.

None knew it more certainly than Robert Bailey. Why else would the Luftwaffe drop bombs on *him*? At this hour on that Saturday evening, Bailey had some of his 100 sheep in a pen beside the garden, shears poised for clipping, when the bombers roared overhead. Now, as he stood transfixed, a sheep in his arms, he heard Vera call from the house: 'Are they Germans, Robert? If they are, you'd better come in.' Bailey could see no good reason. 'It's not likely they'll drop anything on us – they're heading for Hawkinge.' He was still holding the sheep, craning upwards to count the planes, when the first bombs came whistling.

87. The Cockney Spirit – cheerful at all times, despite being bombed out.

Suddenly the sloping canyon of the valley, flanked by the tall groves of beech trees, was like a battle-field; the ground shook as if an earthquake threatened, and then chalk and earth were founting. Inside Ladwood Farmhouse, the kitchen ceiling rained plaster dust and wooden beams, and Vera Bailey staggered out, groping towards her husband. For a moment both she and Robert stumbled as if in a fog; the whole valley was filled with choking smoke. At this moment, it didn't strike Bailey or any of them that German bombers, faced with trouble, were jettisoning their loads. To them it seemed the end of Ladwood, the prelude to invasion.

From the High Command down, the belief was common: this was H-Hour. At 8.07 pm Brigadier John Swayne, unable to locate his chief, Lieutenant-General Alan Brooke, had issued the code-word 'Cromwell', signifying Alert No. One to Eastern and Southern Commands – 'Invasion imminent and probable within twelve hours.' At Gosport Army Co-operation Station, on Portsmouth Harbour, Pilot Officer 'Nobby' Clarke, in a Skua target-towing plane, had word: 'Get cracking – light all the points, working from east to west.' From Weymouth 150 miles east to Beachy Head, Clarke knew that on

182

every available landing-beach petrol pipelines jutted almost level with the water's surface. Now his task was to dive-bomb each with incendiaries, to transform the inshore waters into a raging cauldron of fire.

On the main roads leading inland to Canterbury, Maidstone and Horsham, troops stood grimly by 600-gallon tanks sited ten feet above road level, ready to spray a petrol and gas-oil mixture on the advancing Germans – at thirty gallons a minute, to burn at a heat of 500 degrees Fahrenheit. Professor Lindemann, Winston Churchill's scientific adviser, had grimly assured the Premier: 'Nothing could live in it for two minutes.'

But why had the Germans delayed? Flying east towards Littlehampton, Pilot Officer Clarke could see no invasion barges: only the grey wash of the sea at sundown, white surf creaming on the sand. Then abruptly his radio-telephone crackled. Without explanation he was recalled to Gosport.

Along the coast confusion multiplied. At Folkestone's Hotel Mecca, panicky officials whipped out Mrs Lillian Ivory's telephone, then remembered her boarding house was Intelligence Corps Headquarters; hastily they brought it back again. On a night drive from Brighton to Worthing, Miss Vera Arlett kept her pass at the ready; bayonets glinted eerily at every checkpoint. At Dover, bugles sounded along the white cliffs; in a score of villages from Portsmouth to Swansea, Home Guardsmen, unbidden, rang the church bells to warn against invasion, a lonely tolling over dark fields. In Reg Cooke's little coastguard cottage at Pett, Sussex, the telephone shrilled and the Home Guard was on the line. 'They've landed at Lydd.' Peering east through the darkness, Cooke could see nothing – and in any case he had only a duck-gun. He and his wife Lydia went to bed.

All that night, the Home Guard stood by, alerted for the first threat of invasion since Napoleon's time, gripping a weird armoury of weapons – from assegais to four dozen rusty Lee-Enfield rifles, relics of a spectacle, supplied by London's Drury Lane Theatre. Around Southampton, troops of the 4th Division dozed in motor coaches, fully clothed, rifles by their sides. At Stubbington, Hampshire, Colonel Barrow told his Home Guard company: 'They may be landing paratroops behind you, but there will be no turning back.' Doggedly his farm-workers and shepherds agreed – though only one among them had a .22 rifle; the rest had stout sticks.

Some units had word early. At Gosport, Pilot Officer Clarke and his fellow pilots stood by all night with four bombed-up Roc target-towing planes, only one of them fully armed or equipped with wireless. Others knew nothing until dawn; although Fighter Command's signal, A 443, was issued at 9.50 pm, it was, ironically, one of the night's few cipher messages to be allotted no priority. Some units did not even decode their copy until 10.30 am on Sunday, September 8.

Then, as the full impact struck home, station commanders jumped to it. At Middle Wallop, Red Tobin and the pilots of 609 sat strapped in their cockpits, engines turning over, facing downwind. At Hornchurch, airmen at 603's dispersal heard Wing Commander Cecil Bouchier rasp over the tannoy loudspeaker: 'Stand by – be ready to draw rifles and ammunition from the armoury.' Bouchier was now at his wits' end: his instructions were to wreck all electrical transformers, gut the hangars, blow up the water supply and defend the airfield to the death – but whether before or after demolition, Bouchier didn't know. In the end he did nothing.

In Folkestone, the people numbered Dover's fate in hours: the Germans had completed a cross-Channel tunnel and were preparing to launch bombs against Dover torpedo-fashion. Dover knew the worst about Folkestone: because their ground defences had caved in, German planes had launched that London raid from Hawkinge. Worthing's citizens thought they knew well enough why no bombs had come their way – Goebbels' mother lived there. Croydon had the buzz that Göring was striking at food supplies: thirty milkmen had been machine-gunned in the streets.

Ironically, however, it seemed to the Germans that with every sortie the British got stronger: the unopposed flights of September's first days were past now. To battle over England was to battle for life itself. It was as well the British fighting spirit was there for the pilot shortage worsened daily. Faced with a steady drain of 120 men a week, Dowding saw nothing for it: from now on his squadrons must be split into three categories – Category A squadrons, to bear the brunt of the southern fighting, a small operational reserve of B squadrons, C squadrons stripped of every pilot still capable, virtually reduced to training units. Useless against German fighters, these squadrons were no longer fit to tackle anything save unescorted bombers.

If pilots were lacking, so, too, were the planes. All told, twenty-six eight-gun fighters were being written off each day – roughly 800 per month. When Churchill called for explanations, Lord Beaverbrook clarified: in fact, these figures included aircraft sent for repair. Ultimately they would be back in the fighting line – though it might be a matter of weeks. Now, for the first time, Churchill realized the gravity of the situation: the Air Ministry wastage figures he had been studying all the time took no account of damaged planes, only of total losses. The Under Secretary of State for Air, Archibald Sinclair, was forced to admit it: there were only 288 fighters, eleven days' supply, still in reserve. The losses had eaten into Britain's reserves to the tune of 45 per cent. If Britain's aircraft factories and storage units came under concentrated pinpoint attacks by lone bombers, as Generaloberst Hans Jeschonnek, Luftwaffe Chief of Staff, had advocated as recently as September 2, the position would be desperate.

Now Churchill was at his wits' end: was Britain producing steadily more fighter aircraft, as he had been led to believe, or not? Patiently Lindemann explained: it was indeed, but since more squadrons and

185

training units were being created to absorb them, output remained virtually stationary. And Lindemann, a passionate statistician, added his own acid rider: between May 10 and September 12, the Air Ministry's gains and losses calculations involved a cumulative error of 500 aircraft. It was small wonder that Churchill grumbled: 'It is always very difficult to deal with the Air Ministry because of the variety of the figures they give.'

The Air Ministry had statistical problems of its own. To Dowding's anger, their crash investigators raised sceptical eyebrows over Fighter Command's claims; checking wrecks over a sample area of Kent, they just couldn't find planes enough to support the figures. At once Archibald Sinclair sent for Dowding, urging, 'Look here, you must give us accurate figures – the neutral countries aren't being convinced which side is telling the truth.' Replying, Dowding was glacial: 'All I can say, sir, is that this war isn't being fought for the benefit of the neutral countries – it's being fought for the survival of civilization.'

Hour by hour, Dowding's pilots were living for the day, and their nerves were at full stretch. At Tangmere, Pilot Officer Frank Carey recalled, the morale of No. 43 Squadron 'was really slipping' – and to 607 Squadron, moving in as their relief, it seemed that 43's pilots 'couldn't leave Tangmere fast enough'.

Some men experienced a frightening sense of disorientation. On leave in rural Buckinghamshire, Sergeant Ronnie Hamlyn tried vainly to check himself; one tinkle of a bicycle bell, so akin to the dispersal telephone, set him running like a hare. Pilot Officer Bill Read knew the same primal fear; let an ambulance bell jangle and he took wildly to his heels. At Croydon, Pilot Officer Christopher Currant, 605 Squadron, cursed unrestrainedly at any airman who hastened by; there was that awful jungle compulsion to run, too.

Fearing for his men at Digby, in Lincolnshire, was Squadron Leader James McComb. Word had arrived that the pilots of 611 Squadron must, for the first time, patrol south, over London – yet now, as they stood by at dispersal, there came the solemn, disquieting notes of Chopin's Funeral March. A hard-drinking pilot of No. 29 night-fighter Squadron had crashed fatally two nights earlier; by cruel mischance, the funeral cortège, complete with band, was passing within feet of where McComb's pilots stood bow-taut at attention. Covertly, McComb stole a glance at Pilot Officer Colin MacFie beside him: for this gentle nineteen-year-old, such an ordeal pre-

88. Battle of Britain Polish 'aces'. Sqn Ldr Witold Urbanowicz; Jan Zumbach; Miroslaw Feric; and Zdzislaw Henneberg – seen here on 15 December 1940 after each had been decorated with a British DFC award.

facing his first sortie could prove too much. Momentarily he saw MacFie's face crumple, then knew a blessed relief; the boy was battle-hardened before even a shot was fired. As the gun-carriage passed, MacFie, lips barely moving, muttered: 'First time he's been on the wagon in weeks.'

The tension wasn't surprising. On all sides men saw their comrades die tragically and sensed the precious fragility of life. Near Westerham, Sergeant Stefan Wojtowicz, one of the first Poles to die, crashed in the deep abyss of a chalk-pit; the heat beat up the cliff-face like flames up a chimney flue, and the firemen couldn't reach him. Over Weybridge in Surrey, on their second patrol, every 611 pilot saw Sergeant Frederick Shepherd's Spitfire, hit by ack-ack, plunge flaming into the youngster's parachute, catapulting him to the ground.

This was September 11, when Fighter Command lost twenty-nine aircraft and seventeen pilots, with another six men wounded. As Red Tobin put it to Andy Mamedoff: 'The death of one experienced guy is worth ten Spitfires.'

Off-duty, each man fought against the pressures as best he could. It was the same in every squadron. All night Pilot Officer Bill Assheton, 222 Squadron, screamed from a pit of nightmare, but when the squadron took over the bandstand at Southend's Palace Hotel, he was always first to seize the mike, ad-libbing combat chatter as

187

Squadron Leader Johnnie Hill pounded the drums: 'Achtung, Spitfire – 109s to starboard.' For most, sleep was time ill-spent; when Air Chief Marshal Dowding warned 249 Squadron at North Weald: 'The need for you to rest is paramount – soon we may have to fight for thirty-six hours non-stop', Squadron Leader John Grandy and his pilots were of one mind: 'Christ, let's get to London for a party.'

It wasn't all living it up; with the cornered courage of men whose backs were to the wall, the RAF were growing wary. From September 5 on, Air Vice-Marshal Park was operating every squadron in pairs – the agile Spitfires to deal with the fighter screen, the sturdier, less manoeuvrable Hurricanes to tackle the bombers. And most, now conscious that the Germans' morning raids came from the south-east with the sun behind them, from the west in the afternoon, took care to place themselves up-sun before they dived.

At Duxford, a No. 12 Group station west of Cambridge, the legless Squadron Leader Douglas Bader had carried Park's idea a stage further: why not meet strength with strength? A formation of three squadrons, flying as a wing, was a better match for 100-plus Germans than a scant twelve planes. For 11 Group squadrons, covering the approaches south of London, such formations just weren't practicable: one squadron, quickly airborne, could hinder deliberate precision bombing while a wing meant committing all one's machines against a possible German feint.

But Air Vice-Marshal Trafford Leigh-Mallory, Air Officer Commanding No. 12 Group, had nothing to lose: his airfields lay north of London and in East Anglia, which allowed precious time for a wing to manoeuvre. And though there were teething troubles – thirty-nine fighters could scramble in three minutes flat but it took ten minutes, climbing hard, to get them as high as 2,000 feet – Bader was persevering. On September 14, he planned to lead an armed pack of sixty fighters into the air for the first time.

Although Fighter Command had issued no contrary orders, many pilots now hotly questioned the wisdom of those tight-packed V-shaped formations. At 66 Squadron's Kenley dispersal, young Robert Oxspring, learning fast, was the centre of nightly heated arguments; surely the losses were a pointer towards scrapping the whole formation. When some argued that the height of a battle was no time to switch tactics, Oxspring countered: 'The Guards don't go into battle as if they're Trooping the Colour – they fight from trenches. We're trying to fight a battle like an air display.' Confronted with the standard Fighter Command attacks, Oxspring was withering: 'That book's a criminal document – the whole formation sticks out like a dog's balls.'

All through this week, in the warm, smoky twilight of the pubs they used, the pilots thrashed out the tactics that could wrest victory from defeat. Expertise was the currency. At 28,000 feet, nearing the height of Mount Everest, where the 109s lurked, the grease in your guns might freeze solid and you couldn't fire a shot. If you took off in wet boots, your feet, even 3,000 feet below that height, could freeze to the rudder pedal. At Westhampnett, 602's pilots found that a sliced potato rubbed over the bullet-proof windscreen was the sure way to stop it icing up. At Croydon, 605's pilots teased one flight commander unmercifully: forced on the edge of the stratosphere to relieve the needs of nature, he hit his compass in error, watched in horror as it promptly froze up, leaving him completely lost.

Those who had tips for survival passed them on – to others who listened because their lives depended on them. One pressure of the thumb on the gun button might push the control column slightly forward, depressing the plane's nose – so to aim true, first lock the stick with your left hand, then fire with your right. See that those last fifty rounds in your guns were glinting tracer – then you would know you were running short. Use your mirror to watch your rear like a canny motorist – the top brass hadn't incorporated them in fighter planes, but wise men fitted their own. Prudent men nursed their eyesight too: the man who saw farthest shot first. At Middle Wallop, 609's Poles, Novierski and Ostazewski, sat for hours, inert as zombies – staring at flies on a faraway wall to strengthen the muscles of the eyeball. And at Hornchurch, tyros listened open-mouthed to Pilot Officer George Bennions, 41 Squadron's Yorkshire-born dead-shot: 'You want to be slightly above them or just under their bellies, lad – dead astern, at two hundred yards range, and you just can't miss. . . .'

Around 9 am on Thursday, September 12, Winston Churchill was indeed hoping that the RAF couldn't miss. Now, only 1,381 pilots of Dowding's force stood between England and annihilation. On the face of it Churchill was as buoyant as ever – as if challenge was meat and drink to him. Fearing the worst, his bodyguard, Inspector Walter Thompson, had begged him to consider his own safety; now the London raids had begun, anything could happen. For answer, Churchill, quivering with indignation, had poked his stick towards the

189

worn grey façade of 10 Downing Street: 'Thompson, the Prime Minister of the country lives and works in that house – and until Hitler puts it on the ground, I work there.' Then, despite all Thompson's admonitions concerning security, he posed patiently on the front steps for a group of press photographers. Gently he chided his bodyguard: 'They have to get some copy, Thompson – they're all God's children, you know.'

And this morning, at London's Holborn Viaduct Station, awaiting the Prime Minister's special train that would carry them to Shorncliffe in Kent, Thompson witnessed one of the war's most moving sights. As Churchill, deep in conversation with Lieutenant-General Sir John Dill, Chief of the Imperial General Staff, Lieutenant-General Alan Brooke and Admiral Sir Dudley Pound, the First Sea Lord, paced the station platform, a horde of office workers, streaming

from suburban trains, suddenly espied Churchill across the tracks. In that moment, it was as if a skilled stage director had pulled the strings; the concourse halted, and a great impromptu cry rang out over the whole station: 'Thank God for the guns.' Deeply stirred, Churchill raised his right hand in his famous victory gesture, to rally them: 'And for every bomb they drop we will give them back ten.'

Churchill had a busy day ahead of him. There had been alarming reports of the vulnerability of the Dover guns and he wanted to see for himself. On the way down, he talked long and earnestly with Lieutenant-General Brooke on the defence of the Narrows, then he made a searching inspection of the coastal guns at Dungeness, then went on to Dover to lunch at the Castle with Admiral Sir Bertram Ramsay, Flag Officer Commanding. Yet hectic as the day had been, Brooke noted the Prime Minister had been as piqued as a youngster who had missed a birthday treat: the front had stayed quiet and there hadn't been a single air battle for him to see.

Neither Churchill nor his party knew it, but Fate would recompense them. The greatest air battle of all time was just seventy-two hours away.

89. A Heinkel He 111 crew walk away, under escort, from their burning aircraft; shot down by a Spitfire at Burmarsh, Kent, on 11 September 1940.

90. (*Over the page*) All that was left of the Dornier Do 17Z-2 of Staffel 5/KG3 piloted by Hauptmann Ernst Püttmann, which crashed in the forecourt of Victoria rail station, London, on September 15, after being attacked by Sgt Holmes of 501 Squadron, AAF.

191

9. Battle Over London

September 15

Winston Churchill often dropped into 'The Hole' at Uxbridge – a bomb-proof nerve-centre fifty feet below ground, camouflaged from above by gaily-striped deck chairs, and green lawns merging unobtrusively into the nine-hole Hillingdon Golf Course beyond. This was the first focal point of every battle, where the duty controller, sifting information from radar stations and observer posts already processed by Dowding's Filter Room, allotted incoming raids by sectors – planning the opening gambits like a gigantic game of chess until the squadrons were airborne. At 10.30 am on Sunday, September 15, Churchill's party trooped down sixty-three blackened stone steps to 11 Group's Ops Room, and Air Vice-Marshal Keith Park wondered if Churchill was hoping there would be a good bag. It seemed prudent to warn him: 'I don't know whether anything will happen today, sir. At present all is quiet.'

All over the airfields of southern England, from Hornchurch in the east to Warmwell in the west, the pilots shared Park's feelings: if trouble was afoot, there was no sign of it as yet. It had still been cold and dark when Pilot Officer Red Tobin, sleeping off a late night at The Black Swan with Shorty Keough, awoke to find Pilot Officer John Dundas shaking his shoulder: 'Better wake up.' When Red, irate, demanded why, Dundas, yawning, replied: 'I'm not quite sure, old boy – they say there's an invasion on or something.' Hastily Red had scrambled from bed – just how calm could an Englishman get? – but outside there was nothing but goblin wraiths of mist above the chestnut trees, the measured thud of the bowsers refuelling the planes, and the Spitfires' silhouettes, dark against the dawn, like some weird immobile flight of prehistoric birds.

There was that same relaxed air at every squadron dispersal – as if each pilot sought relief from tension in calm workaday routine. At 229's dispersal, Northolt, Squadron Leader John Banham sat as stiff as a statue while the famous war artist Cuthbert Orde limned a swift portrait in charcoal, then relaxed thankfully as Orde first sprayed the

194

sketch with fixative, then dated it – September 15, 1940. For neither man then could this date hold significance.

At Debden, the pilots of 73 Squadron were agog over a current sweepstake: the sex of Flight Lieutenant Mike Beytagh's forth-coming baby. At Croydon, 605's pilots, sprawled in deck chairs in the gardens of commandeered villas along the airfield perimeter, were absorbed in calculations of their own: how many rose-bushes and cigarette butts would their voracious billy goat, brought south as a mascot, eat before breakfast this morning?

Despite the outward gaiety, a few squadron commanders sensed an aching tension beneath. At Biggin Hill, Flight Lieutenant Brian Kingcombe rallied the incorrigibles of 92 Squadron: 'Any of you chaps war-weary, want a posting? If so, speak now, or for ever hold your water.' At Duxford, the legless Squadron Leader Douglas Bader, making the rounds of his sixty-strong fighter wing, quietly assured the Poles of 302 Squadron: 'You'll soon be back in Warsaw.'

For others it was a time of dedication. Many men, in later years, would recall this morning's services, and how the chaplains, with uncanny prescience, had picked their text from the 139th Psalm: 'If I take the wings of the morning, and dwell in the uttermost parts of the sea; even there shall thy hand lead me.' At Northolt, Zdzislaw Kras-nodebski's Poles voiced a poignant prayer of their own: 'It does not matter that so many must perish on the way, that our hearts are eaten up by longing . . . we believe that You have not forsaken Poland.'

In the Ops Room at HQ 11 Group, Winston Churchill felt this tension, too. To Churchill, the compact, two-storeyed underground room, sixty feet across, was for all the world like a small private theatre, the controller's daïs on which he sat sited roughly where the dress circle would have been. Beside him, on a green, leather-covered swivel chair, Wing Commander Eric Douglas-Jones kept a sharp eye on the battery of six telephones linking him with the fighter sectors – and on the six bulb-lit panels covering the opposite wall, charting the state of every sector's squadrons. The thought crossed his mind: at least the lacquer-red telephone which marked the 'hot-line' to 10 Downing Street would stay silent this morning. Whatever danger threatened, the Prime Minister was here to see for himself.

And to Churchill and every man on watch it was plain that trouble *was* now imminent. Already the WAAF plotters at the map below, earphones adjusted, were expertly piloting the coloured discs with their long croupier's rods: forty-plus coming in from Dieppe, corrected swiftly to sixty-plus. Seconds later, eighty-plus, this time direction Calais. Even Douglas-Jones, a seasoned controller, now felt the brooding sense of crisis. A dead cigar gripped in his teeth – though he yearned to smoke, Keith Park had tactfully explained to him that the air conditioning just wasn't equipped to cope – Churchill now broke the silence. 'There appear to be many aircraft coming in.' Just as calmly, Park reassured him: 'There'll be someone there to meet them.'

All along the coastline of southern England, 50,000 men and women – the watchers of the Observer Corps – binoculars levelled, peered intently towards the mist-shrouded sky, striving to interpret the danger signs – then, as the faint specks grew in number, their officers, prone among yellow gorse on the chalky clifftops, lifted their field-telephones. Their warnings, speeding inland, lent weight to the reports from the radar stations, along the low-lying marshes. At Pevensey, Rye, Swinggate and Poling, the German formations had swum into focus: wide, deep, steadily-beating echoes, arising from the mists of the morning.

From Rye Radar Station, Corporal Daphne Griffiths reported urgently to Fighter Command: 'Hullo, Stanmore, Hostile Six is now at fifteen miles, height fifteen thousand.' At once Stanmore queried, 'How many, Rye?' and swiftly the answer flashed back: 'Fifty-plus. Plot coming up. Read.' Still, in 11 Group's Ops Room, Wing Commander Douglas-Jones made no move. Behind him, Keith Park stood immobile: no man to interfere with his controllers, Park's sole hint of his presence was never more than a firm hand placed quietly on the shoulder, a token of encouragement. For one long second, Douglas-Jones, hesitated. The squadrons needed height and sun – but supposing, as so often happened, this was a German feint? But at 11.03 am he could wait no longer. The lighted bulbs showed every squadron standing by, some men already in their cockpits, and Fighter Command had warned both 10 and 12 Fighter Groups to be alerted, too. He reached for the first of six telephones and automatically, thirty-five miles away, a bulb glowed on the desk of Squadron Leader Roger Frankland, controlling at Biggin Hill.

As Douglas-Jones, using the direct secret line, ordered: 'Seventy-two and Ninety-two Squadrons to patrol Canterbury, angels twenty', Frankland seized his microphone. Simultaneously identical instructions, further coded to fox German fighters, volleyed across Biggin Hill airfield: 'Gannic squadron, scramble, – Gannic squadron,

1. Dad's Army – some f the original LDV Local Defence olunteers) from which e Home Guard was erived, seen here being ained on American ease-Lend P.17 rifles.

scramble. . . .' To the first pilots airborne, it seemed that this morning the Luftwaffe, as never before, held the sky. Twenty feet over Canterbury Cathedral, craning over his Spitfire's starboard wing, Pilot Officer Anthony Bartley, 92 Squadron, noted small, black, cottonwool puffs of flak staining the sky and at once saw why. A vast gaggle of bombers was winging inland, evading the guns with ease, closely escorted by Me 109s, 3,000 feet below and astern. Awed, he muttered: 'Jeepers, where the hell do we start on this lot?'

At 11.15 am Wing Commander Douglas-Jones had alerted Debden's controller: Hurricane Squadrons 17 and 73, this minute airborne, were to patrol over Chelmsford, Essex. Fifteen minutes later two more Hurricane squadrons, Krasnodebski's Poles and John Banham's 229 Squadron, got wind at Northolt: scramble and orbit Biggin Hill. Simultaneously Hurricane Squadrons 253 and 501 were climbing steeply from Kenley, heading for Maidstone at 18,000 feet. Five minutes later, at 11.25, learning that every 11 Group squadron was now in action, Duxford's station commander, Wing Commander Woodhall, sent Douglas Bader's 60-strong 12 Group wing speeding to lend support over London.

At HQ 11 Group, Winston Churchill watched with growing dismay: twenty-one squadrons were airborne now, and on every squadron panel a red bulb glowed ominously beside the legend 'Enemy intercepted'. Now he asked Douglas-Jones: 'Good Lord, man, all your forces are in the air – what do we do now?' Replying, Douglas-Jones strove to sound more confident than he felt: 'Well, sir, we can just hope that the squadrons will refuel as quickly as possible and get up again. The fighter stations will report immediately when any aircraft are available.'

In fact, the position, in many squadrons, was worse than Churchill could know: the hard-pressed 501 Squadron, at Kenley, could this morning muster only two planes serviceable. It was worse for 73 Squadron at Debden: twenty-four hours earlier, their thirteen Hurricanes had been savagely trounced by a squadron of trigger-happy Spitfire pilots. One life – and six aircraft – had been lost before this last great battle was ever joined.

And still the Luftwaffe streamed across the Channel, slim loggerheaded Dorniers, glinting shark-nosed 109s, slow scantily-armed Heinkel 111s, many of them decorated with insignia as colourful as any air force had ever boasted – the green dragon signifying Hauptmann Hans von Hahn's 1st Wing, 3rd Fighter Group, picked out by a high and watery sun, Major Adolf Galland's Mickey Mouse, armed with gun and hatchet, puffing a cigar strangely like Galland's own, the eagle's head of Werner Mölders, Major von Cramon-Taubadel's jet-black ace of spades.

Outside the Receiver Block at Rye Radar Station, Corporal Daphne Griffiths, shielding her eyes against the glare, watched now in silent awe the very planes that she herself had plotted roaring overhead – as if a dense black swarm of insects was advancing upon her, each one trailing ever-lengthening miles of white ribbon. Minute by minute the swarm grew denser, the morning sun gilding yet more legends and emblems; the green heart of Major Hannes Trautloft's 54th Fighter Group, the white-and-red lightning flashes of *Kampfgeschwader* 3, the poised black sledgehammer that marked Oberst Johannes Fink's Dorniers, the bared shark's teeth of No. 2 Wing, Zerstörer Group 76.

High above London's grey huddled rooftops, Pilot Officer Red Tobin, watching them come, knew a strange relief: almost since dawn 609 Squadron had patrolled over the city, first at 25,000 feet, then at 20,000, then up to 25,000 feet once more, the Controller heartlessly juggling the heights like a puppeteer, until half an hour had passed. Then suddenly they saw them – 100-plus German planes – and mercifully the suspense was broken.

Peering skywards, Red Tobin saw, 4,000 feet above them, fifty hovering 109s; but to the right and 1,000 feet below were also twenty-five Dornier bombers, and these Flight Commander Frank Howell was readying to attack. He called to Red: 'O.K., Charlie, come on in.' In this last moment, feral instinct once more saved Red Tobin's life. In the second of closing in, something prompted him to make one last check, swinging the Spitfire violently to port, and as he swung back on the last weave of all he saw, almost dead astern, three yellow-nosed Messerschmitt 109s. Red's voice, 'loud enough to be heard in Kansas', blasted in Howell's eardrum:'Danger, Red Section, danger, danger, danger!'

In that instant, he saw Howell break frenziedly to starboard, down towards the bombers, while the No. 2 man did a tight turn to port, and Red himself, reefing his Spitfire into a steep 360-degree turn, threw on the emergency boost, slamming his propeller into high pitch as he spun round. Again instinct was a screaming voice: keep chasing your own tail and they can't touch you. They're too fast to pull out of that dive.

Red was right. Engines snarling at full throttle the 109s hurtled past at upwards of 400 miles an hour, and Tobin was in turn the pursuer, sending long bursts of tracer hammering in their wake. Smoke bellied from the last plane's motor, then all three were gone, streaking for the anonymity of cloud-cover. Suddenly, dead ahead of him, Tobin saw a slim cigar-shaped Dornier nose into a shallow dive, heading for cloud-cover, and he dived again, thinking: if he makes the cloud, he's lost, so get him now. And with this thought he thumbed the firing button. Tracer broke in a chain of sparks against the bomber's port motor, and abruptly white smoke was bannering. The radiator was hit – or maybe the glycol tank.

Gingerly Tobin eased the Spitfire round, waiting until the port wing was steady in the gunsights, firing again until the aileron collapsed and fragments of wing fluttered emptily through space. As it gained cloud-sanctuary, he momentarily lost sight of it, then plunging through, he was in time to see it crash-land shakily, grinding to a halt, across a wide meadow.

All twenty-one squadrons airborne since 11 am had intercepted, though not all of them had met with marked success. At 18,000 feet

over Biggin Hill, Squadron Leader McNab's Canadians never saw the group of 109s that slashed at them from the sun: only two of the Hurricanes even closed with the raiders. It was the same with 41 Squadron over Gravesend; baulked equally by 109s, they watched yet more bombers slide through to London.

As Big Ben boomed noon on September 15, 148 German bombers arrived undeterred over central London, showering bombs to south-west and south-east, landing one bomb, unexploded, in King George VI's back-garden at Buckingham Palace. Yet from the ground, few civilians witnessed this historic combat: thick white clouds hung low above the city's spires. Fifteen-year-old Roy Owen

Barnes wrote it down as the most disappointing day on record: this morning, as always, he had thrilled to the sound of the siren, yet now, peering at the clouds above Catford, South London, his aircraft recognition booklets were no help at all.

It was easier for Squadron Leader Douglas Bader and the fifty-nine pilots of the Duxford wing. Arriving later over London from the north, they swiftly spotted the bombers five miles distant, 'like drilled black flies sliding towards the naked city'. As they gave chase to the west, they little by little gained height and sun – and suddenly, miraculously, the bombers turned, sweeping into their sights.

Now the radio-telephone was an urgent pandemonium; at the spearhead of No. 302 (Polish) Squadron, Squadron Leader Jack Satchell heard Bader shout: 'Weigh-in, everyone for himself.' Ten thousand feet above, where 12 Group's Spitfires waited to tackle the fighters, Flight Lieutenant Jack Leather chuckled to hear Bader explode: 'There are the buggers – come on, let's get at the bastards.' Promptly, the soothing voice of Wing Commander Woodhall sounded from Duxford's Ops Room: 'Douglas, remember there are ladies in the Ops Room this morning.'

Twenty-seven thousand feet over London, Squadron Leader James McComb, of Bader's Spitfire force, throttled back his machine with mounting impatience. At this height the intense cobalt blue of the sky, the sun's fiery radiance, his breath condensing like frosted glass on the cockpit canopy, were among the most exhilarating sights he had ever seen. But though his Spitfires had waited for seven long minutes to engage the hovering 109s, the German fighters had made no move. Most of them, with growing apprehension, were watching their fuel gauges, knowing that the moment to break for the Channel must come within seconds. McComb didn't divine this, but down below he saw that Bader's Hurricanes had the monopoly of the action. At fever-pitch, McComb broke radio silence: 'To hell with this – we're coming down! Squadron echelon port – St George for Merrie England, rah-rah-rah.' And down they went.

The sky became a wheeling, snarling saraband of warplanes – as Bader later recalled it, 'the finest shambles I'd ever been in'. Flame and black smoke spewed from a Dornier's bursting engines. Aircraft spun everywhere in blurred and fleeting confusion. On his first sortie with 302 Squadron, Flying Officer Julian Kowalski watched two of his comrades fall like stones; though his Hurricane was riddled with seventy-six bullets, he alone survived from his section.

In a combat so frenzied, few men could know with certainty who fired at whom – or with what results. Sergeant Ray Holmes, a Hurricane pilot of 504 Squadron, hot on the trail of a bomb-shedding Dornier, was convinced it was the very plane that had bombed Buckingham Palace; no sooner had it blown up than Holmes himself, his Hurricane hit, baled out. Landing in a dustbin in Ebury Bridge Road, South London, he phoned his home-base, Hendon, with an interim bulletin: his victim had crashed with spectacular force in the forecourt of Victoria Station.

To the Germans, both fighters and bombers, the morning run-up to the target seemed a veritable ambuscade. Oberleutnant Ernst Dullberg, a young 109 pilot, never forgot the eerie sensation of crossing the coast escorted by a silent phalanx of Spitfires – the contrails streaking the sky far above his unit, keeping pace all the way to London. Worse by far was the gauntlet run by Oberst Johannes Fink's scantily-armed Dorniers, a sortie culminating in unmanned guns, with the dead and wounded sprawled out on the floor. Horrified, Fink saw one Dornier fall from the sky before a shot was even fired, knowing its pilot had reached the peak where the strain could be borne no longer. As Fink recalls September 15: 'No man could be asked to bear more tension – mental or physical.'

And many men, gripped by the heat of battle, became all of a sudden primal. Swooping above the black shape of a slowly-descending German pilot, Squadron Leader Bryan Lane, one of Bader's wingmen, watched gleefully as his Spitfire's slipstream rocked the parachute violently towards the topmost branches of a wood, screaming, 'I hope that breaks your neck, you bloody swine!' Above Rotherfield, Sussex, dozens, homeward bound from morning service, watched horror stricken as a Dornier trailed fire towards their village – the gunner's parachute snagged hopelessly on the tailplane, a flight of Hurricanes in pursuit raking him relentlessly with bullets. Chastened, Major Hannes Trautloft confided to his diary: 'Who'd know that it was Sunday if it hadn't been announced on the radio?'

By 12.29 pm the Observer Corps' 19 Group HQ at Bromley, Kent, could report no further raids coming in, only a slow ebb of Channel-bound planes high above the oast-houses and apple orchards. Though the sky was scarred with contrails, and burning metal pulsed and flickered amid the stubble, the last great wave had receded.

The lull would not last long. Even now, on the airfields of northern France, the Germans, determined that the morning's score should

93. Post-mortem – Luftwaffe supremo, Hermann Göring expresses his displeasure to the Luftwaffe crews who 'failed him'.

somehow be reversed, were refuelling and bombing-up for the biggest sorties of all.

In this last effort to force the RAF into a fight to extinction, the Luftwaffe committed every plane they could muster – and to meet the challenge, any RAF plane still serviceable was sent airborne to join the fray. At HQ 11 Group, Winston Churchill himself, noting that every red bulb now glowed ominously, asked Air Vice-Marshal Park: 'What other reserves have we?' Park had to admit it: 'There are none.' His face a graven mask, Churchill said nothing, but his thoughts were anguished. If refuelling planes were caught on the ground by other raids of forty- or fifty-plus, the chances for the RAF were minimal.

Now, in the breathless moments of early afternoon, Sector Controllers all over southern England were marshalling their squadrons according to instructions from 11 Group, and the radio-telephones

crackled with urgent call-signs. All along the south coast, hundreds craning upwards saw the last classic interception of the Luftwaffe by Dowding's fighters: tiny black specks, flashing silver as the sun's rays caught them, machine-guns rattling, as if a boy ran a stick along a line of palings, the white drifting motes of parachutists pulling on their guide lines, like the first faint flakes of a snowfall.

To Major Adolf Galland, the spearhead of this mighty force, whose task was to clear the skies over Maidstone, it seemed that fresh, larger-than-life squadrons had suddenly been conjured from the ground. For ten hectic minutes – one of the longest combats he could ever remember – Galland wheeled in battle with Hurricanes and Spitfires – to achieve precisely nothing. Then, sighting a squadron of Hurricanes, 2,500 feet below, he swooped to test his skill anew, launching a lightning attack from the rear at the last plane on the port flank, closing to within ramming distance. Chunks of molten metal beat a fierce tattoo on his windscreen and now, as he tore past and above, he was, for one fearful instant, penned in on all sides by the Hurricanes. Again he attacked, an onslaught so stunning that not one Hurricane opened fire, and then the whole formation had burst apart, plane after plane peeling skywards and downwards, and 1,500 feet below, Galland saw two pilots bale out.

For most German fighters this whole afternoon proved to be a vicious circle of frustration. Leutnant Hellmuth Ostermann, of the 54th Fighter Group, knew he had never felt more impotent; tugging like a man berserk at the controls of his Me 109, he could feel the very fuselage shaking, yet still the bright blue bellies of the RAF fighters stayed tantalizingly out of range, diving and firing each time the bombers turned, while the 109s, forbidden to pursue, looked helplessly on.

To a few bombers, shorn of fighter-escort, it seemed fruitless even to attempt the journey. Airborne from Juvaincourt in a Junkers 88 of the 77th Bomber Group, Oberleutnant Dietrich Peltz found the whole sky empty of 109s; without hesitation he sent the whole 4,000-pound bomb load tumbling towards the Channel. And other bomber pilots saw the gesture as eminently practical; the piled clouds ruled out all hope of precision bombing, and everywhere the RAF were waiting.

With aces like Galland bemused by the whirl of fighters, it was small wonder the bombers of the afternoon wave paid a bitter price: almost a quarter of all those engaged, with many more seriously damaged. The crucial two hours' delay had given the RAF time to refuel and re-arm, and, even more, to stir men to epic endeavour. Those who had known success that morning knew they just couldn't miss – and those who had failed hitherto were out for blood.

Ever since that tragic August 24 encounter with the Blenheims, Squadron Leader Ernest McNab's Canadians had ached to acquit themselves in battle – and over Biggin Hill, at 2.30 pm on September 15, their chance had come. Diving like angry eagles on a formation of twenty Heinkel bombers, eleven Hurricanes cut them to ribbons – to McNab, the white plumed exhausts of the wheeling aircraft were suddenly 'like sky-writing gone mad'. From the carnage, one Canadian, Flying Officer Phil Lochman of Ottawa, emerged to fulfil ambitions of his own. Belly-landing his Hurricane beside a crashed

94. Some of the 'Few'. 249 Squadron pilots at North Weald, 1940. *L–R*: P. R. F. Burton; A. R. H. Barton; A. G. Lewis; Crossie; T. F. Neil; J. Beazley; Sqn Ldr John Grandy (OC); G. Barclay; K. Lofts. John Grandy in later years became Chief of the Air Staff, RAF.

bomber in the mud-flats of the Thames Estuary, he personally escorted the crew from the aircraft – one of the few fighter pilots ever to take a prisoner.

The battle was now a clawing, stalling mass of fighters bent on destruction, within a cube over southern England eighty miles long by thirty broad, more than five miles high: a battle that within thirty minutes would number above 200 individual combats. So crowded was the sky that Sergeant James 'Ginger' Lacey, a twenty-two-year-old Hurricane pilot, happily tagging on to a flight of 109s, painstakingly shot down two before they even spotted him. As a Dornier's port wing flashed over his cockpit, veteran Squadron Leader Bryan Lane, ducking involuntarily, breathed: 'Why, it's the whole Luftwaffe.' Pilot Officer Patrick Barthropp, operational for the first time that day, felt as awed. After the morning's sortie, he noted in his log-book: 'Thousands of them.' This afternoon, he returned to note again: '*Still* thousands of them.'

With sun and height at last in their favour, few RAF pilots any longer thought of the risks. Pilot Officer Miroslaw Feric, one of Krasnodebski's Poles, sending an Me 110 flaring towards the sea, felt a savage exultation; on the third day of war a German fighter had shot away his control column at the base, leaving him petrified with fear, but accounts had been squared now. Flying Officer Witor Urbanowicz, seeing a Dornier on the point of force-landing, saw no good reason why the crew should survive; one lethal blast across the cockpit sealed the bomber's fate. And Sergeant Stanislaw Karubin, his ammunition exhausted, was still determined to finish off the Messerschmitt that had assailed him; he flew head-on at the plane like a suddenly-loosed torpedo, breaking to reef his Hurricane a yard above the cockpit hood. For a second he glimpsed the German's face distorted in mortal terror – and the man's hand on the controls gave one fatal tremor. A mighty muffled crash sounded from far below, as the Messerschmitt hit a meadow in a rending all-out dive, tearing the body of the plane apart, scattering the wings 100 yards across the pasture.

The battle was only fifteen minutes old, yet already so many parachutes blossomed across the sky that one cheerful Pole, floating down, yelled a warning: 'They'll take us for a bloody parachute division.'

96. (*Over the page*) The skies were clear –
Hurricanes of 85 Squadron, led by Peter
Townsend, skimming across a silver cloudscape
in late October 1940. Although fighting
continued into November, by now the Battle of
Britain had been virtually won conclusively.

Final Encounters

September 15 and After

At 2.30 pm on that mellow September Sunday, the British fighters seemed more numerous and fresh than ever. The truth was that Air Chief Marshal Sir Hugh Dowding was still 170 pilots under strength – but at this eleventh hour a fierce elation had seized every man airborne. Squadron Leader James McComb still recalled seeing his second-in-command, Jack Leather, airborne on the second September 15 sortie, 'grinning hugely, his hood open, German bullets ripping past his flying helmet'. Many took risks that it later turned them cold to think about.

Most were so afire with the chase that all thoughts of time and place were suspended. Implacable Sergeant Janos Jeka, a Polish Hurricane pilot, pursued a 110 so close to the earth his bullets literally scythed up yards of turf. Sergeant David Cox, a Spitfire pilot, chasing a 109 all the way to France, only turned back when his oil temperature went right off the clock. Sub-Lieutenant George Blake, Fleet Air Arm, took his Spitfire so close to a Dornier 'it was like Nelson firing a broadside at Trafalgar'.

Curiously, few pilots this afternoon were notching up top scores; it was teamwork from first to last – and so numerous were the crippled bombers that few men could miss. Over the English Channel, leading 609 Squadron in pursuit of two limping Dorniers, Flying Officer Michael Appleby, deciding the time was propitious to launch one of Fighter Command's classic attacks, rapped out: 'Number One attack, Number One attack, go.' To Appleby's mortification, nobody even heeded him. Without waiting for instructions, Andy Mamedoff, Shorty and the rest had all dived blindly to attack, blasting the bombers to pieces in mid-air, each man duly claiming 'one-sixth of a Dornier'.

To some, it seemed the most routine day ever. Pilot Officer Vernon Simmonds, 238 Squadron, sailed through a barrage of ack-ack over London, blew up the starboard engine of a Heinkel 111, realized that cannon had riddled his own tailplane, and was back at Middle Wallop in fifteen minutes flat. To Sergeant Cyril Babbage, the day spelt

210

tedium all the way. Abandoning his Spitfire over Shoreham, Sussex, shortly before noon, he found the battle so disrupting rail traffic that it took five hours to cover the twenty-five miles from Shoreham to 602 Squadron's dispersal at Westhampnett airfield.

It was a day of stark tragedy for others. Far below the swirl of the battle, at Hanns Farm, Bilsington, a village above the Romney Marshes, thirty-one-year-old Alice Daw was getting her small daughter Vera ready for an outing. Her husband, William, who farmed the smallholding, had promised them both a run in the car, and four-year-old Vera was on tiptoe with excitement. Aerial dog-fights in this part of Kent were now so commonplace that few villagers even bothered to take shelter. At this moment, tinkering with his old rattle-trap inside the barn, Daw wasn't even conscious that there was a plane overhead – or that Oberstleutnant Hassel von Wedel, the Luftwaffe's official historian and World War I comrade of Göring, was in dire trouble. At 6,000 feet over Maidstone, von Wedel never even saw the Hurricane that riddled his yellow-nosed Messerschmitt 109 with bullets. Circling frantically, losing height by the minute, it was cruel misfortune that his engine seized up as he glided over Hanns Farm.

In the barn below, Farmer Daw heard nothing; he was still servicing the car when the Messerschmitt ploughed through the roof of the barn above his head, knocking him unconscious and reducing the car to scrap metal, strewing its severed wings across a field nearby, fatally fracturing Alice Daw's skull as she ran from the cottage, and killing four-year-old Vera outright.

The first men on the scene, the local Fire Brigade, found von Wedel unhurt, his fall from his plane broken by a pile of manure, yet plainly the bald, eagle-faced man was on the verge of crack-up. Near to tears, he could only repeat, 'I've killed a woman, I've killed a woman', over and over again. As one of the Fire Brigade hastened to the farmhouse to brew the stricken pilot a cup of tea, somehow no one had the heart to break the news concerning the child.

A few would always see the day as one of total failure. At Duxford, Squadron Leader Douglas Bader was cursing like a trooper; the scramble had come too late, the Germans had the height on the 12 Group wing all the way, the controlling had been inept from start to finish. Given expert guidance, his pilots could have shot down every raider that crossed the coast – and from now on this was Bader's insatiable ambition.

To the newsmen, by contrast, it seemed a day for tributes. *The New York Times*'s Robert Post reported: 'The German loss of air crews is tremendous.' The London *Daily Express* was sardonic: 'Göring may reflect that this is no way to run an invasion.' The London *Times* was cautiously confident: 'The figures . . . give grounds for sober satisfaction.'

Yet, at top level, many felt concern. At 3.50 pm, as the all-clear sounded at HQ 11 Group, Air Vice-Marshal Park confessed to Winston Churchill that in the last twenty minutes of the raid, Control had been so swamped with information they had not been able to handle it all. Nor had the interception been by any means fool-proof; everywhere the German bombers had broken through. Still, Churchill felt moved to praise Wing Commander Douglas-Jones, clapping him on the shoulder with an unexpected 'Good show, old boy.' It was some hours, however, before Fighter Command knew the extent of their losses – twenty-six planes, thirteen pilots – but it was known that many planes had taken a cruel beating. If the Germans came again in such force, could the RAF still contrive to stem the tide?

At many airfields, they were wondering too. At Northolt, the plight of Zdzislaw Krasnodebski's 303 Squadron was typical of many. By the day's end, only four aircraft remained serviceable. Ten others had cables cut, control surfaces shot away, radiators smashed, wings and engines riddled, one with its main wing spar nearly broken at the junction with the fuselage. Without more ado, the servicing flight, under Flying Officer Wiorkiewicz, a Warsaw factory engineer, settled to a gruelling all-night vigil, nourished only by cups of tea, to present twelve planes serviceable by first light. It was the same on airfield after airfield.

Nobody among Dowding's pilots thought in terms of a final victory. If many messes held parties that night, it was because the nerves demanded one to relax the aching tension, for no man knew now which party might be his last. 73 Squadron's pilots packed out the Fox and Hounds at Steeple Bumstead, Essex, for just one reason: they had found a cunning way of sabotaging the clock to allow an hour's extra drinking.

Only at 8 pm did there seem some cause for jubilation. At Chequers, Winston Churchill, peeling away the black satin eyeband he always wore for sleeping, was just waking from a nap; it had been 4.30 when he had arrived back from 11 Group and the drama had tired him out. He rang the bell, and Principal Private Secretary John

Martin brought a dismal budget of news – the Italians were advancing on Alexandria and fifty British tankers had been destroyed. Then Martin wound up: 'However, all is redeemed by the air. We have shot down one hundred and eighty-three for a loss of under forty.'

Within days, Flight Lieutenant Michael Golovine's crash investigators had arrived at the truth; the German losses totalled no more than fifty-six. In addition to twenty-four ill-fated Dorniers and ten Heinkel 111s, the RAF had accounted for eighteen Messerschmitt 109s, three Me 110s and one Junkers 88. Yet within days too, further truths were emerging; the German attempts were slackening as the Luftwaffe tried to thrash out some feasible way of continuing the assault.

From August, through September, the German losses had totalled some 1,140 planes of all types – and at such a rate the force would surely bleed to death. Even isolated fighter units, like 54th Group's 1st Wing, after losing fourteen pilots in two months, were being pulled from the line. Crimson with rage, Göring summoned his commanders for a stormy September 16 conference, charging furiously: 'The fighters have failed.' In vain, Oberst Theo Osterkamp defended them; if they were restricted to escorting bombers, how *could* they fulfil their original function? Then, too, the British were employing new tactics, gathering large numbers of fighters with express orders to concentrate on the bombers. For answer, Göring could only roar: 'If they come in large numbers, we should be pleased – they can be shot down in large numbers.'

Osterkamp was silent. In the face of Göring's irrational outbursts, there was no more that any man could usefully say. Attacks by single fighters, rendered clumsy by 500-kilo bomb-loads would drag on until December – their losses spiralling as the surprise element that Hauptmann Walter Rubensdörffer had pioneered was lost altogether. The Battle of Britain might be over – but the battle between Göring in Berlin and the Luftwaffe commanders in the west could only intensify from now on.

In any case, air supremacy was no longer geared to the logistics of 'Operation Sea-Lion'. A day earlier, in Berlin, Hitler had stressed that 'Four to five days good weather are required to achieve decisive results.' But, by September 17, Gross-Admiral Raeder had dictated for the War Diary, 'The enemy air force is by no means defeated. On the contrary, it shows increasing activity. The Führer therefore decides to postpone "Sea-Lion" indefinitely.' Within two months,

Hitler's resolve was crystallized – the onslaught on Russia, 'Operation Barbarossa', assumed full priority.

Reichsmarschall Hermann Göring veered from the frustrated to the philosophical. On September 14, at his hunting lodge in the Rominterheide, East Prussia, he assured Hauptmann 'Assi' Hahn at the height of a stag hunt: 'Two weeks more and Britain will be forced to her knees.' Within days he confessed ruefully to General Kurt Student: 'We'd forgotten that the English fight best with their backs to the wall.'

It was not an admission he would make at all levels. When Generalfeldmarschall Albert Kesselring suggested that it was high time to concentrate solely on night bombing, Göring exploded: 'Night raids? What insanity! I can finish the air war without that.' But, within days, he saw that this solution was the one way of breaking down British morale, reasoning: 'After all, man isn't a nocturnal animal.' He rallied the disillusioned Oberst Johannes Fink: 'You must give the German people air superiority as a Christmas present to hang on their trees.'

All this lay in the future. For most people, as September 15 drew to a close, it was a matter of overwhelming relief that after six fateful weeks they were still alive and free.

Pilot Officer Geoffrey Page lay in a clean white hospital bed, not moving, not speaking. By now he knew well enough what the battle had done to his face and hands. Fifteen major surgical operations were to be endured before Page, through bitter determination, fought his way back to operational flying, vowing to take one German life for every operation he had undergone. Only once this was achieved would the bitterness drain from him, leaving him void and spent, but this was not yet. There was nothing in his heart now but hate.

Zdzislaw Krasnodebski, at thirty-seven, could summon up more philosophy. Barely conscious at the Queen Victoria Hospital, East Grinsphead, he blessed the opiates that dulled his pain. The noise of the last great air battle seemed very far away, but he knew that until he flew again his stewardship had not been in vain. Each time Jan Zumbach and young Ludwig Paszkiewicz came to visit him, the squadron had eclipsed its past endeavour.

For most pilots, the evening of September 15 was as uneventful as any other. Young Barrie Heath, a 611 Spitfire pilot, got back late to

215

his rented flat neat Digby airfield to make his peace with his wife. It wasn't only combat that kept him so long; they had had a few drinks in the mess. When Joy Heath chided him: '*I do* wish you'd let me know if you're going to be late for dinner', the young pilot apologized meekly. The cast-iron excuse – that he had been fighting for his country – never occurred to him until later.

For some, there were other worries to be settled. At Gravesend, Pilot Officer Robert Oxspring couldn't face a drink until he had first rung the Rochester police. Had the house wrecked by his very first German victim been tenanted or empty? The police were reassuring and he felt better. Only twenty-five years later did he learn they had spared his feelings, that a woman and child had died.

For Red Tobin and the pilots of 609, it was a routine evening at The Black Swan, Monxton, except that he drank that much harder to forget the day's events. Three days from now, he, Andy and Shorty would go north as pilots of the first Eagle Squadron, forming at Church Fenton, Yorkshire. He would miss the British right enough, but maybe action with the new outfit would be rougher yet. As Andy always said: 'Time will tell.'

In northern France, the Germans, as yet, had no inkling that the invasion was off. Only gradually would that realization sink in, and some would know relief, others regret. Major Hannes Trautloft, a diarist to the end, noted: 'It seems very unlikely we shall end the war against Britain this year – and who knows what will happen next spring?' At Sempy, in the Pas de Calais, Major the Baron Günther von Maltzahn voiced what some perhaps already felt: 'We're never going to win this war; we can't.' At Guines, Major Martin Mettig, hearing of the cancellation, asked the officers assembled in the Casino: 'What were all the deaths for then, eh?' and nobody could answer him.

Adolf Galland was in Lille, playing ragtime on a café piano, a score of others clustered round. It was long past midnight, but when the provost's men strode disapprovingly in to check on his papers, Galland just played faster than ever, black cigar still clenched in his teeth. He said: 'Just look in the *Berliner Illustrierte* – front page.' It featured his latest decoration, as large as life. At this moment, he hated provosts as much as staff-officers, anybody who wasn't a pilot, the whole stinking war.

Back across the Channel, in southern England, the night seemed mercifully quiet. Outside Ladwood Farmhouse, Robert Bailey was

100. (*Right*) Oberleutnant Karl Fischer of 7./JG27 dive on two unarmed Avro Anson trainers on 30 September 1940, but stalled on a steep turn and crashed in Windso Great Park.

101. (*Far right*) Fligh Lieutenant John Dundas, DFC, who claimed Major Helmu Wick, the 56-victory commander of JG2 as h thirteenth victim, on 2 November 1940. Only seconds later Dundas was killed by Wick's wing-man.

102. (*Right*) Squadron Leader Roland Robert Stanford Tuck, DSO, DFC, leader of 257 Squadron by Novembe 1940. Credited with twenty-nine victories, thirtieth victim was onl positively identified as recently as 1977.

103. (*Far right*) Robe Wardlow Oxspring – 'Oxo' – who flew with 6 Squadron in 1940; a un commanded in World War One by his father Oxspring survived the war and remained in th RAF, rising to Group Captain.

216

Nigeria
OYO PROVIN

lost in thought. It had been the usual quiet evening at Swingfield Baptist Chapel, and he and Vera had been home well in time to hear the BBC's 9 pm bulletin, when announcer Alvar Lidell read the news: 'Wave after wave of raiders tried to approach the capital . . . some planes got through, but the rest were harassed and shot to pieces by our Spitfires and Hurricanes.' Bailey dimmed the oil-lamp and stood quietly in the darkness. The news seemed more cheering, but who knew how much the public were told? Some of the Swaffers' children, clustered behind him in the porch, heard some bombers, and one asked timidly: 'Is that a German?' 'No,' Bailey said quickly, 'they're ours. Don't worry. They're ours.'

It was quiet on the airfields too. Wing Commander Cecil Bouchier was still in the Ops Room at Hornchurch, writing citations and sifting combat reports: in days like these it seemed the only time a station commander had to catch up. Soon the trucks would race past like fire-engines, bearing the pilots to dispersal, but that would be the dawn of another day.

Through the darkened corridors of Fighter Command, Air Chief Marshal Sir Hugh Dowding threaded his way like a ghost. Current Air Ministry propaganda was suggesting that his command was stronger now, towards the end of the battle, than at the beginning, and the false emphasis made Dowding angry: it hardly took into account the victories that had been achieved at the cost of pilots killed or wounded – or that many fighter squadrons were now little more than training units. It had been a long and awful struggle, and so much lay ahead.

It was late at Chequers, too, when Winston Churchill at last left his study. Outside the door, Inspector Walter Thompson was almost dropping on his feet, and Churchill, concerned, peered through the gloom: 'You're tired out, Thompson.' Thompson admitted it: 'Yes, I am, sir.' He remembered that day because it was the first time Churchill had ever put an arm round his shoulder. Then Churchill said: 'It will be worth it in the end. We're going to win, you know.' They walked along the corridor like that, the Prime Minister's arm still round the shoulder of his faithful shadow.

At Biggin Hill, Corporal Elspeth Henderson was going off-duty. Northwards, the sky glowed with driven fires as 180 bombers pounded London and the ack-ack barrage studded the night with golden sparks. Pausing for a word with the sentry, Elspeth wondered just how crowded the public air-raid shelter would prove at this hour; it

218

was too stifling to sleep in the little room above the butcher's shop that was now Biggin's Emergency Ops Room, and meanwhile, their old billets were still unrepaired. To the problems of feeding and keeping clean was added now the problem of sleeping.

Ahead lay the long nights of bombing. The day battles were all but over, but Elspeth Henderson did not know that then. Tomorrow would be just another working day. Slowly, her trim resolute figure passed from the sentry's view. The darkness swallowed up the sound of her footfalls.

Order of Battle

August 13, 1940

EAGLE DAY: THE RAF
Fighter Command

HEADQUARTERS, FIGHTER COMMAND. Bentley Priory, Stanmore, Middlesex
> *Air Officer Commanding-in-Chief:*
> Air Chief Marshal Sir Hugh Dowding

HEADQUARTERS, No. 10 GROUP. Rudloe Manor, Box, Wiltshire
> *Air Officer Commanding:*
> Air Vice-Marshal Sir Christopher Brand

PEMBREY SECTOR STATION
Wing Commander J. H. Hutchinson
No. 92 Spitfire Squadron – Squadron Leader P. J. Sanders (to Biggin Hill, 9/8/40)

FILTON SECTOR STATION
Group Captain Robert Hanmer
No. 87 Hurricane Squadron – Squadron Leader T. G. Lovell-Gregg; Squadron Leader R. S. Mills (from 18/8/40)
(based at Exeter Satellite Station, then to Bibury)
No. 213 Hurricane Squadron – Squadron Leader H. D. McGregor
(based at Exeter Satellite Station; to Tangmere on 7/9/40)

ST. EVAL SECTOR STATION (Coastal Command)
Fighter Section HQ: Group Captain L. G. le B. Croke
No. 234 Spitfire Squadron – Squadron Leader J. S. O'Brien; Flight Lieutenant C. L. Page
(to Middle Wallop on 14/8/40, returning to St. Eval 11/9/40)
No. 247 Gladiator Squadron – Flight Lieutenant H. A. Chater
(One flight only, operating from Roborough Fleet Air Arm Station)

MIDDLE WALLOP SECTOR STATION
Wing Commander David Roberts

No. 238 Hurricane Squadron – Squadron Leader Harold Fenton; Flight Lieutenant Minden Blake (acting CO until 15/9/40)
  (to St. Eval on 14/8/40, returning Middle Wallop 9/9/40)

No. 609 Spitfire Squadron – Squadron Leader Horace Darley
  (also operating from Warmwell Satellite Station: Wing Commander George Howard)

No. 604 Blenheim Squadron – Squadron Leader Michael Anderson

No. 152 Spitfire Squadron – Squadron Leader Peter Devitt
  (also operating from Warmwell)

HEADQUARTERS, No. 11 GROUP. Hillingdon House, Uxbridge, Middlesex
  Air Officer Commanding:
  Air Vice-Marshal Keith Park

DEBDEN SECTOR STATION
Wing Commander Laurence Fuller-Good

No. 17 Hurricane Squadron – Squadron Leader C. W. Williams; Squadron Leader A. G. Miller (from 29/8/40)
  (detached Tangmere 19/8/40, returning Debden 2/9/40)

No. 85 Hurricane Squadron – Squadron Leader Peter Townsend
  (to Croydon from 19/8/40, returning Castle Camps, Debden Satellite, 3/9/40, thence to Church Fenton)

NORTH WEALD SECTOR STATION
Wing Commander Victor Beamish

No. 56 Hurricane Squadron – Squadron Leader G. A. Manton
  (also operating from Rochford Satellite Station; transferred Boscombe Down 1/9/40)

No. 151 Hurricane Squadron – Squadron Leader J. A. Gordon; Squadron Leader Eric King (from 21/8/40); Squadron Leader H. West (from 4/9/40)
  (to Stapleford Satellite Station on 29/8/40; thence to Digby 1/9/40)

HORNCHURCH SECTOR STATION
Wing Commander Cecil Bouchier

No. 54 Spitfire Squadron – Squadron Leader James Leathart; Squadron Leader Donald Finlay (from 26/8/40 to 28/8/40 only); Squadron Leader Pat Dunworth (from 6/9/40)
  (also operated from Manston; transferred Catterick 3/9/40)

No. 65 Spitfire Squadron – Squadron Leader A. L. Holland
(also operated from Manston; transferred Turnhouse 27/8/40)

No. 74 Spitfire Squadron – Squadron Leader Francis White; Flight
Lieutenant Adolph Malan (from 28/8/40)
(to Wittering on 14/8/40, thence to Kirton-in-Lindsey, from 21/8/40, and
Coltishall, from 10/9/40)

No. 266 Spitfire Squadron – Squadron Leader R. L. Wilkinson
(detached to Eastchurch Coastal Command Station during 13/8/40;
operated from Hornchurch and Manston until 21/8/40; then to Wittering)

No. 600 Blenheim Squadron – Squadron Leader David Clark
(based at Manston, for night-readiness only; transferred Hornchurch
24/8/40; thence to Redhill, forward airfield for Kenley, from 15/9/40)

BIGGIN HILL SECTOR STATION
Group Captain Richard Grice

No. 32 Hurricane Squadron – Squadron Leader John Worrall; Squadron
Leader Michael Crossley (from 16/8/40)
(to Acklington 28/8/40)

No. 610 Spitfire Squadron – Squadron Leader John Ellis
(to Acklington 31/8/40)

No. 501 Hurricane Squadron – Squadron Leader Harry Hogan
(operating at Gravesend Satellite Station, then to Kenley from 10/9/40)

Other forward bases in the Biggin Hill Sector were:
Hawkinge – Squadron Leader E. E. Arnold
Lympne (the emergency landing field) – Squadron Leader D. H. Montgomery

KENLEY SECTOR STATION
Wing Commander Tom Prickman

No. 615 Hurricane Squadron – Squadron Leader Joseph Kayll
(to Prestwick 29/8/40)

No. 64 Spitfire Squadron – Squadron Leader Aeneas MacDonell
(to Leconfield and Ringway, 19/8/40)

No. 111 Hurricane Squadron – Squadron Leader John Thompson
(operating from Croydon Satellite Station until 19/8/40; transferred to
Debden until 3/9/40; returning to Croydon 7/9/40; thence to Drem)

No. 1 (RCAF) Hurricane Squadron – Squadron Leader Ernest McNab
(based at Croydon, non-operational until 16/8/40; transferred to Northolt
Sector, fully operational 17/8/40)

NORTHOLT SECTOR STATION
Group Captain Stanley Vincent

No. 1 (RAF) Hurricane Squadron – Squadron Leader D. A. Pemberton
(to Wittering 9/9/40)

No. 303 (Polish) Hurricane Squadron – Squadron Leader Zdzislaw Krasnodebski (until 6/9/40); Squadron Leader Ronald Kellett (non-operational until 31/8/40)

No. 257 Hurricane Squadron – Squadron Leader H. Harkness (until 12/9/40); Flight Lieutenant Robert Stanford Tuck (to Debden 15/8/40; from 5/9/40 operating from Martlesham Heath Satellite Station)

TANGMERE SECTOR STATION
Wing Commander Jack Boret

No. 43 Hurricane Squadron – Squadron Leader John 'Tubby' Badger; Squadron Leader Caesar Hull (from 1/9/40); Squadron Leader Tom Dalton-Morgan (from 16/9/40) (to Usworth 8/9/40)

No. 145 Hurricane Squadron – Squadron Leader John Peel (operating from Westhampnett Satellite Station; to Montrose Flying Training Command Station and Dyce Coastal Command Station on 14/8/40)

No. 601 Hurricane Squadron – Squadron Leader the Hon. Edward Ward; Flight Lieutenant Sir Archibald Hope, Bt. (from 16/8/40) (to Debden 19/8/40, returning Tangmere 2/9/40; thence to Exeter, 7/9/40)

HEADQUARTERS, No. 12 GROUP. Watnall, near Nottingham, Nottinghamshire
Air Officer Commanding:
Air Vice-Marshal Trafford Leigh-Mallory

CHURCH FENTON SECTOR
Group Captain C. F. Horsley

No. 73 Hurricane Squadron – Squadron Leader M. W. Robinson (to Debden 5/9/40)

No. 249 Hurricane Squadron – Squadron Leader Eric King; Squadron Leader John Grandy (from 21/8/40) (to Boscombe Down 14/8/40; transferred to North Weald 1/9/40)

No. 616 Spitfire Squadron – Squadron Leader Marcus Robinson; Squadron Leader H. E. Burton (from 3/9/40) (operating from Leconfield Satellite Station; to Kenley 20/8/40; to Coltishall, then Kirton-in-Lindsey from 3/9/40)

No. 302 (Polish) Hurricane Squadron – Squadron Leader Jack Satchell and Squadron Leader Mumler (non-operational until 20/8/40; attached Duxford 13/9/40)

Wing Commander S. H. Hardy
No. 222 Spitfire Squadron – Squadron Leader Johnnie Hill
  (to Hornchurch 30/8/40)
No. 264 Defiant Squadron – Squadron Leader Philip Hunter; Squadron
  Leader Desmond Garvin (from 24/8/40)
  (to Hornchurch 22/8/40; withdrawn to Kirton-in-Lindsey 28/8/40)

DIGBY SECTOR STATION
Wing Commander Ian Parker
No. 46 Hurricane Squadron – Squadron Leader J. R. MacLachlan
  (to Stapleford Satellite Station, North Weald Sector, 1/9/40)
No. 611 Spitfire Squadron – Squadron Leader James McComb
  (operating from Fowlmere Satellite Station, Duxford Sector, from
  11/9/40)
No. 29 Blenheim Squadron – Squadron Leader S. C. Widdows

COLTISHALL SECTOR STATION
Wing Commander W. K. Beisiegel
No. 242 Hurricane Squadron – Squadron Leader Douglas Bader
  (to Duxford 2/9/40)
No. 66 Spitfire Squadron – Squadron Leader Rupert Leigh
  (to Kenley 3/9/40, then to Gravesend from 11/9/40)

WITTERING SECTOR STATION
Wing Commander Harry Broadhurst
No. 229 Hurricane Squadron – Squadron Leader H. J. Maguire; Squadron
  Leader John Banham (from 7/9/40)
  (to Northolt 9/9/40)
No. 23 Blenheim Squadron – Squadron Leader G. Heycock
  (from Colly Weston Satellite 16/8/40; to Middle Wallop and Ford (Fleet
  Air Arm Station) 13/9/40)

DUXFORD SECTOR STATION
Wing Commander A. B. Woodhall
No. 19 Spitfire Squadron – Squadron Leader P. C. Pinkham; Squadron
  Leader Bryan Lane (from 5/9/40)
  (operating also from Fowlmere Satellite Station)
No. 310 (Czech) Hurricane Squadron – Squadron Leader Douglas Black-
  wood; Squadron Leader Sasha Hess
  (non-operational until 18/8/40)

HEADQUARTERS, No. 13 GROUP. Blakelaw Estate, Ponteland Road,
 Newcastle-on-Tyne, Northumberland
  Air Officer Commanding:
  Air Vice-Marshal Richard Saul

CATTERICK SECTOR STATION
Wing Commander G. L. Carter

No. 219 Blenheim Squadron – Squadron Leader J. H. Little
No. 41 Spitfire Squadron – Squadron Leader H. R. L. Hood; Squadron
 Leader Lister (from 8/9/40)
 (to Hornchurch 3/9/40)

USWORTH SECTOR STATION
Wing Commander Brian Thynne

No. 607 Hurricane Squadron – Squadron Leader James Vick
 (to Tangmere 9/9/40)
No. 72 Spitfire Squadron – Squadron Leader A. R. Collins; Wing Commander Ronald Lees (for 2/9/40 only); Flight Lieutenant Edward Graham
 (operating from Acklington Satellite Station; to Biggin Hill on 31/8/40;
 operational from Croydon after 1/9/40)
No. 79 Spitfire Squadron – Squadron Leader Hervey Hayworth
 (operating from Acklington; to Biggin Hill 27/8/40; transferred to Pembrey 8/9/40)

WICK SECTOR STATION (Coastal Command)
Fighter Section HQ: Wing Commander Geoffrey Ambler

No. 3 Hurricane Squadron – Squadron Leader S. F. Godden
 (to Castletown 7/9/40)
No. 504 Hurricane Squadron – Squadron Leader John Sample
 (operating from Castletown Satellite Station; to Hendon, under Northolt
 Sector control 6/9/40)
No. 232 Hurricane Squadron – Squadron Leader M. M. Stephens
 (operating from Sumburgh Satellite Station on half-squadron basis only)

DYCE SECTOR STATION (Coastal Command)
Fighter Section HQ: Group Captain F. Crerar

No. 603 Spitfire Squadron – Squadron Leader George Denholm
 (operating with one Flight at Montrose (Flying Training Command); to
 Hornchurch 27/8/40)

Wing Commander the Duke of Hamilton and Bradon

No. 605 Hurricane Squadron – Squadron Leader Walter Churchill; Flight Lieutenant Archie McKellar (from 11/9/40)
(operating from Drem Satellite Station; to Croydon 7/9/40)

No. 602 Spitfire Squadron – Squadron Leader A. V. R. 'Sandy' Johnstone (from Drem Satellite Station to Westhampnett, Tangmere Sector, 13/8/40)

No. 253 Hurricane Squadron – Squadron Leader Tom Gleave and Squadron Leader H. M. Starr (until 31/8/40); Squadron Leader Gerry Edge (partially operational from Prestwick (Flying Training Command); to Kenley 30/8/40)

No. 141 Defiant Squadron – Squadron Leader W. A. Richardson

No. 245 Hurricane Squadron
(based at Aldergrove, Northern Ireland, station administered from Air Ministry)

EAGLE DAY: THE LUFTWAFFE

AIR FLEET FIVE. Stavanger, Norway
  Generaloberst Hans-Jürgen Stumpff

X FLYING CORPS
General Geisler

Long-range bombers

KG 26	*Heinkel 111*	
Staff Flight	Oberstleutnant Fuchs	Stavanger
I	Major Busch	Stavanger
III	Major von Lossberg	Stavanger

KG 30	*Junkers 88*	
Staff Flight	Oberstleutnant Loebel	Aalborg, Denmark
I	Major Doensch	Aalborg, Denmark
III	Hauptmann Kellewe	Aalborg, Denmark

Fighters

ZG 76	*ME 110*	
I	Hauptmann Werner Restemeyer	Stavanger
JG 77	*ME 109*	
II	Hauptmann Hentschel	Stavanger, Drontheim

plus coastal reconnaissance, long-range reconnaissance and mine-laying units

AIR FLEET TWO. Brussels
  Generalfeldmarschall Albert Kesselring

I FLYING CORPS

Generaloberst Grauert

Long-range bombers

KG 1	*HE 111 (except 3rd Wing)*	
Staff Flight	Oberstleutnant Exss	Rosières-en-Santerre
I	Major Maier	Montdidier-Clairmont
II	Major Kosch	Montdidier-Nijmegen
III	Major Willibald Fanelsa (DO 17 equipped)	Rosières-en-Santerre
KG 76	*JU 88 – DO 17*	
Staff Flight	Oberstleutnant Froehlich	DO 17 Cormeilles-en-Vexin
I	Hauptmann Lindeiner	DO 17 Beauvais
II	Major Moericke	JU 88 Creil
III	Oberstleutnant Genth	DO 17 Cormeilles-en-Vexin

plus long-range reconnaissance units

II FLYING CORPS

General Bruno Lörzer

Long-range bombers

KG 2	*DO 17*	
Staff Flight	Oberst Johannes Fink	Arras
I	Major Gutzmann	Epinoy
II	Major Paul Weitkus	Arras
III	Major Werner Kreipe; Major Adolf Fuchs (from 13/8/40)	Cambrai
KG 3	*DO 17*	
Staff Flight	Oberst von Chamier-Glisczinski	Le Culot
I	Oberstleutnant Gabelmann	Le Culot
II	Hauptmann Pilger	Antwerp/Deurne
III	Hauptmann Rathmann	Saint-Trond
KG 53	*Heinkel 111*	
Staff Flight	Oberst Stahl	Lille-Nord
I	Major Kaufmann	Lille-Nord
II	Major Winkler	Lille-Nord
III	Major Edler von Braun	Lille-Nord

Dive-bombers
II (St) G 1	*JU 87*	
	Hauptmann Keil	Pas-de-Calais
IV (St) LG 1	Hauptmann von Brauchitsch	Tramecourt

Fighter-bombers
Erpro-bungsgr.	*Me 109 – Me 110*	
(Test Group) 210	Hauptmann Walter Rubens-dörffer; Oberleutnant Martin Lutz (from 15/8/40)	Calais-Marck Monchy-Bréton
II/LG 2	Hauptmann Weiss	St. Omer

IX FLYING DIVISION (*later* IX FLYING CORPS)
General Coeler

Long-range bombers
KG 4	*HE 111 – JU 88*		
Staff Flight	Oberstleutnant Rath	HE 111	Soesterberg
I	Hauptmann Meissner	HE 111	Soesterberg
II	Major Dr. Wolff	HE 111	Eindhoven
III	Hauptmann Bloedorn	JU 88	Amsterdam/Schipol

KG 100	*HE 111*	
	Hauptmann Friedrich Carol Aschenbrenner (transferred to IV Flying Corps, Air Fleet Three, from 17/8/40)	Vannes, Brittany

plus mine-laying, coastal reconnaissance, naval co-operation and long-range reconnaissance units

JAFU 2
Regional Fighter Commander: Oberst Theo Osterkamp Wissant

Fighters
JG 3	*ME 109*	
	Oberstleutnant Carl Viek;	Samer (from 14/8/40)
	Major Gunther Lützow; Hauptmann Hans von Hahn	Colombert (from 21/8/40)

II	Hauptmann Erich von Selle;	Samer (from 14/8/40)
III	Hauptmann Walter Kienitz (from 8/8/40); Hauptmann Wilhelm Balthasar	Desvres
JG 26 Staff Flight	*ME 109* Major Gotthard Handrick; Major Adolf Galland (from 21/8/40)	Audembert
I	Hauptmann Fischer; Hauptmann Rolf Pingel (from 21/8/40)	Audembert
II	Hauptmann Karl Ebbighausen; Hauptmann Erich Bode (from 17/8/40)	Marquise
III	Major Adolf Galland; Hauptmann Gerhard Schöpfel (from 21/8/40)	Caffiers
JG 51	*ME 109* Major Werner Mölders (from 21/8/40)	Wissant; Pihen
I	Hauptmann Hans-Heinrich Brustellin	Wissant; Pihen
II	Hauptmann Günther Matthes	Desvres; Marquise
III	Major Hannes Trautloft; Hauptmann Walter Oesau (from 25/8/40)	St. Omer
IV (1/77)	Hauptmann Johannes Janke (from 25/8/40)	St. Omer
JG 52 Staff Flight	*ME 109* Major von Merhart; Major Hans Trübenbach	Coquelles
I	Hauptmann Siegfried von Eschwege; Hauptmann Ewald;	Coquelles
II	Hauptmann von Kornatzki; Hauptmann Ensslen (to Jever from 18/8/40)	Peuplingne
III	Hauptmann Alex von Winterfeld (withdrawn from Coquelles, 1/8/40)	

I/LG 2	Major Hans Trübenbach; Hauptmann Herbert Ihlefeld	Calais-Marck
JG 54 Staff Flight	*ME 109* Major Martin Mettig; Major Hannes Trautloft (from 25/8/40)	Campagne; Guines
I	Hauptmann Hubertus von Bonin	Guines
II	Hauptmann Winterer; Haupt- mann Dietrich Hrabak (from 30/8/40)	Hermalinghen
III	Hauptmann Ultsch; Hauptmann Scholz (from 6/9/40)	Guines
ZG 26 Staff Flight	*ME 110* Oberstleutnant Joachim Huth	Lille
I	Hauptmann Macrocki	Yvrench-St. Omer
II	Hauptmann Ralph von Rettberg	Crécy-St. Omer
III	Hauptmann Schalk	Barley-Arques
ZG 76 Staff Flight	*ME 110* Major Walter Grabmann	Laval
II	Hauptmann Max Groth	Abbéville-Yvrench
III	Hauptmann Dickoré; Hauptmann Kaldrack	Laval

AIR FLEET THREE. Paris
Generalfeldmarschall Hugo Sperrle

VIII FLYING CORPS
General the Baron von Richthofen

Dive-bombers

St G 1 Staff Flight	*JU 87* Major Hagen (incl. DO 17)	Angers
I	Major Paul Hozzel	Angers
III	Hauptmann Mahlke	Angers
St G 2 Staff Flight	*JU 87* Major Oscar Dinort (incl. DO 17)	St. Malo
I	Hauptmann Hubertus Hitschold	St. Malo
II	Major Walter Enneccerus	Lannion

St G 77

Staff Flight	Major Graf Schonborn (incl. DO 17)	Caen
I	Hauptmann Freiherr von Dalwick	Caen
II	Hauptmann Plewig	Caen
III	Hauptmann Bode	Caen

Fighters

V(Z) LG 1	*ME 110*	
	Hauptmann Liensberger	Caen

plus DO 17 and JU 88 reconnaissance units

V FLYING CORPS

General Ritter von Greim

Long-range bombers

KG 51	*JU 88*	
Staff Flight	Oberstleutnant Fisser	Orly
I	Major Schulz-Hein	Melun
II	Major Winkler	Orly
III	Major Marienfeld	Etampes
KG 54	*JU 88*	
Staff Flight	Oberstleutnant Hoehne	Evreux
I	Hauptmann Heydebreck	Evreux
II	Oberstleutnant Koester	St. André-de-L'Eure
KG 55	*HE 111*	
Staff Flight	Oberst Alois Stöckl; Major Korte (from 14/8/40)	Villacoublay
I	Major Korte	Dreux
II	Major von Lachemaier	Chartres
III	Major Schlemell	Villacoublay

IV FLYING CORPS

General Pflugbeil

Long-range bombers

LG 1	*JU 88*	
Staff Flight	Oberst Alfred Bülowius	Orléans/Bricy
I	Hauptmann Wilhelm Kern	Orléans/Bricy
II	Major Debratz	Orléans/Bricy
III	Major Bormann	Chateaudun
IV	Hauptmann Hans-Joachim Helbig	Orléans/Bricy

KG 27	*HE 111*	
Staff Flight	Oberst Behrendt	Tours
I	Major Ulbrich	Tours
II	Major Schlichting	Dinard; Bourges
III	Major Freiherr Speck von Sternberg	Rennes

plus naval co-operation and long-range reconnaissance units

JAFU 3

Oberst Werner Junck – Cherbourg, then Wissant from 29/8/40

Fighters
[*Transferred to Air Fleet Two from 24/8/40*]

JG 2	*ME 109*	
Staff Flight	Oberstleutnant Harry von Bülow, Major Schellmann	Evreux; Beaumont-le-Roger; Mardyck
I	Major Hennig Strümpell; Major Helmut Wick	Beaumont-le-Roger; Mardyck
II	Major Schellmann; Hauptmann Griesert	Beaumont-le-Roger; Mardyck
III	Hauptmann Dr. Erich Mix; Hauptmann Otto Bertram	Le Havre; Oye Plage

JG 27	*ME 109*	
Staff Flight	Major Max Ibel	Cherbourg-West; Guines
I	Hauptmann Eduard Neumann	Plumetot; Guines
II	Hauptmann Werner Andres; Hauptmann Lippert (from 8/8/40)	Crépon; Fiennes
III	Hauptmann Joachim Schlichting; Hauptmann Max Dobislav	Carquebut; Guines

JG 53	*ME 109*	
Staff Flight	Major Hans-Jürgen Cramon-Taubadel; Major Freiherr von Maltzahn	Cherbourg; Étaples
I	Hauptmann Blumensaat;	Rennes; Le Touquet

234

II III	Hauptmann Hans Mayer Major Freiherr von Maltzahn Hauptmann Hans-Joachim Harder; Hauptmann Wolf-Dietrich Wilcke	Dinan, Guernsey Sempy; Brest; Le Touquet
ZG 2 Staff Flight	*ME 110* Oberstleutnant Freidrich Vollbracht	Toussée-le- Noble; St. Aubin
I II	Hauptmann Ott; Hauptmann Henlein Hauptmann Carl; Hauptmann Karlheinz Lessman	Amiens; Berck-sur-Mer Guyancourt; Berck-sur-Mer

Acknowledgments

Over pre-lunch drinks in the pillared hush of the RAF Club, London, an oberstleutnant of the new Luftwaffe dropped his bombshell. A Battle of Britain veteran, like his host Group Captain Peter Brothers, RAF, he looked back wryly to that summer of 1940 – when many Luftwaffe aces like himself vowed that their first drink on British soil would be taken here in this bar. Now, though contrary to all known club etiquette, he sought a favour: for auld lang syne, he'd like to buy a drink for every man in the house.

An unprecedented request – but then hadn't it been an unprecedented campaign? So promptly the group captain went into a huddle with the club's secretary, who in turn cajoled a quorum of committee members into reaching a drumhead decision. For a former adversary and a Battle of Britain survivor, anything was possible – and shortly the oberstleutnant, in the chair, was standing treat to an imposing cross-section of that year's Air Force List.

The story – and the sentiment – are typical. Air chief marshals, generals, pilots of every grade, flight mechanics, farmers, fishermen – 505 people in all, throughout Britain, the Commonwealth, Germany and the United States – showed similar generosity during the compilation of this book. All of them unselfishly gave up countless hours of time, to ensure that this human record of the Battle might be as complete as could be.

The chivalrous jousting of the skies seems to have engendered this universal mood: nothing is ever too much trouble. It is symbolized, in many ways, by three unique associations: the Battle of Britain Association, the *Gemeinschaft der Jagdflieger,* and the *Gemeinschaft der Kampfflieger,* and to the officials of all three go my undying thanks – most especially to Air Commodore Aeneas MacDonell and Group Captain Tom Gleave, in London; to Herr Hans Ring, Herr Werner Andres and Herr Hans-Joachim Jabs, representing the German fighter pilots and to Oberst Robert Kowalewski, who fixed up many bomber interviews. They made possible contacts which I and my research team would never otherwise have made, and to Hans Ring I am forever indebted for permission to draw freely from his work, *The German Fighter Forces in World War Two.* And many others, rifling through old diaries and address books, furnished valuable introductions: General-leutnant Adolf Galland, Group Captain Peter Brothers, Oberst Freiherr Fritz von Schroetter, Wing Commander Robert Wright, Wing Commander

236

John Cherry, Oberst Erik Hartmann, and Wing Commander Robert Stanford Tuck, in whose house some of the first crucial problems were thrashed out.

To the secretaries of many squadron associations, too, goes my deepest gratitude for their help in tracing literally scores of survivors. In particular, the help furnished by G. J. Rothwell (17 Squadron), Dennis Fox-Male (152), Ken Battrick (600), W. J. Cornish (601), G. Greenwood (605), Wing Commander Francis Blackadder (607) and Wing Commander Kenneth Stoddart (611) saved endless time and trouble. Lieutenant Earl Boebert, USAAF, and Bill Matthews, both of the American Aviation Historical Society, cut many corners in tracing the first United States fliers. On the WAAF side I had help beyond price from Wing Officer Margaret Green, Mrs Violet Hime and Mrs Daphne Carne (then Griffiths) who initiated me into the mysteries of those 1940 radar stations.

Many survivors went far beyond the scope of the book to help get a better feeling of what it was all like. You sense how infinitely precious life was then when Group Captain Zdzislaw Krasnodebski, now re-united with Wanda in a quiet Toronto apartment, recalls the electric excitement of young Ludwig Paszkiewicz's first combat, and the comradeship of those long-ago nights at The Orchard restaurant . . . when Wing Commander Geoffrey Page, now a top aircraft company executive, shows the livid scars that the fires of battle imprinted on his hands . . . when Mrs McWatt Green (then Elspeth Henderson) beside her pin-neat rock-garden in Craiglockhart, Edinburgh, recalls the simple problem of getting a good night's rest at Biggin Hill. For a moment her eyes glow as she re-lives the danger, the sense of purpose, the fun of being a pretty young WAAF in England's front-line.

Superficially, most of these people can look back to that far-off summer with detachment – it's almost as if somebody else's snapshot had been pasted in their album. Yet all of them, having come close to death, seem to have achieved a greater maturity, a deeper understanding of their fellow men, than falls to many – most often in their readiness to laugh. Leaning on his five-barred gate, Robert Bailey chuckles and confesses ruefully: 'I'd give anything to see a dog-fight up there again – provided nobody got hurt.' From the streamlined ease of an executive suite in Bonn, Germany, Adolf Galland stresses that life with JG 26 wasn't all combat – sometimes there were parties where you could always sober the fuddled one with a roar of 'Achtung, Spitfire!' Oberstleutnant Herbert Kaminski, of the new Luftwaffe, recalls those days, too. 'There was more discipline then,' muses 'The Last of the Prussians', 'you didn't have to ask a general's permission to put a private on kitchen fatigue.'

To these and many other survivors I am truly grateful, for without their help this book could not have been written. To record even part of the story was a task equalling nine years' research: a 30,000 miles journey by a team thirteen-strong throughout 230 cities, towns and villages in Great Britain, Germany, Canada and the United States. The testimony of 434 eye-witnesses was the raw material from which this book was fashioned.

I must stress that none of the people here acknowledged necessarily agree with all – or in some cases with any – of my conclusions. For the views expressed or implicit in the course of the narrative, for any errors that may have crept in, I alone am responsible.

Despite personal testimony, this book is founded essentially on the hard core of records: on war diaries, flying log-books, police blotters, private diaries and contemporary letters. In this respect I am lucky enough to have been the first Battle of Britain writer to have had access to the invaluable studies of the United States Strategic Bombing Survey, and to the private papers of Lord Cherwell (then Professor Frederick Lindemann), Winston Churchill's scientific adviser. My deepest thanks thus go to the many archivists who made records available or suggested contacts: to Victor Gondos, Jr., Elmer O. Parker and John E. Taylor, of the National Archives and Records Services, Washington; to Sir Donald MacDougall and Miss Christine Kennedy of Nuffield College, Oxford; to Mr L. A. Jackets, Chief of the Air Ministry Historical Branch, London, and to Mr W. J. Taunton, Mr E. H. Turner, Mr S. H. Bostock, and Mrs G. A. Fowles, of that department; to Chris Coles, of the Ministry of Defence's Air Information Department; above all, to Generalleutnant Panitzki, Brigadegeneral Rudolph Jennett, Oberstleutnant Technau and Dr Lupke, for their generous long-term loan of many records from the Führungsakademie, Hamburg.

How the Battle reacted on the people of southern England has remained, for the most part, a closed book; a special word of thanks, therefore, to Dennis Knight and Peter Foote who generously made available the private archive they had amassed over seven years. Their painstaking transcription of police registers, Civil Defence occurrence books, borough and rural district council records amounted to a veritable repository of unplumbed local lore. Time and again Messrs Knight and Foote emerged as the men who could pinpoint to the second when a plane crashed, where, what happened thereafter.

Others, too, worked like beavers to fill in blank passages in the narrative. Wing Commander R. V. Manning, Director of Air Force History, RCAF, Ottawa, proved the final authority on all things Canadian; Mr W. W. Wybraniec of the Polish Air Force Association in Great Britain, and most especially Major L. W. Bienkowski, lent essential colour to the Polish narrative; Mr I. Quimby Tobin and Mrs Phyllis Harrington went to untold trouble in furnishing the private diary of the late Pilot Officer Eugene Tobin as well as answering a host of supplementary questions. Generous help came, also, from Mr James Lucas, Mr Vernon Rigby and Mr John Sutters, of the Imperial War Museum; from Leonard England and Mary Taylor, of

Mass Observation Ltd, from Herr Ziggel and Dr Schmalz, untiring in their help at the Bundesarchiv, Koblenz; from Mr L. G. Hart and E. J. Grove of Post Office Headquarters, London, and Malcolm Miles and C. A. Allen of the Royal Air Force Association.

At the British Broadcasting Corporation, G. A. Hollingworth and P. G. Curtis miraculously unearthed the text of the original BBC news bulletin broadcast at 9 am on September 15, 1940; Jackie Robertson, of Scottish Television, most kindly lent a set of shooting scripts covering the war story of 602 Squadron; Bill Herbert and Norman McBain, respectively of the Canadian Broadcasting Corporation's Vancouver and Montreal offices, dug out useful tapes. Vexed questions on Battle of Britain weather were the province of the Meteorological Office's John Grindley at Bracknell. At the outset Mrs Ilse R. Wolff, of the Wiener Library, London, provided useful leads.

On the RAF side I was lucky enough to have valuable consultations at Fighter Command level with Air Chief Marshal Lord Dowding and his former deputy Air Chief Marshal Sir Douglas Evill. At Bomber Command, Air Chief Marshal Sir John Grandy proved a gracious host; Air Chief Marshal Sir Keith Park sent a cogent narrative all the way from New Zealand; Air Vice-Marshal Sir Cecil Bouchier spent hours recalling the triumphs and tribulations of life at Hornchurch. Air Vice-Marshal George Chamberlain and Air Vice-Marshal Laurence Fuller-Good provided useful written accounts. Others who afforded sterling help were Air Vice-Marshal Harry Hogan, Air Vice-Marshal Frank Hopps, Air Vice-Marshal Stanley Vincent, Air Vice-Marshal John Worrall; Air Commodore Harold Bird-Wilson, Air Commodore James Coward, Air Commodore Robert Deacon-Elliott, Air Commodore Alan Deere and Air Commodore Desmond Hughes. And Air Commodore John Thompson not only took the time to talk about 111 Squadron, he arranged an intriguing, on-the-spot tour of the now disused 11 Group Ops Room, from where Winston Churchill watched the last great battle.

In Germany I had valuable advice and encouragement from first to last – notably from General Alfred Bülowius, General Paul Deichmann, an ever-present help, General Johannes Fink, General Martin Harlinghausen, General Max Ibel, General Werner Kreipe, General Hans Seidemann, and General Hannes Trautloft, an indefatigable diarist even in the heat of combat. The exemplary patience of Brigadegeneral Walter Enneccerus, Brigadegeneral Paul Hozzel, Brigadegeneral Karl Kessel and Brigadegeneral Johannes Steinhoff deserves special mention, too.

Many others spent far more time and trouble than I had a right to expect – in suggesting untapped sources, in authenticating dates, in helping locate survivors. On the lifeboats, K. F. Speakman and H. B. Fleet gave indispensable guidance in Ramsgate and Margate. H. R. Pratt Boorman, *The Kent*

Messenger's director, and Tony Arnold, of the Dover bureau, helped enormously by making public my appeal for survivors. Peter Williams, of Southern Television, and Arthur Streatfield were equally towers of strength . . . Peter Corbell and Christopher Elliott freely lent long-out-of-print books and papers . . . Derek Wood selflessly devoted a hard-won Saturday to sorting through nuggets omitted from his mammoth study, *The Narrow Margin* . . . David Irving not only gave sterling leads but lent generously from his unique private collection of German and American microfilms.

Finally, the uncomplaining hours put in by my own research team deserve a chapter all their own. Joan St. George Saunders and her researchers provided enough solid fact to nourish a hungry computer; Marguerita Adey's contribution, though brief, was telling; Lila Duckworth's pioneer translations saw the German side of things proceeding smoothly from the start. Marise Dutton's coverage of the Vancouver scene was as exceptional as Jean Farrer's work across 6,000 miles of Great Britain – of inestimable value in assembling the jigsaw.

Pamela Hoskins proved all over again that the fact – or the eye-witness – which can elude her is rare indeed. Dennis Knight and Peter Foote worked back and forth like beavers across southern England . . . Elisabeth Leslie filed invaluable transcripts with the habitual serenity that took her undaunted through a blizzard in the Pass of Glencoe. Robin McKown weighed in from New York. In Los Angeles and throughout 5,000 miles of Germany, Nadia Radowitz made an untold contribution, standing in as interpreter at upwards of seventy interviews before devoting six months to translating bales of German documents. The finished work would have been poorer without her.

Above all, my deepest debt is to my wife, who handled almost all of the Canadian and United States research, beside card-indexing, conducting many other interviews, typing the final draft and offering the moral support that saw it through. Hers was the hardest task of all – for she had to live through the writing.

Bibliography

PUBLISHED SOURCES

Acutt, D. G. F. *Brigade in Action: the History of the St. John Ambulance Brigade in Weymouth, 1939–45.* Weymouth: Sherren & Son, 1945.

Adam, Ronald. *Readiness at Dawn.* London: Victor Gollancz, 1941.

Allingham, Margery. *The Oaken Heart.* London: Hutchinson, 1941.

Among the Few; Canadian Airmen in the Battle of Britain. Ottawa: R.C.A.F. Historical Section, 1948.

Ansel, Walter. *Hitler Confronts England.* Durham, N.C.: Duke University Press, 1960.

Anthony, C. 'From Spads to Spitfires', *Air Mail,* n.s., Vol. 5, No. 2, 1953.

Anthony, Gordon, and Macadam, John. *Air Aces.* London: Home and Van Thal, 1944.

Armitage, Squadron Leader Dennis. 'The Battle of Britain,' *The Elevator,* Journal of the Lancashire Aero Club, Spring–Autumn, 1958.

Austin, A. B. *Fighter Command.* London: Victor Gollancz, 1941.

Baley, Stephen. *Two Septembers.* London: George Allen & Unwin, 1941.

Barker, Felix. 'Twenty-four Hours That Saved Britain,' *London Evening News,* September 12–17, 1960.

Barrymaine, Norman. *The Story of Peter Townsend.* London: Peter Davies, 1958.

Bartz, Karl. *Swastika in the Air.* London: William Kimber, 1956.

'The Battle of Britain,' *The Wire,* Journal of the Royal Signal Corps, Vol. XXI, No. 247.

Baumbach, Werner, 'Why We Lost,' *The Royal Air Force Review,* Vol. 7, No. 12, 1952–53.

—. *Broken Swastika.* London: Robert Hale, 1960.

Beckles, Gordon. *Birth of a Spitfire.* London: William Collins, 1941.

Bekker, Cajus, *Radar-Duell im Dunkel.* Oldenburg-Hamburg: Gerhard Stalling Verlag, 1958.

—. *Angriffshöhe 4000.* Oldenburg-Hamburg: Gerhard Stalling Verlag, 1964.

Bell, Reginald, *The Bull's Eye.* London: Cassell, 1943.

Bickers, Richard T. *Ginger Lacey, Fighter Pilot.* London: Robert Hale, 1962.

Birkenhead, Lord. *The Prof in Two Worlds.* London: William Collins, 1961.

Bishop, Edward. *The Battle of Britain.* London: George Allen & Unwin, 1960.

Blackstone, Geoffrey. *History of the British Fire Service.* London: Routledge, 1957.

Boebert, Earl. 'The Eagle Squadrons', *American Aviation Historical Society Journal,* Spring, 1964.

Bolitho, Hector. *Combat Report,* London: Batsford, 1943.

—. *A Penguin in the Eyrie.* London: Hutchinson, 1955.

Bonnell, J. S. *Britons Under Fire.* New York: Harper, 1941.

Boorman, H. R. Pratt. *Hell's Corner, 1940.* Maidstone: Kent Messenger Office, 1942.

Bowman, Gerald. *Jump for It.* London: Evans Bros., 1955.

Braham, Wing Commander J. R. D. *'Scramble!'* London: Frederick Muller, 1961.

Braybrooke, Keith, *Wingspan: a History of R.A.F. Debden.* Saffron Walden: Hart, 1956.

Brickhill, Paul. *Reach for the Sky.* London: William Collins, 1954.

Brittain, Vera. *England's Hour.* London: Macmillan, 1941.

Bryant, Sir Arthur (ed.). *The Alanbrooke Diaries.* London: William Collins, 1957.

Buchan, William. *The R.A.F. at War.* London: John Murray, 1941.

Bullmore, Francis. *The Dark Haven.* London: Jonathan Cape, 1956.

Burt, Kendal, and Leasor, James. *The One That Got Away.* London: Michael Joseph & William Collins, 1956.

Butler, Ewan, and Young, Gordon. *Marshal Without Glory.* London: Hodder & Stoughton, 1951.

Capka, Jo. *Red Sky at Night.* London: Anthony Blond, 1958.

Carne, Daphne. *The Eyes of the Few.* London: P. R. Macmillan, 1960.

Carter, E. *Grim Glory.* London: Humphries, 1941.

Charlton, L. E. O. *Britain at War: The Royal Air Force, September, 1939– September, 1945.* London: Hutchinson (5 vols) 1941–1947.

Childers, James Saxon. *War Eagles.* New York: D. Appleton-Century Company, Inc., 1943.

Churchill, Sir Winston. *The Second World War, Vol. II: Their Finest Hour.* London: Cassell, 1949.

Clifton, P. 'Top-Score Fighter,' *The R.A.F. Flying Review,* Vol. 8, No. 12, 1953.

Clout, Charles. 'Swastika Over Sussex,' *Air Britain Digest,* March, 1965.

Collier, Basil, *The Defence of the United Kingdom.* London: H.M. Stationery Office, 1957.

—. *The Leader of the Few.* London: Jarrolds, 1957.

—. *The Battle of Britain.* London: Batsford, 1962.

Cook, Raymond. *Shellfire Corner Carries On.* London: Headley Bros., 1942.

Corbell, Peter M. 'R.A.F. Station, Hornchurch,' *Air Britain Digest,* Vol. III, Nos. 9 and 10.

Crook, D. M. *Spitfire Pilot.*London: Faber & Faber, 1942.

Darwin, Bernard. *War on the Line.* London: Southern Railway, 1946.

De Bunsen, Mary. *Mount Up with Wings.* London: Hutchinson, 1960.

Deere, Alan. *Nine Lives.* London: Hodder & Stoughton, 1959.

Deighton, Len. *Fighter.* London: Cape, 1977.

Dempster, Derek, and Wood, Derek. *The Narrow Margin.* London: Hutchinson, 1961.

'Demu,' 'Ops Rooms. A Footnote to the History of the R.A.F. in the Battle of Britain,' *The Fighting Forces,* October, 1946.

Destiny Can Wait: the Polish Air Force in the Second World War. London: William Heinemann, 1949.

Dickson, Lovat. *Richard Hillary.* London: Macmillan, 1950.

Dietrich, Otto. *The Hitler I Knew.* London: Methuen, 1957.

Dixon, J. L. *In All Things First: a History of No. 1 Squadron.* Orpington: The Orpington Press, 1954.

—. *A Brief History of No. 19 Squadron.* Driffield: Registration Record, 1954.

Donahue, A. G. *Tally-Ho! – Yankee in a Spitfire.* London: Macmillan, 1943.

Dowding, Air Chief Marshal the Lord. *The Battle of Britain,* a supplement to the *London Gazette,* September 10, 1946.

E. B. B. (ed.). *Winged Words: our airmen speak for themselves.* London: William Heinemann, 1941.

Eeles, Lt.-Col. H. S. *History of the 17th Light Ack-Ack Regt., R.A.* Tunbridge Wells: Courier Co. Ltd., 1946.

Eichelbaum, Dr. (ed.). *Das Jahrbuch von Der Luftwaffe, 1940,* Berlin: Verlaghaus Bong, 1941.

Ellan, Squadron Leader B. J. *Spitfire.* London: John Murray, 1942.

Embry, Sir Basil. *Mission Completed.* London: Methuen, 1957.

Fahrten and Flüge gegen England. Berlin: Zeitesgeschichte-Verlag, 1941.

Faircloth, N. W. *New Zealanders in the Battle of Britain.* Wellington, N. Z.: War History Branch, Dept. of Internal Affairs, 1950.

Farrer, David. *The Sky's the Limit: the Story of Beaverbrook at MA.P.* London: Hutchinson, 1943.

Farson, Negley. *Bomber's Moon.* London: Victor Gollancz, 1941.

Fiedler, Arkady, *Squadron 303: the Story of the Polish Fighter Squadron with the R.A.F.* London: Peter Davies, 1942.

Field, Peter J. *Canada's Wings.* London: John Lane, The Bodley Head, 1942.

'The Fifteenth of August,' by a Pilot, *R.A.F. Quarterly,* Vol. 13, No. 4.

Finnie, G. K. 'Lessons of the Battle of Britain,' *Roundel,* Vol. II, No. 6.

'The First Great Air Battle,' *Air Mail,* Vol. 6, No. 5.

Fleming, Peter. *Invasion 1940.* London: Rupert Hart-Davis, 1957.

Forbes, Wing Commander Athol, and Allen, Squadron Leader Hubert. *Ten Fighter Boys.* London: William Collins, 1942.

Forell, Fritz von. *Mölders und Seine Männer.* Graz: Steirische Verlags-anstalt, 1941.

—. *Mölders.* Saltzburg: Sirius-Verlag, 1951.

Forrester, Larry. *Fly for Your Life.* London: Frederick Muller, 1956.

Foster, Reginald. *Dover Front.* London: Secker & Warburg, 1941.

Friedin, Seymour (ed.). *The Fatal Decisions.* New York: William Sloane, 1956.

Front-Line Folkestone. Folkestone: Folkestone, Hythe & District Herald, 1945.

Galland, Adolf. *The First and the Last.* London: Methuen, 1953.

—. 'La Bataille d'Angleterre,' *Forces Aériennes Françaises,* Nos. 61–65, August–September, 1955.

Gallico, Paul. *The Hurricane Story.* London: Michael Joseph, 1959.

Garnett, David. *War in the Air.* London: Chatto & Windus, 1941.

Gibbs, Air Vice-Marshal Gerald. *A Survivor's Story.* London: Hutchinson, 1956.

—. 'The Battle of Britain,' *Journal of the United Services Institution of India,* Vol. LXXXIII, No. 352–53.

Gleave, Group Captain Thomas. *I Had a Row with a German.* London: Macmillan, 1941.

Gleed, Ian. *Arise to Conquer.* London: Victor Gollancz, 1942.

Graves, Charles. *The Home Guard of Britain.* London: Hutchinson, 1943.

—. *The Thin Blue Line.* London: Hutchinson, 1941.

Green, Dennis W. *Famous Fighters of the Second World War.* London: MacDonald, 1962.

Gribble, Leonard. *Heroes of the Fighting R.A.F.* London: George G. Harrap, 1941.

Griffith, Hubert. *R.A.F. Occasions.* London: The Cresset Press, 1941.

Gritzbach, Erich. *Hermann Göring: The Man and His Work.* London: Hurst and Blackett, 1939.

Hagedorn, Hermann. *Sunwards I've Climbed.* New York: Macmillan, 1942.

Hanna, A. M. 'Fighter Command Communications,' *The Post Office Electrical Engineers Journal,* Vol. 38, Part 4.

Harbottle, H. R. 'The Network of Telephone Circuits and the Defence Telecommunications Control,' *The Post Office Electrical Engineers Journal,* Vol. 38, Part 4.

Hayson, G. D. L. 'The Battle of Britain,' *South African Air Force Journal,* Vol. II, No. 4.

—. 'How the Few Saved the Many,' *Wings,* Vol. 9, No. 10, September, 1950.

Herlin, Hans. *Udet: a Man's Life.* London: MacDonald, 1960.

Hill, Air Marshal Sir Roderic. 'The Air Defence of Great Britain,' *Journal of the Royal United Services Institution,* May, 1946.

—.'The Fighters' Greatest Day,' *Journal of the Royal Air Forces,* Vol. 3, No. 5.

Hillary, Richard. *The Last Enemy.* London: Macmillan, 1942.

'Hitler's Battle of Britain Plan', *The R.A.F. Flying Review,* Vol. 15, No. 2.

Hocklin, John. 'The Air Defence of the Port of London,' *Port of London Association Monthly,* May, 1945.

Hoffmann, Heinrich. *Hitler Was My Friend.* London: Burke Publishing Co., 1955.

Hollis, Gen. Sir Leslie, and Leasor, James. *War at the Top.* London: Michael Joseph, 1959.

Houart, Capitaine. 'Les Aviateurs Belges à la Bataille d'Angleterre,' *Vici,* October 17, 1955.

Illingworth, Frank. *Britain Under Shellfire.* London: Hutchinson, 1942.

Ingham, Harold S. (ed.). *Fire and Water: an Anthology.* London: Lindsay Drummond, 1942.

Ismay, Lord. *Memoirs of General the Lord Ismay.* London: Heinemann, 1960.

Johnson, Air Vice-Marshal J. E. *Full Circle.* London: Chatto & Windus, 1964.

Joubert, Air Chief Marshal Sir Philip. 'How the Way Was Paved for the Battle of Britain,' *The R.A.F. Flying Review,* Vol. 5, No. 2, 1949.

—. *The Forgotten Ones.* London: Hutchinson, 1961.

Keeping Them Flying. London: Air Force Publications, 1943.

Kemp, L.-Cdr. P. K. *Victory at Sea.* London: Frederick Muller, 1957.

Kempe, A. B. C. *'Midst Bands and Bombs.* Maidstone: Kent Messenger Office, 1946.

Kennedy, A. Scott, *'Gin Ye Daur': 603 (City of Edinburgh) Fighter Squadron.* Edinburgh: Pillans and Wilson, 1943.

Kent, Group Captain John. 'The Battle of Britain: extracts from a personal diary,' *The Polish Airmen's Weekly Review,* June, 1957.

Kesselring, Generalfeldmarschall Albert. *Memoirs.* London: William Kimber, 1953.

Knight, G. *Five Hundred Hours in the Blitz.* (Typescript MS, British Museum Reading Room, London.)

Knoke, Heinz. *I Flew for the Führer.* London: Evan Bros., 1953.

Kohl, Hermann, *Wir fliegen gegen England.* Reutlingen: Ansellin und Laiblin Verlag, 1941.

Lanchbery, Edward. *Against the Sun.* London: Cassell, 1955.

Lecerf, J. L. 'La Bataille Aérienne d'Angleterre,' *Forces Aériennes Françaises,* 10 Année, No. 107.

Lee, Asher. *The German Air Force.* London: Duckworth, 1946.

—. 'When Adler Angriff Went Off Half-Cock,' *The R.A.F. Flying Review,* Vol. 8, No. 12.

Le Page, M. 'Memories of the Luftwaffe in the Channel Islands,' *Air Britain Digest,* Vol. II, No. 1.

Lewey, F. R. *Cockney Campaign,* London: Stanley Paul, 1947.

Lewis, J. H. 'London Diary, 1940,' *Air Britain Digest,* Vol. V, No. 5, 1953.

Lloyd, F. H. M. *Hurricane: the Story of a Great Fighter.* London: Harborough Publishing Co., 1945.

Lowe, Frank, 'Twenty Years Ago They Broke The Luftwaffe,' *The Montreal Star Weekend Magazine,* September 10, 1960.

Lyall, Gavin, and Knight, Dennis. 'The Air War', *The London Sunday Times Magazine,* May 30–June 6, 1965.

M-M S. *Together We Fly.* London: Geoffrey Bles, 1941.

McCrary, John R. (Tex), and Scheman, David E. *First of the Many.* New York: Simon & Schuster, 1944.

McKee, Alexander, *Strike from the Sky.* London: Souvenir Press, 1960.

Mackersey, Ian, 'Tally Ho! cried John Peel,' *The R.A.F. Flying Review,* Vol. V, No. 2.

—. *Into the Silk.* London: Robert Hale, 1956.

Macmillan, Wing Co-Commander Norman. *The Royal Air Force in the World War,* Vol. I–II. London: George Harrap, 1942–44.

Manstein, Field Marshal Erich von. *Lost Victories.* London: Methuen, 1958.

Marchant, Hilde. *Woman and Children Last: a Woman Reporter's Account of the Battle of Britain.* London: Victor Gollancz, 1941.

Marchant, P. R., and Heron, K. M. 'Post Office Equipment for Radar,' *The Post Office Electrical Engineers Journal,* Vol. 38, Part 4.

Marrs, Pilot Officer Eric. '152 Squadron: A Personal Diary of the Battle of Britain,' *The Aeroplane,* October 12, 1945.

Marsh, L. G. *Polish Wings Over Britain.* London: Max Love Publishing Co., 1943.

Masters, David, *'So Few'* (8th ed.). London: Eyre and Spottiswoode, 1946.

Mathias, Joachim. *Deutsche Flieger über England.* Berlin: Steiniger Verlag, 1940.

Mee, Arthur. *1940.* London: Hodder & Stoughton, 1941.

Middleton, Drew. *The Sky Suspended.* London: Secker & Warburg, 1960.

Milne, Duncan Grinnell. *Silent Victory.* London: The Bodley Head, 1958.

Mitchell, Alan W. *New Zealanders in the Air War.* London: George Harrap, 1945.

Moggridge, 'Jackie.' *Woman Pilot.* London: Michael Joseph, 1957.

Möller-Witten, Hanns. *Mit den Eichenlaub zum Ritterkreutz.* Rastatt: Erich Pabel Verlag, 1962.

Murrow, Edward R. *This Is London.* London: Cassell, 1941.

Nancarrow, F. E. 'The Defence Teleprinter Network,' *The Post Office Electrical Engineers Journal,* Vol. 38, Part 4.

Nancarrow, Fred G. *Glasgow Fighter Squadron.* London: William Collins, 1942.

Narracott, A. H. (ed.). *In Praise of the Few: an Anthology.* London: Frederick Muller, 1947.

—. *How the R.A.F. Works.* London: Frederick Muller, 1941.

Newton, John H. *The Story of No. 11 Group, R.O.C.* Lincoln: Lincolnshire Chronicle Office, 1946.

'Night Shift.' 'The Work of A.A. Searchlights in the Last War,' *Journal of the Royal Artillery,* Vol. LXXV, No. 11.

Nixon, B. *Bombers Overhead.* London: Lindsay Drummond, 1943.

Nockolds, Harold. *The Magic of a Name.* London: G. T. Foulis, 1950.

Norris, G. McKellar. 'Scottish Ace,' *The R.A.F. Flying Review,* Vol. XV, No. 8.

O'Brien. T. H. *Civil Defence.* London: H. M. Stationery Office and Longmans Green, 1955.

Offenberg, Jean. *Lonely Warrior.* New York: Taplinger, 1958.

Osterkamp, Theo. *Durch Höhen und Tiefen jagt ein Herz.* Heidelberg: Vowinckel Verlag, 1952.

Parham, H. J., and Belfield, E. M. G. *Unarmed Into Battle.* Winchester: Warrens and Sons, 1956.

Park, Air Chief Marshal Sir Keith. 'Background to the Blitz,' *The Hawker-Siddeley Review,* December, 1951.

Pawle, Gerald. *The War and Colonel Warden.* London: George Harrap, 1963.

Pile, General Sir Frederick. *Ack-Ack.* London: George Harrap, 1949.

Pollard, Captain A. O. *Epic Deeds of the R.A.F.* London: Hutchinson, 1940.

Postan, Professor M. M. *British War Production.* London: H.M. Stationery Office and Longmans Green, 1952.

Powell, Henry P. *Men With Wings.* London: Allan Wingate, 1957.

Priller, Josef. *Geschichte eines Jagdgeschwaders* (Das JG 26, 1937—45). Heidelberg: Vowinckel Verlag, 1962.

Quednau, Horst. 'I Bombed Britain', *The R.A.F. Flying Review,* Vol. VI, No. 12.

R. J. S. *Czechoslovak Wings.* London: Czechoslovak Publications, 1944.

Raeder, Grand-Admiral Erich. *Struggle for the Sea.* London: William Kimber, 1959.

Ramsay, L. F. *West Wittering in the Front Line.* Eastbourne: Sussex County Magazine, 1946.

Randle-Ford, J. M. *A Dorset Village's War Effort.* Bournemouth: Roman Press, 1945.

Rawnsley, C. F., and Wright, Robert. *Night Fighter.* London: William Collins, 1957.

Reid, J. P. M. *Some of the Few.* London: MacDonald, 1960.

—. *The Battle of Britain.* London: H.M. Stationery Office, 1960.

Reynolds, Quentin. *The Wounded Don't Cry.* London: Cassell, 1941.

Richards, Denis. *Royal Air Force, 1939–45. Vol. I, The Fight at Odds,* London: H.M. Stationery Office, 1953.

Rieckhoff, Lt.-Gen. H. J. *Trumpf oder Bluff.* Geneva: Interavia SA., 1945.

Ries, Karl, Jr. *Markierungen und Tarnanstriche der Luftwaffe im 2 Weltkrieg.* Finthen bei Mainz: Verlag Dieter Hoffmann, 1963.

Robbins, Gordon. *Fleet Street Blitzkrieg Diary.* London: Ernest Benn, 1944.

Roberts, L. *Canada's War in the Air.* Montreal: A. M. Beatty Publications, 1943.

Robertson, Ben. *I Saw England.* London: Jarrold, 1941.

Robertson, Bruce. *Spitfire. The Story of a Famous Fighter.* Letchworth: Harleyford Publications, 1960.

Roof Over Britain. London: H.M. Stationery Office, 1943.

Roper, H. R. Trevor. *Hitler's Table Talk.* London: Weidenfeld and Nicolson, 1953.

The Royal Canadian Air Force Overseas. Vol. I. Toronto: O.U.P., 1944.

Rüdel, Hans. *Stuka Pilot.* London: Transworld Publications. 1957.

Sands, R. P. D. *Treble One: the Story of No. 111 Squadron.* North Weald: privately printed, 1957.

Sansom, William. *Westminster at War.* London: Faber & Faber, 1947.

Sargent, E. *The Royal Air Force.* London: Sampson, Low and Marston, 1944.

Saundby, Air Marshal Sir Robert. 'Preparations for the Battle of Britain,' *The Listening Post,* Vol. XXXI, No. 11, March, 1958.

Saunders, Hilary St. George. *The Battle of Britain.* London: H.M. Stationery Office, 1941.

Sayers, W. Berwick (ed.). *Croydon Corporation in the Second World War.* Croydon: Roffey and Clark, for Croydon Corporation, 1949.

Schmidt, Dr. Paul. *Hitler's Interpreter.* London: William Heinemann, 1951.

Sheean, Vincent. *Between the Thunder and the Sun.* London: Macmillan, 1943.

Shirer, William. *Berlin Diary.* London: Hamish Hamilton, 1941.

60 Group Radar Bulletin. Welwyn Garden City: Broadwater Press, 1945.

Slessor, Marshal of the R.A.F. Sir John. *The Central Blue.* London: Cassell, 1956.

Smitten City: the Story of Portsmouth Under Blitz. Portsmouth: Evening News, n.d.

Smythe, D. C. 'On the Direct Bomber Route,' *Our Empire To-Day,* Vol. XXV, No. i-iv.

Spaight, J. M. *The Battle of Britain.* London: Geoffrey Bles, 1941.

—. *The Sky Is the Limit.* London: Hodder & Stoughton, 1940.

Sprigg, T. S. 'The Battle of Britain,' *United Services Review,* July 8, 1946.

—. *The War Story of Fighter Command.* London: William Collins, 1941.

Stewart, Oliver. 'An Air Battle Over the English Channel,' *London Calling,* No. 50.

Student, Gen. Kurt. 'Hitler's Secrets,' *Kommando,* Vol. 3, No. 20.

Sutton, Barry. *The Way of a Pilot.* London: Macmillan, 1942.

Sutton, H. T. *Raider's Approach.* Aldershot: Gale and Polden, 1956.

Taylor, J. W. R., and Allward, M. F. *Spitfire.* London: Harborough Publishing Co., 1946.

Terry, John. 'Eleven for Danger,' *Air Mail,* Vol. 2. No. 24. 1950.

—. 'Their Greatest Day,' *Air Mail,* Vol. 3, No. 35, 1951.

Thetford, O. G. 'No. 600 (City of London) Squadron,' *Air Reserve Gazette,* Vol. X, No. 1, 1948.

—. 'No. 603 (City of Edinburgh) Squadron,' *Air Reserve Gazette,* Vol. X, No. 4, 1948.

—. 'Twenty-Five Part-Time Years,' *The R.A.F. Flying Review,* Vol. VI, No. 4, 1950.

Thomas, R. L. *The Kent Police Centenary: recollections of a hundred years.* Maidstone: privately printed, 1957.

Thompson, Wing Commander H. L. *New Zealanders with the Royal Air Force, Vol. I.* London: Oxford University Press, for the War History Branch, Department of Internal Affairs, New Zealand, 1953.

Thompson, R. J. *Battle Over Essex.* Walthamstow: Guardian Press, 1944.

Tobin, Eugene, with Low, Robert. 'Yankee Eagle Over London,' *Liberty Magazine,* March–April, 1941.

Uderstadt, E. R. *Das Jahr VII.* Berlin: Schmidt Verlag, 1941.

Urbanek, Walther. *Fliegerhorst Ostmark.* Innsbruck: Gauverlag und Druckerei, 1941.

'The Victory of Britain,' *Faugh-A-Ballagh,* Journal of the Royal Irish Fusiliers, Vol. XXXIV, No. 152.

Walker, Oliver. *Sailor Malan.* London: Cassell, 1953.

Walker, Ronald. *Flight to Victory.* London: Penguin Books, 1941.

Wallace, Graham. *R.A.F. Biggin Hill.* London: Putnam, 1957.

Walwyn, E. H. Sheppeard. *Purleigh in Wartime.* Chelmsford: The Tindal Press, 1946.

War in East Sussex. Lewes: Sussex Express & County Herald, 1945.

Weber, Dr. Theo. *Die Luftschlacht um England.* Fraunfeld: Huber, 1956.

Wendel, Else. *Hausfrau at War.* London: Odhams, 1957.

Weymouth, Anthony. *Plague Year.* London: George Harrap, 1942.

Wheatley, Ronald. *Operation Sea Lion.* London: O.U.P., 1958.

Whitty, H. Ramsden (ed.). *An Observer's Tale.* London: Roland, 1950.

Williams, Peter. 'The Fateful Fifteenth,' *The R.A.F. Flying Review,* Vol. II, No. 11.

Williams, R. 'Twelve Years Ago,' *The R.A.F. Flying Review,* Vol. VII, No. 12, 1952– 53.

Willis, J. *It Stopped At London.* London: Hurst & Blackett, 1944.

Wilmot, Chester. *The Struggle for Europe.* London: William Collins, 1954.

—. 'Why Hitler Failed to Invade,' *Stand-To,* Vol I, No. 1, January, 1950.

Wilson, A. J. *Sky Sweepers.* London: Jarrold, 1942.

Winslow, T. E. *Forewarned is Forearmed.* Edinburgh: William Hodge, 1947.

Wooldridge, John de L. *Low Attack.* London: Sampson Low and Marston, 1944.

Woon, Basil. *Hell Came to London.* London: Peter Davies, 1941.

Wright, Robert. *Dowding and the Battle of Britain.* London: Macdonald, 1969.

Wykeham, Air Vice-Marshal Peter. *Fighter Command.* London: Putnam, 1960.

Yoxall, John. 'No. 65 (East India) Squadron,' *Flight,* Vol. 65, 1954.

—. *The Queen's Squadron.* London: Iliffe, 1949.

MANUSCRIPT SOURCES

Except in the case of public archives, the sources listed here are contemporary, privately prepared accounts, the property of the owners, to whom I am deeply indebted for making them available.

Air Ministry, Directorate of Public Relations. *German Air Force Operations Against Britain: Tactics and Lessons Learned* (Imperial War Museum, London, S.E. 1).

Bailey, Robert. *An Account of Ladwood Farm in the Battle of Britain.*

Beecroft, Pamela. *A Biggin Hill Diary* (Courtesy Mrs. D. H. Grice).

Crossley, Wing Commander Michael. *Diary of 32 Squadron.*

Deacon-Elliott, Air Commodore. *No. 72 Squadron,* a private diary.

Deichmann, General Paul. *Actions of No. 11 Flying Corps in the Battle of Britain* (Karlsruhe Collection, Hamburg). Translated by Nadia Radowitz.

—. *German Attacks on R.A.F. Ground Targets,* 13/8/40–6/9/40: a study (Karlsruhe Collection, Hamburg). Translated by Nadia Radowitz.

—. *Mass Day Attacks on London: a monograph* (Karlsruhe Collection, Hamburg). Translated by Nadia Radowitz.

—. *Some Reasons for the Switch to Night Bombing; an appreciation* (Karlsruhe Collection, Hamburg). Translated by Nadia Radowitz.

—. *The Struggle for Air Superiority During Phase 1 of the Battle of Britain* (Karlsruhe Collection, Hamburg). Translated by Nadia Radowitz.

Donaghue, L. *No. 54 Squadron, R.A.F.* (Air Ministry Public Relations typescript).

—. *No. 19 Squadron, R.A.F.* (Air Ministry Public Relations typescript).

—. *No. 65 Squadron, R.A.F.* (Air Ministry Public Relations typescript).

Elliott, Donald V. *No. 66 Squadron, a private diary* (Courtesy Christopher Elliott).

Féric, Pilot Officer Miroslaw. *Extracts from the Memoirs of a 'Kosciuszko' Pilot: the story of 303 (Polish) Squadron,* unpublished MS. (Courtesy Major L. W. Bienkowski, owner and translator).

First Flying Corps, Luftwaffe: Operational Orders for Attacks 'Sea of Light' and 'Loge' (Karlsruhe Collection, Hamburg). Translated by Nadia Radowitz.

Gefechtskalendar, Air Fleets Two and Three, 1/8/40–15/9/40 (Karlsruhe Collection, Hamburg). Translated by Nadia Radowitz.

Göring, Reichsmarschall Herman. *Conference Decisions of 21st July, 1st, 3rd, 15th and 19th August* (Karlsruhe Collection, Hamburg). Translated by Nadia Radowitz.

Grabmann, General Walter. *The Fighters' Role in the Battle of Britain,* a study (Karlsruhe Collection, Hamburg). Translated by Nadia Radowitz,

Greiner, Helmuth. *The Battle of Britain,* 4/9/40–7/9/40 (Karlsruhe Collection, Hamburg). Translated by Nadia Radowitz.

Ibel, General Max. *The 27th Fighter Group, Luftwaffe,* a private diary. Translated by Nadia Radowitz.

Jacobs, Squadron Leader Henry. *Jacob's Ladder,* an unpublished autobiography.

Lindemann, Professor Frederick (Lord Cherwell). *The Cherwell Papers* (Courtesy Nuffield College, Oxford).

Mann, E. L. *Recollections of 1940,* an essay.

Matthes, Günther. *The 2nd Wing, 51st Fighter Group,* a private diary. Translated by Nadia Radowitz.

Milch, Generalfeldmarschall Erhard. *Report of the Inspector General of the Luftwaffe,* 25/8/40 (Karlsruhe Collection, Hamburg). (Translated by Nadia Radowitz.)

Ministry of Information: Observers' Regional Reports on Morale, 1/8/40–9/9/40 (Courtesy Mass Observation Ltd., London, S.W. 7).

Osterkamp, General Theo. *Experiences as Fighter Leader 2 on the Channel* (Karlsruhe Collection, Hamburg). Translated by Nadia Radowitz.

Page, Wing Commander Geoffrey. *Autobiography,* an unpublished MS.

Richthofen, General the Baron von. *Private Diary* (Karlsruhe Collection, Hamburg). Translated by Nadia Radowitz.

Ring, Hans. *The German Fighter Forces in World War Two,* a study, in preparation. Translated by Nadia Radowitz.

Satchell, Group Captain W. A. J. *The First Polish Fighter Squadron, R.A.F.,* an unpublished history of No. 302 Squadron.

Seidemann, General Hans. *Actions of No. VIII Flying Corps on the Channel Coast* (Karlsruhe Collection, Hamburg). Translated by Nadia Radowitz.

Tobin, Pilot Officer Eugene. *Private diary* (Courtesy Mr. I. Quimby Tobin).

Trautloft, General Hannes. *The 54th Fighter Group,* a private diary.

United States Strategic Bombing Survey Records: including *Record Group 243:* interrogations of General Karl Koller, Professor Messerschmitt, Dr. Albert Speer, General Werner Junck, Dr. Kurt Tank, Generalfeldmarschall Sperrle, General Werner Kreipe, General Halder, General Goldbeck, Generalfeldmarschall Albert Kesselring, Feldmarschall Wilhelm Keitel, General Adolf Galland (Courtesy David Irving). Microcopy T–321: *Records of H.Q. O.K.L. (Oberkommando Der Luftwaffe),* German Air Force High Command (United States National Archives, Washington, D.C.).

Photograph Credits

All photographs are from the Chaz Bowyer Collection. Individual sources are acknowledged gratefully hereunder.

1 FOX Photo Agency
2 Author's Collection (CB)
3 Archiv Schliephake
4 CB Collection
5 FLIGHT INTERNATIONAL
6 CB Collection
7 Grp Capt C. F. Gray, DSO, DFC
8 G. Fischbach Archiv
9 Beaumont Aviation
10 Archiv Schliephake
11 K. Munson
12 CB Collection
13 CB Collection
14 Bippa

15 CB Collection
16 CB Collection
17 Courtesy OC 56 Squadron, RAF
18 CB Collection
19 CB Collection
20 Imperial War Museum
21 CB Collection
22 CB Collection
23 CB Collection

24 CB Collection
25 CB Collection
26 Archiv Schliephake
27 G. Fischbach Archiv
28 Via M. Sargent
29 CB Collection
30 Imperial War Museum
31 Imperial War Museum
32 Sqn Ldr C. P. O. Bartlett, DSC
33 CB Collection
34 Imperial War Museum
35 CB Collection

36 CB Collection
37 CB Collection
38 C. E. Brown
39 Imperial War Museum

40 K. Munson
41 K. Munson
42 CB Collection
43 CB Collection
44 CB Collection
45 CB Collection
46 CB Collection
47 Courtesy OC 74 Squadron, RAF
48 Imperial War Museum
49 CB Collection
50 Director Publicity, Wellington, NZ

51 M. Sargent
52 M. Sargent
53 CB Collection
54 CB Collection
55 Imperial War Museum
56 PN Agencies
57 CB Collection
58 CB Collection
59 CB Collection
60 CB Collection
61 FOX Photo Agency

62 CB Collection
63 CB Collection
64 Public Archives of Canada
65 Via M. Sargent
66 CB Collection
67 M. Sargent
68 CB Collection via J. Bushby
69 CB Collection
70 Hawker Siddeley Aviation

71 R. F. Watson via N. L. R. Franks
72 M. Sargent
73 J. B. Cynk
74 Imperial War Museum
75 CB Collection
76 M. Sargent
77 Public Archives of Canada
78 R. C. B. Ashworth
79 R. F. Watson via N. L. R. Franks
80 CB Collection
81 J. B. Cynk

82 Archiv Schliephake
83 CB Collection
84 CB Collection
85 CB Collection
86 Public Archives of Canada
87 CB Collection
88 J. B. Cynk
89 CB Collection

90 CB Collection
91 CB Collection
92 CB Collection
93 CB Collection
94 CB Collection
95 CB Collection

96 Imperial War Museum
97 CB Collection
98 Grp Capt C. F. Gray, DSO, DFC
99 CB Collection
100 CB Collection
101 PN Agencies
102 CB Collection
103 British Official

Index